# WRITING HOME

# ELI GOLDBLATT

---

# WRITING
# HOME

---

## A Literacy
## Autobiography

*For Angela + her family —*
*So good to meet together today*
*— whenever we meet.*
*Much joy —*
*El Goldblatt*
*8/30/2024*

Southern Illinois University Press
*Carbondale and Edwardsville*

Lyrics from "It's Alright, Ma (I'm Only Bleeding),"
by Bob Dylan, and "A Hard Rain's A-Gonna Fall,"
by Bob Dylan, copyright © 1965 by Warner Bros.
Inc., renewed 1993 by Special Rider Music, all
rights reserved, international copyright secured,
reprinted by permission. Lyrics from "Tangled
Up in Blue" by Bob Dylan, copyright © 1965
by Warner Bros. Inc., renewed 1993 by Rams
Horn Music, all rights reserved, international
copyright secured, reprinted by permission.
**Help Me Make It Through The Night**
Words and Music by Kris Kristofferson
© 1970 (Renewed 1998) TEMI COMBINE INC.
All Rights Controlled by COMBINE MUSIC CORP. and
Administered by EMI BLACKWOOD MUSIC INC.
All Rights Reserved    International Copyright
Secured    Used by Permission
*Reprinted by permission of Hal Leonard Corporation*

Library of Congress Cataloging-in-Publication Data
Goldblatt, Eli.
Writing home : a literacy autobiography / Eli Goldblatt.
    p. cm.
Includes bibliographical references.
ISBN-13: 978-0-8093-3085-0 (pbk. : alk. paper)
ISBN-10: 0-8093-3085-7 (pbk. : alk. paper)
ISBN-13: 978-0-8093-3086-7 (ebook)
ISBN-10: 0-8093-3086-5 (ebook)
1. Literacy—Social aspects—United States.
2. Education—Biographical methods. 3. Goldblatt, Eli.
4. College teachers—United States—Biography. I. Title.
LC151.G653 2012
302.2'244—dc23                    2011028067

*For Harry and Selma Goldblatt*

The concept of a present as a divider, or a mirror with past and future reaching out from a neutral vanishing point, denies the authority of the mind, which is only alive now.

—Gil Ott, *Traffic*

In all areas of life and ideological activity, our speech is filled to overflowing with other people's words.

—Mikhail Bakhtin, *The Dialogic Imagination*

# Contents

Acknowledgments    xi

Introduction: From Garret to Tree House    1

1. Tour of Duty    8

2. The Right to Mourn    32

3. Into the Daedalean Dreamscape    60

4. Following Williams    78

5. Dry Creek Road    102

6. White Coat    113

7. Entering Philadelphia    142

8. Beyond the Fathers    176

9. *Viajeros, Extranjeros*    197

10. High Five at Second Base    235

Bibliography    257

*Gallery follows page 112*

# Acknowledgments

I'VE BEEN WRITING A message to my father about my thoughts and decisions, my accomplishments and misdeeds, my loves and disappointments ever since I saw him laid out in his red turtleneck and white jeans on the floor of our apartment in Silver Spring, surrounded by emergency workers and neighbors trying to revive him. They couldn't bring him back, and neither can my poems or essays or studies or letters or emails. At the same time, the fact that I write rather than act or paint may be largely due to my mother. With her sharp eye for contradictions and unsubstantiated claims, I continue to scan my writing, especially when I'm addressing an academic or administrative audience. Her death in 2002 has hardly weakened her criticism of my prose. At early stages of my drafting process, I have to exclude her from my imagined audience because she represents that reasonable, logical mind I admire but need to disengage when I start composing. Every sentence I revise successfully, however, owes its solidity and snap to her. The mistakes are certainly mine.

I have too many friends to thank for this book and the experiences it attempts to reflect and explore. I simply ask forgiveness from those I don't name. Among high school friends who helped, I'm grateful to Vicki Bor, Dave DuGoff, Liz Symonds, Bob Baum, and especially Ruth Greenspan, John Gussman, and Joe Pavlock. I hope the stories reflect my immense gratitude to Joel Gordon, Paul Bernier, David McAleavey, John Landreau, and Bill Lamme; these men brought great richness and perspective into my life. Abby Ruder was gracious and helpful in reading parts of the manuscript. David Bushnell provided crucial perspective and friendship as he read and commented on every chapter. I could not have gotten through the writing without Herb Cohen's wise counsel. I did some major revisions at the wonderful Costa Rican home of George Cisneros and Jeff Halvorsen. Other supportive friends include Len Rieser, Chris and Ellen Hill, Julia Blumenreich, Robin

Semer, Jacques Wilmore, Mark Lyons, Charles Alexander, and David Kannerstein, as well as my baseball companions Alan Symonette and Fred Day. Of professional friends I must especially thank Keith Gilyard for invaluable suggestions and Linda Adler-Kassner, Russel Durst, and Michael Smith for consistent support. Steve Parks and I share stories of our military childhoods as we spin out our plans for community projects. My wonderful colleagues at Temple include Michael Kaufmann; Sue Wells and her husband, Hugh Grady; Steve Newman and his wife, Keely McCarthy; and my chair, Shannon Miller. I'm grateful to Temple's College of Liberal Arts for the study leave that allowed me to draft much of the book. Editor-in-Chief Karl Kageff of Southern Illinois University Press was extremely encouraging, and copyeditor Julie Bush improved my prose. The anonymous readers added significantly to tone and point of view in the final draft.

Most of the events I recount here happened before I met my wife, Wendy Osterweil. She's heard all the stories, listened to my dreams as I relived difficult memories, and read much of the manuscript, but that is not how she most contributed to this work. Her presence—intelligence, imagination, and unfailing humor—sustains me at times I doubt myself. We travel well together, no matter whether we stay or go. I hope I indicate a little of what our son, Leo, means to me, but I must thank him for sharing his view of school and the new world. Wendy brought a great extended family into my life, and I thank them all for accepting me in their unfolding history. The dearness of my brother, Aaron, and my sister, Sharon, is evident throughout the narrative. I thank Aaron and his wife, Laura, for their concern as I trudged through these recollections. Aaron in particular knows what home has meant to us both.

# WRITING HOME

# From Garret to Tree House

ONE LATE FALL AFTERNOON, I was talking to friends at Tree House Books, a small nonprofit bookstore and literary center off the Temple campus. I'm on the board of Tree House, and we were planning programs for the spring, considering what workshops the children in the neighborhood needed and what events would draw adults. Suddenly a couple of police cars raced past the front door, sirens wailing. Then three more passed, along with a pack of cops on bicycles. When the seventh patrol car screamed by, Barbara—a longtime activist and resident in this neighborhood of North Philadelphia—remarked grimly, "There has to be a cop down." Within a few minutes, Barbara had a call from her sister saying that indeed two policemen had been shot, and one had died. The shooter, who had been in trouble with the law nearly all his life, also lay dead on the street.

The K–8 school on the next block was locked down, and people were standing in small groups before their row homes. We returned to our meeting in a changed mood and quickly decided to call a meeting of local anti-violence activists, police representatives, and residents to talk about violence in the community. Forty people showed up at Tree House two weeks later to tell their stories and discuss how to move forward. We decided to host a regular monthly event where we showed documentaries or invited speakers to raise issues crucial to the life of the people in the immediate vicinity, hoping that our books and space would foster ideas about how those in the neighborhood could draw closer and gather power for themselves to challenge the problems that face them all: guns and drugs, low employment and poorly maintained housing, schools that need more money and love. We can't change much quickly, but every new person who comes across the threshold represents a little more strength for the job.

Why is an English professor spending time planning programs at a local bookstore? Why isn't he writing books or teaching undergraduates to read poetry? Why isn't he directing writing across the curriculum or chairing a tenure committee? I'm a traditional professor with an office and rank, committee assignments and papers to read. But my roles at the university never seem sufficient for the vision I have of literacy. I don't think English stops at the edge of the campus; literature, rhetoric, and linguistics grow poorer when they remain purely academic studies. If English majors go on to careers in finance or law but children just outside the campus can't read at grade level, what system have I perpetuated? If my graduate students get faculty positions but a teenager a block from my office is shot on his way home from a pick-up ball game, what order of justice do I serve? I can't solve all the problems inside my own college, let alone right the inequities in the city around us, and yet my educational theory seems flawed if I pay attention to one category of student but ignore the learners pressed up against glass walls that seal off my university's oversized buildings and wide plazas from the hope-starved schools and ghetto-priced corner stores at the edges of our splendid precinct. My North Philadelphia neighbors lose out on jobs every day because they don't have the credentials or training or social capital to compete for work in corporate headquarters fifteen blocks away, where our alumni hold responsible positions. A hundred yards from a subsidized housing project, my college grants PhDs to people who have come from El Paso and Prague. How do we wake from this dream of contradictions that comforts some and crushes others?

I can't deny my deep investment in an institution—indeed, my complicity in a vast educational system—that feeds me and my family, allows me the opportunity to work with hopeful students every semester, offers me the means to develop productive projects in my city. I have many friends among the colleagues and administrators in my school, and the university rewards me for what I do. Yet I never feel exactly at home in our concrete and steel campus among the beautiful young people walking from class to class. Indeed, I never feel exactly at home anywhere, even in the city where I have lived for twenty-eight of the last thirty-four years. My first marriage fell apart and my second grew and matured in Philadelphia. Here I helped start a poetry reading series in a bar and learned to teach in a school where the roof leaked till the ceiling fell down. I cheered in two World Series parades for the Phillies and coached a kids' baseball team in my Mt. Airy neighborhood to a league championship. I watched my son become bar mitzvah, graduate from high school, and move into his first college apartment. I danced at my brother's two weddings. I sat with my mother as she died in her Center City apartment, and we buried her ashes under a cherry tree in our yard. Philadelphia is my home if any place can be, and yet, because I grew up moving from military post to post, following the orders the army handed my dad, Philadelphia still feels at times provisional to me, a place that cannot call me native. In one part of my mind, I'll always be passing through.

I have often asked my undergraduate and graduate students over the years to write literacy autobiographies in order to help them see the intimate ways that reading and writing influence their lives. Teachers should be prepared to undergo the same trials they set for their students, and so I decided I needed to write a literacy autobiography myself. This book traces my attitudes toward reading and writing—in school, but mostly outside of school—across many cities and towns, primarily over my first thirty years. It records my search for home and my growing recognition that only in my writing life could I feel born within and borne upon the words forming the world I inhabit. My childhood, during which I traveled with my family from Cleveland to Boston to San Antonio and beyond, taught me to value relationship over geography, learning over possessions. My father's death in 1965, on the weekend before my thirteenth birthday, taught me that even the people we need most can suddenly disappear. The written word persists, though it can be made to lie and torture, to obfuscate and satirize. A story of changing occupations, broken loves, and restless travels in the United States and Latin America isn't so unusual for my generation, but my little story stands in harmony and counterpoint to the larger stories of the Cold War, civil rights, Vietnam, and Latin American revolutions. Above all, this is a story about two competing and coinciding concepts of literacy: the individualist ideology of Western literary tradition in contrast with the broader social meaning of literacy that defines a group's identity or a nation's character. As a young poet I felt I had to write alone, but over time I recognized that other people shared this moment on the planet. I slowly redefined what I meant by "writing" and the work I regarded as mine because I reimagined the audience and purpose for written words in different genres.

I hope this book will appeal to writers and educators, as well as to artists and activists. I can't separate these various roles in my own life.

*Writing Home* has very little explicit theory in it and depends on narrative to make my case for an understanding of literacy as embedded in a single person's ambitions and hopes as well as in the multiple relationships that bound and expand a life. Let me point out one dynamic, however, that emerged for me in the telling: the clash between and coexistence of the traditional Western view of the individual poet striving alone and the more recent social conception of the writer in relationship to other writers and readers. As the drama of my own literacy unfolded, these two versions of writing seldom shared the stage at the same time until recently. Indeed, when I was first learning to write poetry, I could see nothing but the solitary writer. During a year away from college in 1971–72, I moved to the Amherst area in Massachusetts to work in a print shop. The first week there, I rented a room in Northampton on the top floor of a large, unkempt Victorian house, mostly because it reminded me of a writer's garret in Paris of the 1920s. Only a bare light bulb hung from the ceiling, the window was a dormer so shaded by trees that no light came in, the bed took up most of the floor space, and everything creaked. I was overjoyed at the idea I could write in such isolation, and I cleared a little space on a makeshift desk to begin writing that evening. But as the evening came on, I became more and more lonely and nervous. The moldy air stuck in my lungs. Old men coughed in the rented rooms below. I didn't feel much like opening my journal, and the light was too dim to see what I might scrawl anyway. I wandered in town until I got hungry enough to stop for a hamburger at a local diner and talk to the waitress. In the middle of the night, I ventured downstairs to the communal bathroom and met in the hallway an enormous and nearly naked man who looked like a sleepwalking sumo wrestler. I retreated upstairs, left the apartment early the next morning, and never went back, losing my week's deposit. My glorious dream of the poet laboring in a garret dissipated slowly over the next few years, but I realized then that contracting tuberculosis wouldn't make me Keats.

The social view of literacy pictures writing and authorship in an entirely different way. Since the early 1970s, composition scholars have emphasized group acceptance of fundamental contexts for literacy: the conventions for academic discourse; the unspoken expectations about genre; the assumed attitudes toward people, ideas, and events in school training. Even poetry teachers, seemingly the keepers of individualist ideology, have framed clever classroom activities to generate individual and group poems since the early days of "writers in the school" and Kenneth Koch's wonderful 1970 book on teaching kids, *Wishes, Lies, and Dreams*. Writing classes of every mode use peer review or group critiques to emphasize the real rhetorical demands that audiences make on writers. At the macro level, writing in schools makes no sense if it isn't connected to writing outside school. I can no longer conceive of writing across the curriculum unless I also think of writing beyond curricula, or what others call "writing across communities." The shooting near Tree House reminded me that violence done in my city is violence done to my family and me as well, and this insistent reality must be reflected in my writing and teaching life somehow.

Despite this recognition that writing is social, my experience as a writer suggests that writers must and do write alone, no matter how many spirits and social realities and word etymologies and reader expectations populate the writing room. Sometimes a kid from the projects needs to write herself out of her neighborhood, even if eventually she writes herself back in later. The most political interpretations of literacy, deeply cognizant of the power of the State and capitalist economy to shape private proclivities, cannot erase the intimate and idiosyncratic feelings attached to the act of composing. We are always alone, even as we are ever in community with contemporaries and history. A detailed account of any writer's multiple pathways will bear out that slant and piquant truth about the indefinable human activity named by the clinical-smelling term "literacy."

I can't end this beginning without a note about gender and sexuality. This literacy narrative is very much a heterosexual boy's story. Until my first encounters with feminism, I was strongly influenced by male writers, mentors, friends, and a few unfriendly characters. My mother's mark is everywhere to be seen in my writing and my life, but I myself didn't notice her influence for a very long time. As a young man, I tried to turn a different direction whenever I saw traces of her language in my words. Girls and women often shook my firmly male worldview, but I was less than conscious of female forces in my drive to have my say in a world of literature and ideas that was so dominated by Great Men. My childhood of military police and baseball caps didn't quite prepare me to see poetry as man's work, and I initially responded to Ezra Pound's swaggering prose in part because he preached that verse making could be a manly art.

Women were both love objects and close friends, but I needed to prove myself to men, especially to the father I'd lost. My most precious memories of my father come from the few moments when we sat at the dinner table after the shabbas meal and argued about an invention I had in mind or the nature of the God in our holiday blessings. No matter what I said, my ideas never convinced him—my understanding of Judaism or science couldn't match his—but I felt he approved of my passionate attempts to disagree with him. His father had taught him chess with the warning that the day the son won a game would be the last day they played, and the day did indeed come. Dad told me that story in jest when he taught me to play, but he didn't live long enough for me to test whether he would have broken the tradition.

My simple gender polarity splintered badly in the breakup with my first wife, whom I call Sylvie in this book. Feminism charged every social gesture—indeed, every domestic and foreign space from the kitchen to the moon—with high-energy sex and gender politics. My consciousness about race and class, just opening up in those years after college, turned inside-out with the collapse of my marriage: suddenly a political position became more personal than skin. I could no longer take social or intimate motivations for granted, and the heat from that broken bond seared my eyes open. What official culture celebrated as settled and sacrosanct, I now recognized as fluid and provisional. I left for Central America after we separated, unsure what or who I was, but the combination of Maya ruins and modern revolution somehow helped settle me again into my job as a writer, recomposing myself in the welter of Spanish and English. As my foreman Paul in the California vineyards might have said, I learned how to "pay attention" that year away from America.

Teaching provides me the bridge between individual and communal senses of self in language. Learning happens both inside the mind and inside the group; the teacher manages the learning environment. My sojourn in medicine proved to me that I might have made a home in public hospitals and free clinics, but doctoring focused too much on information and intervention and not enough on the small, wild voices of distinct men and women, boys and girls. In medical school, I re-encountered my father and his history; a year was enough to learn that I had to release my life from his. Teaching requires attention to others in a way I find congenial but constantly challenging, humbling but always renewing. My second marriage, a joyful collaboration with my dear friend Wendy Osterweil, started with a long first phone conversation that centered mostly on teaching. She was finishing her second year in the classroom, and I was in my fourth. We simply had too much to say to each other about our students, our work, our pleasure watching others grow. That conversation goes on unabated today. We raised our son, and along the way I coached or watched him play in hundreds of games in three sports, and that too provided an education about how kids learn. All the while, writing formed my foundation, as art did for Wendy, and engaging with neighborhood arts and literacy projects became an arena to challenge what we thought we knew about composing and design.

I chose storytelling as the methodology for this exploration of my literacy. It has taken me well over a decade to bring this version of my narrative to the form you read now. I wouldn't claim the events or players in my story represent models of literacy development, and I don't expect that readers, especially younger readers, will "identify" with me, whatever that might mean. I do hope readers recognize themselves now and then in the text. My stories involve ancient technologies—typewriters and library card catalogs, letters sent by US post, long-distance phone calls limited by high rates and land lines—and the events take place within a massive historical shift in cultural attitudes over issues that young people today may regard as already settled. But all writing involves technology, and writers must compose through and against the historical moment into which they are born. I wrote this book partly to reconcile certain private tales I've told family and friends over the years with the larger vision of literacy I have slowly pieced together during my academic career. At the same time, I am reaching out beyond my personal circle in the hope that my stories offer solidarity to others who make their homes with written words.

## 1

# Tour of Duty

IN 1962 OR SO, my brother and I were waiting in a clinic to receive shots our pediatrician had ordered as part of a routine checkup. All patients went to a single clinic for simple outpatient procedures in the army hospital on the post where we were stationed in Landstuhl, Germany, not long after the Russians put up the Berlin Wall. We waited among soldiers needing stitches and mothers holding colicky babies for the nurses to call us in to be inoculated. We knew "inoculate" meant they would inflict pain. Aaron was six or seven, and he was worried the shot would make him cry. Being two and a half years older, I couldn't tell him I feared pain at least as much, and so I dragged him around the room, cheering him up with whatever inspiration I could find. That is what a big brother was supposed to do. We looked at the action pictures hung on the walls of the clinic and hospital halls. Each little painting depicted a famous battle or military scenario; each was accompanied by an uplifting caption explaining the scene. The one we lingered at longest showed a young soldier, a trumpeter for the infantry, who volunteered to do a brave and impossible deed with the chipper exclamation, "I'll try, sir!" I convinced Aaron that this should be his motto, and I drilled him on what he would say to himself when he faced the needle. He repeated, "I'll try, sir!" a couple of times to me before they called us in, and I believe both of us got through the ordeal without tears.

I must admit that a year or two before this clinic scene, when Aaron couldn't read at all, I almost convinced him that one postcard in my dinosaur collection read on the back, "The diplodocus is the ancestor of the Goldblatts." I managed to get him to ask my mother if that was what the card really said, and then I had a laugh when he came storming back. In short, I didn't always use my reading ability for my little brother's greater good. I read incessantly about scientists and inventors, especially Tom Swift Jr.—boy inventor and son of an inventor—and biographies of Edison, Pasteur, and Einstein. I dreamed of becoming world-famous like them for a machine I built or a discovery I made. I loved the *All About* book series, especially the volume by Roy Chapman Andrews, dinosaur hunter from the New York Museum of Natural History. I read Hardy Boys mysteries when I didn't have a fresh Tom Swift book at hand. I read books about sports heroes like Christy Mathewson, Babe Ruth, and Dizzy Dean, especially firsthand accounts of great ball games they played in. I read about Indian leaders like Chief Joseph, Sitting Bull, Tecumseh, and Sequoya, creator of the Cherokee alphabet. I read and reread a book about a young brave who changed his name after a vision quest.

Aaron didn't much like to read, maybe in part because I did. We could never favor the same choice, whether in chicken (I was white meat, and he was dark meat) or ice cream (chocolate for me, vanilla for him) or vegetables (he liked green peppers, and so I liked carrots). He looked at pictures in Time/Life books and magazines, but while I read about adventures, he took them. He caught frogs and crawdads with reckless pleasure while I hung back and commented. He jumped from tree limbs even when he was too small to catch the branch we older kids could reach. When we played "gunner" in the playground, Aaron "died" more convincingly than anybody else, whether he'd chosen to be blown from the jungle gym by a pretend grenade or strafed on the sand by an imaginary machine gun. I read the Boy Scout manual on knot-tying and earned my first-aid merit badge, but he was more likely to build a fort in the woods and require medical attention for some cut he got hauling wood. I never broke a bone, but he broke a few and also caught his hand in a door I closed and got the tip of his nose cut off—many times he was injured while doing something with me, but he always played harder and with more abandon. He was impatient, hated waiting on lines, and didn't care as much as I did about saying the right thing. Once, when we were about to get on the army transport ship to Europe, a soldier was checking the family health records and asked, "Are you allergic to anything?" Five-year-old Aaron piped up, "I'm allergic to chipmunks!" I thought sure they would turn us back because my loopy brother had just made up this ailment, but they let us board anyway. Aaron knew I was secretly afraid of touching frogs and only once revealed my weakness to mutual friends. I thought I would never forgive him for that betrayal, but we couldn't afford to stay mad at each other long. Sometimes, when I had one of my nightmares about vampires or werewolves—my greatest fear, the possibility that I would transform into something evil I couldn't control—I'd wake him up and tell him he could sleep in the lower bunk with me. He would dutifully climb down the ladder and sleep at the other end of my bed. Sometimes bullies would pick on him and I would fight to protect him, or I would include him in a game I was playing with guys my age. After all, from post to post and city to city we shared a bedroom, even if we didn't always share enthusiasms.

To grow up in the army means first of all to accommodate to constant change. Between the time my father, Harry, enlisted, when I was not quite four, and the time he died, when I was nearly thirteen, we lived in seven different homes in four US states and Europe. We did own a house in San Antonio for a year when I was five. My father was very proud to set up his family in a home with his new commission as a captain, after earning $600 during his entire first year out of medical school, but my parents must have realized quickly that they couldn't afford to live off the post. I suspect they started off with the idea that they could be IN the army without being OF the army, but they could not resist the identity of the military family. My mother, Selma, may have been a New York Reform Jew with a master's degree in sociology from the University of Chicago, but she was now an army wife. My father may have grown up in Cleveland, the son of a slender little Hungarian Orthodox Jewish scholar who hung wallpaper for a living and studied *kabbalah* in secret, but now his main identity was as an officer in the US Army Medical Corps. Settled civilians just can't understand the pressures of moving every few years, of taking orders to go wherever the command tells you to go, of losing friends at a moment's notice when you are sent away to Ft. Hood, Texas, or Okinawa, Japan, or Ft. Bragg, North Carolina. Nor could my parents protect my brother and sister, Sharon, and me from the life they chose. My mother used to tell the story about the first time a close friend of mine suddenly had to leave town. I was perhaps five, and he was a favorite playmate across the street. I came into the house crying that Billy was gone and I would never have a friend again. She comforted me as we always comforted ourselves: at least we had the family to depend on when others disappeared. After a while, you learn to make friends fast and say good-bye as a matter of course, though it never really stops hurting. Better to be around other military folks who understand impermanence as a dependable element in life.

My mother was in fact my closest friend through those years, and probably in some ways I was hers, too. Except for the ten months of hospital stays and convalescence before my father died, he worked sixty or seventy hours a week as long as I knew him. I remember watching him dress in the dark when I was five, and he always returned in the dark, sometimes well after we went to bed. Occasionally he would go away for training maneuvers, but most of the time he was on the wards or in his hospital office; I lost my first tooth at dinner in the hospital cafeteria on a family visit to see him at work. My mother knew no one in most of the places we moved, and without a husband around it was her job to set up our home wherever we went, often using government-issued furniture in place of personal belongings we had stored or could not afford to buy. She sometimes had to walk long distances for groceries because we had no car or my father needed to drive to work, and I remember great outings where she would pull a red wagon with my baby sister bundled up inside and my brother and me walking next to her as we made our way down a highway and across traffic to the commissary where we could buy food. I would have long talks with her while she hung clothes in the basement laundry room or cooked shabbas dinner on a Friday afternoon. She always took me seriously and entertained any subject, from the latest machine in Tom Swift to the reasons the Russians hated us.

Once my father was gone—she always used the term "gone" rather than "dead"—these talks often turned to her concerns about my brother and sister or plans for family expenditures, but they also involved world politics and the latest struggles in her job as a bureaucrat in Nixon's Health, Education, and Welfare Department during the Vietnam War. Studies say the mental health of a military child depends heavily on the attitudes of the mother toward the service and the strength of the mother/child relationship. She was probably often depressed, worn out, even despairing about her family's situation, but to me she was always warm, intellectually challenging, and hopeful. She had incredibly high standards for my schoolwork, but, unlike my father, she never lost her temper with me or shamed me for not being quick enough. She played piano beautifully and always managed to take the piano along on our moves, but she seldom played for her own pleasure. Her father had spoiled performing for her with his intense drive to make her a classical star, but she couldn't let the instrument go, either. She played only on Jewish holidays or family occasions when we would all sing from the folk songbook that always sat on the music stand. On rare occasions, we would come into the house and find her playing Rachmaninoff or Chopin from complicated sheet music, but she would soon stop and secret the books again inside the piano bench.

A tour of duty may name the whole of a military person's career or it may tag a specific assignment, especially abroad. Landstuhl, Germany, was both the center of our army experience and the representative tour of my childhood. We lived in Cleveland and Boston during Dad's medical school and internship. I was sick in bed with infantile asthma for the year in Boston. That was in fact one reason my father enlisted, because they told him they would send us first to Texas, a place my doctor recommended to clear up my symptoms. Once Dad joined, with promises of special training and accelerated promotions because of his dual degrees in dentistry and medicine, we moved from his general surgery residency in San Antonio to civilian plastic surgery training in St. Louis before being posted to Germany. After Landstuhl, we moved to Ft. Benning, Georgia, briefly, then back to San Antonio when Dad developed a pneumonia that damaged his heart, and finally to Silver Spring, Maryland, where his death ushered us into permanent civilian life. Ft. Sam Houston in Texas was the biggest post, and to a four-year-old it offered the paradise of countless swimming pools, all numbered and in different mysterious configurations. Ft. Benning represented the *real* army because there they emphasize fighting rather than healing; paratroopers and Special Forces outnumber nurses and doctors. Battles among kids in Benning were fierce. Three friends I had in Georgia fought almost every day about which service was best—the US Army, Navy, Marines, or Air Force—and I would get attacked for not taking sides. The gym teacher at the Benning school had us all run twice down a path to a certain rock in a field, and the faster guys were instructed to hit the slower boys as they lapped them coming around the second time.

But little Landstuhl Army Medical Center, or LAMC—surrounded by barbed wire up on a small mountain overlooking a picturesque southeastern German town close to the border of France, and hardly more than an hour from Frankfurt—served as home in my fourth, fifth, and sixth grade years. In Landstuhl, I learned to play baseball, saw my first stolen *Playboy* centerfolds, heard my first curse words, and realized a lot of people didn't like Jews because "jew" was what kids called anybody they didn't like. I began to dream there about becoming an inventor or an astrophysicist, whatever that meant to me. I started asking questions about religion nobody could answer, not even my father or Rabbi Hellman at the air force base in the next town. I developed a habit of cultivating parallel private and public lives. My reading and fantasy life about science grew into a personal, even sacred pursuit in my room (or my half of the room I shared with my brother). My commonplace life involved school, sports, Boy Scouts, and playing in the woods all around the post. I learned about dirty jokes, which formed for years the bulk of my knowledge about female anatomy and adult reproductive behavior. I discovered that a guy could talk with buddies about girls he really liked only late at night on sleep-outs in the backyard. I made deep friendships with kids I would never see again, like the time Kurt and Johnny and I helped Bobby clean out his desk in the middle of the year because his family had suddenly been transferred stateside.

Europe opened up to us on family trips to Scandinavia and Finland, England, and Italy. We saw Tivoli Gardens and the Little Mermaid statue in Copenhagen, Madame Tussauds wax museum and Sherlock Holmes's fabricated apartment in London, Michelangelo's *David* in Florence and the Piazza San Marco in Venice. My brother and I wore green Bavarian felt hats with high crowns and narrow brims, to which we pinned medallions from each place we visited. A snapshot in front of a German salt mine shows us wearing our hats, holding our Brownie cameras (mine was maroon and had a flash; Aaron's was black and had a flip-up viewfinder). Aaron cranes his skinny little neck upward into a big smile, a hummingbird caught momentarily in stasis but never repose. In my chunky GI glasses and posed smile, I look every bit the out-of-place American tourist child of the early 1960s—earnest, staunchly curious, brave in my bewilderment. My sister was a toddler, but in many pictures she is wrapped in a long cloth and wears a makeshift headpiece; Sharon took every opportunity to dress like the princess my father adored. My mother made the sandwiches and navigated; my father always drove and led us on adventures. We once traveled miles and miles into the Norwegian countryside to find a preserved Viking ship. I started to worry we would never find our way home, and we came across no one to help us, including one man who listened to my father talk for minutes in carefully enunciated English and then got on his bike and rode away without a word. We finally did get to see the ship, a tribute to my father's perseverance with three restless kids in the car, and I will not forget the light on the old decaying wooden vessel, the heft of the weaponry they carried, the distance from their day to ours.

Our trips always contained this element of distant awe, for history or "masterpieces" I couldn't comprehend—such as the frescoes in the Sistine Chapel, with all their strangely athletic Christian saints arrayed around a muscular God of babies and bare-breasted women and damned souls. We encountered the sheer geography of a pass through the Alps or chance meetings with fun-loving young travelers in a hostel at the Arctic Circle. Still, we three kids tried to entertain each other at our own scale. Once my brother and I were playing catch with my sister's favorite doll as my father drove our blue '55 Chevy Bel Air station wagon seventy miles an hour down an Italian highway. We were spread out in the back section that my father had converted into a cushioned platform, beneath which he stored all our camping equipment and food. Sharon was crying in my mother's lap. I threw the doll, and Aaron missed it. The doll hit the windshield and landed in my father's lap. He screeched to a halt on the shoulder, called Aaron over first, and hit him hard in the arm. When I wouldn't come, he somehow reached all the way back, dragged me to him, and punched me too. Another time my sister got lost in a campsite beside a rushing river, and my mother and father ran all over the camp screaming her name. I imagined her little head bobbing in the choppy water under the rope stretched out to snag swimmers, but finally my father found her wandering far from the shore, watching other campers set up their tent.

With the exception of a single trip, we traveled through Germany to get to other places in Europe rather than stay in the country to see the sights. But a tour of Berlin was a different story. The Cold War was at its most intense during the years we were in Landstuhl, and military families were trained to prepare for hostilities, which generated a low but constant whisper of fear in children's ears. Soon after our arrival, my parents were briefed on how to walk across Europe in the case of war, how to cook grass and worms if supplies ran low, and what to stock in our private lockers in the basement should there be an emergency or siege. Kids played war games in the woods regularly, and though Nazis were sometimes the enemy, we knew the Communists were always the real bad guys. I never learned much about my father's politics, but my mother always followed the debates of the day, and both of them must have been deeply concerned about the Berlin Wall. My father, I think, saw a trip to the wall as a duty, an obligation, a dubious gift of history. I suspect he felt that, no matter how fearsome, witnessing the divided city of Berlin was an educational opportunity for his children far more crucial than visiting the Louvre or Buckingham Palace. Unlike all our other trips, this one was undertaken grimly, with purpose rather than wonder. When I remember the journey, I remember the silence most. My brother recalls that, on the way to the railroad station, we spied an East German license plate on a car in the street. My father pulled over immediately and reported it because that was what he had been instructed to do if we ever saw such a vehicle. I don't remember the incident, and it sounds like a kid's nightmare now, but that's certainly how we experienced the anxiety of the time.

We took a long train ride to reach Berlin. I suppose we started in Frankfurt or Heidelberg, snug in our own little sitting compartment that turned into a sleeping chamber in the evening with the help of a silent but friendly porter. Late at night the train stopped, and I dimly recall large men in bulky uniforms and big hats moving down the train corridor, checking passports. I didn't understand the geography when my parents explained we had to leave West Germany and pass through an enemy country to get to West Germany's most famous city. We arrived early in the morning and moved as if in slow motion through Berlin. Everything seems mixed up in my mind: the dark colors, the soldiers from Britain and France and the United States and East and West Germany and the Soviet Union. Soldiers watched from their tanks and stood on corners with machine guns and warm hats. Snow was falling. We got out of a bus to see the wall, to see the markers where people had jumped out of buildings to die on the western side. Everywhere people were staring—at us, at the wall, at the monuments surrounded by barbed wire. I don't remember the hotel where we stayed, don't remember taxis or shops or meals, but I remember people walking quietly on snowy streets while guards stood at checkpoints with their guns and dogs under signs written in half a dozen languages.

My father and I were seldom alone together in my childhood. When I was very young, he tried to play catch with me in the backyard, but he always got home near dark, and we would have to go inside when the ball hit me in the face. Once we worked on a model of a cave-man skeleton together, and for a short time he undertook to teach me Hebrew because I wasn't learning enough for him in Sunday school. The summer before I turned thirteen, we went to synagogue together a few times. But in Berlin, he insisted that only I should accompany him on a bus tour of East Berlin. My siblings were too young—my mother had to stay with them—but I was old enough and needed to see this place for myself. This frightened me utterly except that I would be with Dad, men viewing the enemy world together. We got on the bus in the sunlight, but by the time we had passed through Checkpoint Charlie, the notorious entryway to East Germany for Allied military people and diplomats, and rolled through the no-man's-land where eastern escapees had been shot, I remember the weather turned gloomy and thick. Only a short time before, tanks from East and West had faced each other over this tiny space. We waited for our passports to be checked and then rode through the streets on a circuit that passed shops and people. We were not allowed outside the bus. My father and I sat together, but I doubt we spoke. I didn't know what I was supposed to learn, but I gathered we were seeing how poorly the Russians treated the Germans on their side. I don't remember that they seemed shabbier or more forlorn, even though I was trying hard to detect suffering. I remember some relief when we got back to the rest of the family, but I don't think I felt much lighter till we left Berlin altogether and arrived again in Landstuhl. My father and I together had witnessed the oppo-site of freedom, and that was meant to be his gift to me.

The territory of our lives in Germany was defined by the routine practices of the US Army. The military police (MPs) in their speedy little jeeps patrolled the streets and manned the checkpoints as we entered and left the post. Buildings were numbered, though as kids we referred to our three-stairwell, three-story apartment buildings by their colors. Our family lived in the Pink Building, we played Wiffle ball with Italian Mike in the Green Building next door, and across the street was the Yellow Building (in another yellow building farther down the block lived Jeff, fan of the Confederacy and son of a chaplain, and Poochie, an older, brown-skinned African American kid who could pick up any grounder with grace, even on our rocky sandlot field). Some buildings went by initials, like the BOQ (bachelor officers' quarters) and the PX (the post exchange, a military department store that would carry anything except food, which you got at the commissary) and the NCO Club (the social gathering place for "noncommissioned officers," soldiers with the rank of corporal, sergeant, or warrant officer). We had a barber shop, an ice cream counter, a bowling alley, and a movie theater on the post, but every function was housed in a generic building that barely advertised what might be inside. There was a secret satisfaction in knowing the bright promises contained within a drab green block building or a Quonset hut set among barracks and parade grounds.

Post housing was segregated by rank. My family lived in the officers' quarters because my father was a captain and later a major. The medical center employed many middle-ranked commissioned officers, some doctors or other professionals serving short-term military service obligations rather than career stints, which was what my Dad was doing, in for ten years or more. Career officers would sometime differentiate themselves as "real army," as opposed to the drafted sort, but warrant officers, lieutenants, captains, and majors, with their families, all lived together on one curving street perhaps three city blocks long. The small post had only two units in the colonels' quarters; four families lived in each building, and their little area was more amply landscaped and set off from our sector. The generals' quarters contained only two tasteful brick one-story duplexes, more like American houses than the apartment buildings the rest of us lived in. We didn't even ride our bikes around there for fear that MPs would chase us away or the commander himself would come out and yell at us and give our dads demerits. The post was small enough that when we arrived, the commander was not even a general but a senior field officer named Colonel John Tenery, a World War II POW, veteran of the Korean War, and plastic surgeon who had gone into hospital administration. I remember meeting him once at a restaurant. He was tall and courtly and had the leathery look of a longtime soldier, even though he wore civilian clothes. He had chosen my father to take over his old clinical department, and my father treated him with unmistakable respect. Later that year, Dr. Tenery came out of clinical retirement to stitch my brother's nose back together because my father followed the rule that a surgeon never operates on his own family.

Because it wasn't a post with much of a fighting force, not many families of enlisted soldiers lived in Landstuhl. I suppose only the senior NCOs could afford to bring their families with them to Europe. The sergeants' quarters were a small set of apartments between our area and the baseball field. I remember going to visit a classmate there and being surprised that the front door of his stairwell was cracked and didn't close automatically. The light in the hall didn't work, either, and their one playground seemed smaller and rockier than ours. All the buildings were painted the same army beige. I wondered why their quarters seemed so much more run-down than ours, but the logic of rank made differences seem natural. The commanding officer had the big house; privates and corporals without families—including corpsmen who worked at the hospital—lived in the barracks up the hill near the movie theater and the motor pool (where they kept and serviced vehicles, or what civilians would call a garage). The rest of us sorted out in between.

Among kids at school, on the playgrounds, at Little League, or running down the hill after a cowboy movie on a Saturday afternoon, we mixed with little problem. Still, people didn't have to talk about rank to emphasize its importance, and even with silence, the hierarchy showed through. We played marbles and baseball and football and army and cowboys as though we all lived in a small town in Kansas, far from the Germany that lay right outside the post perimeter. We were all afraid of the German kids who would sometimes sneak up into the woods to stare at us through the barbed wire. A few old, formally dressed Germans would walk onto the post on Sunday to visit the mausoleum-like Bismarck Tower. Their weekly pilgrimage seemed a strange intrusion on our resolutely American life.

We most often played with kids who lived near our homes, and that tended to reinforce the separation by rank, but many activities on the post crossed military class lines. My baseball team, the Giants, combined enlisted men's and officers' children and was coached by GIs.

I remember a gruff and portly Sergeant Carmack (I think his nickname was Tex) with a handlebar mustache who coached the team one year. I still have the team ball from that year because I was the opening day catcher and caught the ceremonial first pitch of the season from the commanding officer. Many of the kids who signed it lived in the sergeants' quarters. George, a black kid from an enlisted family, was playing third base on that opening day until I made a mess of catching. I had studied the position in books all spring and knew exactly how to stand and how to throw the ball down to second. But when it came time to don a mask in a live game, it turned out I couldn't see the ball without my glasses and allowed five runs to score before the coach took me out in the first inning. George took over and became a team leader, I played decently at third, and the Giants won the championship that year. But rank haunted us in more formal settings. I remember recognizing vaguely at age eleven or so, when a new boy came into our Boy Scout troop and immediately became the senior patrol leader, that his family had moved into the colonels' quarters.

I fought with an African American boy named Donald in sixth grade, and he scratched my face with a broken bicycle pump. Normally he was my friend, a guy among the guys, but he got upset about something that day. Kids would get like that sometimes—angry, withdrawn, edgy—especially if a family had just gotten orders to move or a father was called away on extended duty. The fight erupted quickly at the end of a school day, and I remember no repercussions afterward. I was aware he lived in the sergeants' quarters, and if I ascribed his sudden outburst to any social factor, it was more likely to be where he lived than his race. Rank was naturally the ruling prejudice of our culture. Military historian Samuel Huntington from the 1950s famously defined an officer as a "manager of violence," and rank reflects the hierarchy of that management structure. Especially on a medical army installation, officers stand farther away from the inherent violence of the military, but in the end they are all committed to the main mission. The chain of command regarding violence is in this sense simple: the general whispers orders, the field officer issues them to his sergeants, the sergeants bark them to their soldiers, and the soldiers fire the weapons and take the grand share of casualties. Thus, overt force is most associated with lower-ranked GIs, even if all are committed to its exercise. In those days of heavy world tension shadowed by the atom bomb, violence under military command was held in check through policies and procedures we kids barely noticed, but violence underlay our conversations, our play scenarios, our schooling. I knew from very early on that firearms and not bandages were the representative tools of my father's employer. That made my father just a little less a soldier in my mind than the GIs who stood guard at the gate to the post.

My father, like all army medical personnel, didn't normally carry a gun on duty. Our family used to laugh about the one picture we had of my father with a gun on his hip because it looked so out of character. My father's job was largely to patch up men who had blown up their hands in a firearm mishap, had their cheeks bitten off in a barroom brawl, or had dived out of a barracks window in some crazy stunt a thousand miles from home. The fact that he could develop operations to repair cleft lips and cleft palates in little babies, his surgical specialty, was largely due to the brooding peace of the moment. Had he been alive for Vietnam, he most certainly would have been sent to set up field hospitals there. He was very interested in early medical interventions to prevent scarring.

I recognized even then that my father identified himself more with medicine than with the military. My mother used to say in later years that the army was a way to practice as he wished, without ever having to perform nose jobs or face-lifts to pay the bills. I certainly saw him as a doctor above all else. He hadn't been a very good student in college, and he started out in dentistry because he could get into that school. He soon found, however, that he needed medical training to fix jaws and faces as he imagined himself doing. Soon after they met in the late 1940s, my mother traveled with him to Israel, serving as his assistant as they drove a truck fitted out with dental equipment from kibbutz to kibbutz in the Negev desert. Once they married, she devoted herself to his career. She helped him apply to medical school and kept the family books and all his army correspondence, in addition to caring for us. In Germany, my father had to prepare hundreds of his cases for his board certification as a plastic surgeon. For what may have been months, he and my mother worked at night and weekends putting his cases together in a big wooden box shaped like a coffin. My mother typed as he dictated, and together they pasted photos of burned arms and flayed faces to the neatly formatted reports. They forbade us to look into the box, but my brother and I peeked long enough to see horrific images that still come to my mind too easily. The Friday night after they finished the box and sent it off to the board, my father added a ritual to our usual Sabbath ceremony before dinner. He sang the kiddush, the long blessing over the wine, as usual after my mother lit shabbas candles. Then he read a new prayer he would repeat thereafter each Friday, a piece from Proverbs: "A woman of worth, who can find? For her price is far above rubies" (Hertz 405). My mother sat at the other end of the table—stunned, I think, by this surprise. Her eyes shined and her nostrils grew wide, the sign that she was proud and happy. As it happened, my father never did earn his certification, though the cases passed review. He went back to the States for the exam but did not pass one particular phase. He had studied the hand exhaustively; they tested him instead on the foot. He died before he had the chance to take the test again.

My parents, I expect, developed their own reaction to a posting in Germany. In San Antonio and St. Louis, my father put all his energies into training as a general surgical resident and then a maxillo-facial surgeon, and my mother was raising three children under the age of eight. But by the time we came to Landstuhl, my father had to head a department. My mother settled into her occupation as an army wife while her husband was largely absent. Few of her neighbors came from New York City or had a college degree, and probably none had, like her, considered joining the Communist Party in the late 1940s. I do know both of them despised being in Germany so soon after the Holocaust. My father in particular made that clear with occasional scowling remarks at typical German scenes like local beer festivals or the crowded public pool. I remember he said once after talking to a German civilian who worked in the hospital, "They all say they fought on the Eastern Front and hated the Nazis. Who do you suppose supported Hitler?" Jewishness alone set us apart from nearly everyone we knew, but my parents seemed determined to act like normal Cold War Americans even while, I suspect, they quietly resisted the politics of rank and race and the McCarthy era they saw around them. I did not understand why my father forbade us to answer the phone "Major Goldblatt's residence" when I tried using that formula in imitation of the way other kids answered the phone. I was very proud that he'd been promoted, but he warned me to make nothing of it with my friends.

In the early 1960s, race operated in complicated ways in the army. The military was among the first major American social institutions to integrate by race. A year and three months after Jackie Robinson played his first game for the Brooklyn Dodgers in 1947, President Truman signed Executive Order 9981, which initiated the process of eliminating racial discrimination in the forces. The military wasn't officially fully integrated until the last all-black unit had been abolished in 1954, but by the time my father joined, the army was still far more integrated than many sectors of the civilian workforce. I went to school with African American kids who lived in officers' as well the sergeants' quarters, but I remember white families were the overwhelming majority in Landstuhl. Racism was still a part of the military culture, just quietly so. One of the most intense experiences of my childhood involved race, though I did not know it at the time.

We were supposed to rotate back to the States in the summer of 1964. I was nearly twelve, and I desperately wanted to return "home." I thought somehow America would be a better place, one with no curse words and no jokes about Jews, where I could visit my grandparents and cousins in New York and Cleveland, where I could go to a school held in a big brick building instead of a temporary hut. I'm not sure what I really sought in this mythical USA. We all felt in exile from the genuine country while we lived in this artificial America set off by barbed wire. The flagpole near the hospital entrance and the ball field down by the PX and the cowboy movies on Saturday reminded us of the country we were supposed to protect from the Russians, but we knew enough to want the real thing. The Pledge of Allegiance held almost mystical meaning for us, and when taps sounded at five in the afternoon, everything on the post stopped cold as the flag came down. I pictured my father halting in mid-stitch during an operation when he heard the trumpet. Sometimes we even stood in the rain and saluted, like the GIs did. Germany lay all around us, filled with red-faced people who smelled of beer and cigarettes and didn't much care for the US presence in their country. Truth be told, kids were mostly scared of the Germans, and on Boy Scout camping trips we told stories about the "Krauts" that just got us more scared.

I don't remember playing baseball that summer of 1964, and perhaps my family didn't let me join a team because they expected to be sent back soon after school ended. Vacation dragged on. We packed a little but did not move. My parents at first told us only that we were waiting for orders and then later that my father's replacement was being held up because he had to testify at a trial in the States. I became very anxious to go back; this seemed somehow an affront to our patriotism, a denial of our freedom, an insult to our family. I drew an American flag with colored pencils and taped it to the head of my bunk bed. I remember nights when I would sing "God Bless America" and cry myself to sleep. Finally in August, we were allowed to leave, and we moved to Columbus, Georgia, in time to start school before our boxes were even fully unpacked. The month we returned to the States, three civil rights workers—Michael Schwerner, Andrew Goodman, and James Chaney— were found murdered in Philadelphia, Mississippi. Race riots in 1964 injured hundreds of people in Philadelphia, Pennsylvania, as well as in Rochester and Harlem, New York. Walt Disney released *Mary Poppins* that year, and it soon became my sister's favorite movie. Johnson was running against Goldwater for president, and in my seventh-grade class the arguments over the election were fierce, led by a very loud girl named Shauna who proclaimed that only Goldwater could save us from the Communists.

Fifteen or so years later, my mother told me her version of the story behind our late departure from Landstuhl. According to her, it had to do with an incident in my sister's nursery school. My mother served on the board of the school, which was independent of the post elementary school and run by the officers' wives association. The board had a rotating position of chairwoman, and the custom was that if the honor came to a wife of an officer of lower rank, she would defer to a higher-ranked woman next on the rolls. Another woman on the board was Mrs. Wright, the wife of a captain who was serving his military obligations as an administrator in the hospital. Captain and Mrs. Wright were African Americans from distinguished, highly educated middle-class families in the District of Columbia. Through my dad and Captain Wright, our two families had become friendly. They had two daughters, both younger than I and both always very well dressed and behaved. I met them again much later in DC where the girls, now young ladies, were going to a private school when I was in high school. In any case, Mrs. Wright's name came up as chair, and despite the fact that the commanding officer's wife was next on the list, Mrs. Wright decided to accept the position and serve. This caused a scandal on the post. Most people either sided with the insulted commanding officer's wife or stayed out of the conflict entirely, but my mother sided with her friend—the Jewish woman and the black woman on the committee against nearly everyone else. Rank, as always, was partly at issue, but race in this case figured as well, the way my mother told the story. My father, instead of disciplining his wife and setting things in order as he was expected to do, sided with my mother against the commanding officer. My mother said no one on the post would talk to her or my father, either out of disgust or fear. My parents felt certain at the time that my father's transfer orders were held up by his superiors to teach him a lesson, as were his promotion to lieutenant colonel and his appointment to direct the surgical unit at Ft. Benning's Martin Army Medical Center.

I don't remember much about school in the army. My earliest distinct school memories are actually from one period we were not living on an army post, during the year in St. Louis when my father was training at Barnes Hospital. I was in third grade, and though Mrs. Graham was a sympathetic teacher, I never seemed to get my work done and spent a lot of time dreaming at my desk. My parents took me to a child psychologist, who made me draw pictures and answer questions. He pronounced me bright but bored and recommended that the teacher assign me special reports on subjects of my choice outside the curriculum. I can remember working on science presentations and standing in front of the class explaining space travel and dinosaurs. The upshot of this was that I learned how to fight. Other boys didn't much like this chubby little new kid—fresh from Texas and the only Jew in the neighborhood—getting special treatment. One day after school I fought two kids all the way down the hill to my house, with a crowd following us and my brother holding my books. I'd throw one boy off and another would jump on top of me until we got to our apartment house and Aaron and I could run inside. My father had forbidden me to use my fists in anger; I never understood if this was a Jewish stricture, his personal idea of non-violence, or a way of protecting my brother

24

(whom I never hit in anger but more than once injured by accident when we were playing too hard). The prohibition added to my unintimidating stature and undiagnosed poor eyesight as distinct disadvantages in a fight. I finally prevailed on Dad to allow me to sign up for wrestling at the local YMCA, where we were already taking swimming. I got hit in the head with a rock behind the Y during a friendly rock fight (the first time I remember my father and I were ever alone was when he stitched me up that night in an empty clinic room), but I did learn enough to feel I could handle bullies after that. I later wrestled in high school, much to my mother's profound disapproval.

Third grade in St. Louis was just before we went to Germany, and the greatest lessons that year were those I learned outside of school. The crises for our family were the questions of where we would go next and would my father be able to travel with us. We had been told unofficially that we were being sent to Okinawa, Japan. My mother signed herself up for scuba diving lessons at the Y, a rare move in doing something entirely for her own pleasure. But then official word came that we were being sent to a landlocked town in southern Germany. This seemed disastrous for the family at first because of my parents' animus against Germans, but we couldn't worry about what we couldn't change, and we had a more immediate challenge to face. We wanted "concurrent travel," permission for the military man to travel with his family, and that became the refrain in our house with every mail delivery. Did we get concurrent travel today? When would travel orders arrive? One evening, my siblings and I were returning home with my mother from the grocery store, and when we opened the front door my father came leaping down the stairs from our apartment, waving papers and calling out, "We got concurrent travel! We got concurrent travel!" I had hardly ever seen him so excited. At seven years old, I knew only that the verdict "concurrent" held the power to allow our father to sail with us across the ocean, and the thought that he'd be with us gave me tremendous comfort.

Europe provided many learning experiences, but few of them came in school. I earned high grades except in handwriting, which brought me not only my sole C but the ignominy of being the last kid in the class allowed to use a pen instead of a pencil to complete assignments. My parents simply expected good grades, and my father pronounced that he saw no need to praise me for what I could obviously do with ease. I think I understood he felt proud of me, but his way of expressing his pride was in the form of jokes about how I had "buffaloed 'em again" when they came home from a positive conference with my teachers. He probably thought he was being supportive by asking why my As weren't A+s, but I took his teasing a little more seriously than he meant it. Doing well was no badge of honor among my peers, either. It was probably a sign of acceptance that I didn't have to fight much in Landstuhl even though I was the "smart" boy in class. My friends tolerated my performance in school because school simply didn't count in our calculus of stature. Catching ground balls, running fast, being able to stand up even when a big kid tackled you, starting a fire with only two matches on a wet camping trip, telling a joke that actually got a laugh, these were what earned you respect. Girls still didn't figure much in our consciousness, but I had the idea that a boy's school skills didn't impress them either.

For most of our tour of duty in Germany, one girl, Jean, was always better than I in school, and for our last year, another girl—Rachel, daughter of a Jewish family we had known briefly before in San Antonio—joined Jean in occupying the spot of smartest pupils. Jean was the daughter of the junior high school principal and not technically an army kid; she seemed always to have the right answer before me. Rachel had the same Jewish pressures at home that I did to do well in school. Both of them had way better handwriting than I did, and despite my reputation for science, they were both better math students. This took the pressure off of me and probably saved my friendships with Kurt and Johnny and others who were just as smart but not particularly motivated by school. I would eagerly have traded my unwished-for ability to answer teachers' questions for Johnny's speed or Kurt's athletic confidence.

Johnny came from a big Appalachian family. I was in their apartment only once, even though they lived across the hall from us the first year in Germany and we played together all the time after school. They had few belongings that stood out among the drab GI furniture we all had in our homes, but a huge picture of their extended family hung above the couch in their living room. I remember Johnny pointing out his grandparents, but I was most impressed that some of the men in the old black and white photograph held rifles. He had one younger brother, Tommy, who seemed a little crazy to the rest of us because he garbled his words and liked to set fire to his toy soldiers. Tommy was the same age as my brother, but Aaron preferred to play with Johnny and me most of the time. They had two sisters, much younger, who mostly stared at us when we all got together, and I don't remember either of them saying a word. His mother was as silent as the girls, and his dad was a very big man with huge hands. Like most dads, he wasn't around very much, but I remember he didn't work in the hospital and might have supervised in the motor pool. I imagined him working on the large "Deuce and a Half" trucks that convoyed American troops and supplies all over Europe at the time. Johnny was pretty quiet himself and certainly never said much in school. He was tall and very skinny, and he could run faster than anybody I knew. We used to call him Crazy Legs because of the way he would run with a football. But what I remember most about Johnny was that he would check out the tallest stack of books from the school library every week, and most weeks he brought the whole stack back so he could get out another load for the next week. Many times he wouldn't show up in school, and I'd get home to find out his mom had made him stay home to watch his sisters. That was OK with him because he had his books. I don't believe Johnny got good grades, but I could talk to him about any of those biographies with orange covers and a silhouette of the subject on the cover. He would know everything about Lincoln or General Patton or Florence Nightingale or whoever it was. Johnny left after fourth grade, as I recall, the year we changed teachers in January because the first teacher had to rotate back to the States with her husband.

One educational experiment in sixth grade put my standing as a boy at risk. In the summer, I had played on the Giants, the post's championship team. Though I hadn't hit very well, I played a serviceable third base and got hit by pitches more than anybody else in the league, all of which earned me standing as a "decent" player. We had been in Landstuhl long enough that I had ridden my bike over every inch of road that kids were allowed to travel, and I had even gone to places in the X-Woods where signs said "unauthorized personnel" were not permitted. I had begun to feel regular. When fall came, our teacher, Mrs. Schoenberg, was not a very effective class manager; the class grew so unruly that once she gave us a little speech and ran out of the room in tears. But she was a kindly person, and her husband was a teacher at the junior high. Whether she came up with this plan or someone else did, Jean, Rachel and I were asked to work with the librarian regularly, reading to the kindergarteners and first-graders who visited the library. We would be called out of class, and the librarian would help us choose picture books to read to the kids, introduce us to the group, and leave us to take kids on a ride on the library's "magic carpet" to the strange world of books. I enjoyed the privilege, the break from routine, and the chance to read aloud in funny voices. Later in the year, the three of us put on a puppet show for kids, writing our own play and huddling together behind a puppet stage to perform. I was grateful my friends couldn't see me taking such pleasure pretending to fly with little kids or making them laugh with our show, but I was mortified when the librarian would say, "Now, girls—oh, sorry—girls and ELI too . . ." I don't remember my friends commenting on my activities outside of class, but I felt the danger every time the librarian called me away, even while I also felt pride. I was actually thrilled to be so close to Jean and Rachel behind the puppet theater because I had never been that near a girl my age before, except in a hated dance class. I had never known that girls smelled different from boys—my little sister certainly didn't count—and the revelation embarrassed me as much as it excited me. But I was adamant in my own mind that I did not "like" these girls, who were after all both my biggest school competition and a threat to my boyhood. With two exceptions—watching my teacher weep and having one of the fathers come into the class in uniform to talk to us about "psychology"—this experiment in coeducational independence is the only school memory I have for that year.

In one way, however, school mattered a great deal to me. Much in our lives made me uneasy, but in class I knew what to do. I did not feel secure in baseball games on the chance I would muff a ground ball and lose the game. In Boy Scouts, where I moved quickly through the ranks because I could learn from books, I worried some adult would ask me to tie a knot I had never learned properly or perform a first-aid maneuver I had forgotten, and they would bust me back to Tenderfoot. Any movie that showed a main character transforming into a monster, even if I watched it through my fingers, gave me nightmares for a month. On car trips, my father used to have me convert kilometers into miles in my head, and I feared I wouldn't remember my times tables fast enough or I'd forget to carry a number while he waited for my answer. Of course, any day I could walk in from playing football in the sandlot and my mother might tell me we had gotten orders to move to Letterman Medical Center in San Francisco or Ft. Knox in Kentucky, places I knew other families went. But despite the fears and instabilities in my life, I always knew how to do school, no matter what city we lived in. I might have to deal with bullies, and I might not know how to get to the new PX, but I could figure out what teachers wanted and read what they assigned. School was safe for me, and it didn't much matter if sometimes it was boring or even pointless. On any given day, I might meet a new friend, find a new library book, or answer a question nobody else could answer. The rhythm of school after a long summer was a dependable pleasure for me that overcame my fear of fitting in or of hearing some older boy call me a kike. School signaled I had a place in the scheme of things on the post.

Perhaps the greatest gift that school in Landstuhl gave me was my first male teacher, Mr. Irvine, in fifth grade. I'm sure he was a serious problem for the administration, because he would often tell us tales of fräuleins and beer and how much he was enjoying himself in Germany. He had a list of Dumb Kids (DKs) and Smart Kids (SKs) on the board, and you could get your name on one or the other list for the slightest infraction or the flimsiest achievement, depending on his mood. He referred to one kid as Cry Baby because his initials were CB and the guy once whined in class. Mr. Irvine forced another kid to read her entire essay aloud, pronouncing the misspelling "lik" for "like" through many comparisons, and we all laughed at her mistake. In short, he was more or less a stinker as a teacher by most standards. But the boys loved Mr. Irvine. He had a crew cut like our fathers. He had a low voice and a wild way of talking about his home in California. In between his stories and jokes and funny expressions, we did some math and reading and spelling. For all his sarcasm and mean names, we felt he loved us in a way we could understand from other men in our lives. We would have followed him anywhere because he was different from all the other teachers and more like us. He was somehow on our side.

When we did a class project about dinosaurs, one of my favorite topics in the world, we all made creatures in a large diorama and everybody got sloppy putting wet newspaper strips on an armature for a giant papier-mâché volcano. Kids prepared reports to give on the day we would unveil our project to the world. The big day came and our narrow room in the Quonset hut for fourth through sixth grades was jammed with mothers and even a few fathers. After all the kids had presented, Mr. Irvine gave a little speech and lit the crater in the top of the volcano. It spluttered, did nothing, and then suddenly burst into flame, catching fire on the side of the mountain as well as inside the tin cup on top. Smoke filled the room, and people spilled out the fire exit and the front door. We yelled and whooped with excitement more than fear. I remember looking back as I left. With smoke thick above his head, Mr. Irvine stood his ground, spraying the fire with an extinguisher and shouting to everyone as they ran out that this had never happened before. Maybe he looked ridiculous, but he also looked like a hero. By the next day, our parents probably wanted him run out of Europe, but my friends and I only loved him more.

Mr. Irvine was the only teacher, except for Mrs. Marblestone in synagogue nursery school, who acknowledged my Jewishness. Sure, when Jewish holidays came around, my teachers would have me go from class to class explaining Rosh Hashanah or Chanukah, but this reduced me to a sideshow attraction, half contortionist and half bearded lady. I took pride in what I knew from my family, but I didn't expect anybody in other classes to pay attention to what I knew—it was just too strange for them. But Mr. Irvine had me write a play for Chanukah, and my friends got to be soldiers in the Maccabee army. I was the narrator, and a girl I liked played my granddaughter sitting at my feet to hear the story of the Festival of Lights. The play came off without disaster, and my friends didn't reject me for writing it. Perhaps because of this attention, my family asked Mr. Irvine to Friday night dinner. Often my father would ask a lonely Jewish soldier to dinner on shabbas, or another Jewish family from the area would join us, but this was the first time a teacher came to our house for my mother's roast chicken. I was so nervous that night that when Dad asked me to sing the blessing over the wine, I suddenly couldn't remember the tune or the words. I'd been singing it every Friday since I started school, and I knew the blessing better than I knew my phone number, but no sound would come out of my mouth. My father looked down the table, pointed to Mr. Irvine, and said sternly to me, "Does that man have your tongue?" The joke was just enough to relax me, and I sang the *bruchah* perfectly.

## 2

## The Right to Mourn

IN THE SUMMER OF 1965, my father and I attended services at a different synagogue every Saturday morning. We had just moved to Silver Spring, Maryland, a near suburb of Washington, DC, from San Antonio, Texas, where he had been in the hospital for months with a damaged heart. I was nearing my thirteenth birthday, and I needed a place to have my bar mitzvah despite the fact that I could sing fewer than a dozen Hebrew prayers I had memorized in services and could sound out unfamiliar words only haltingly. My bar mitzvah preparations consisted of a couple of lessons the previous fall in Ft. Benning from Tsvi, a drafted GI who was the son of a Chasidic rabbi, and a few attempts to chant along by myself with a recording of Torah and Haftorah blessings we had bought in a Judaica store. My father and I knew nothing about the customs of suburban Jews, and each week we were overwhelmed by the lavish buildings, the large crowds of well-dressed worshippers, and the month-long waiting lists to schedule a bar mitzvah, even one with two or three boys at a time.

Jewish congregations in the military had contained perhaps twenty families and a handful of GIs, sometimes more in the larger posts. Services were often held in all-purpose chapels where the rabbi set up a portable ark on Friday nights and took it down on Saturday to accommodate the Protestant and Catholic Sunday services. In Georgia, our congregation had its own space with a more or less permanent ark and two real Torahs, but the shul was in a converted barracks surrounded by dilapidated structures dating from the Second World War. In DC, people dressed up fancy for the Sabbath and drove big cars. Nobody was particularly interested in us when we hung around after services to eat a little challah if they had a reception, but we didn't care very much how they treated us because we were too busy sizing them up ourselves. We would discuss what we liked and didn't about the service, the sermon, the architecture, and the congregation as we drove home to our bare little garden apartment on Piney Branch Road. Sometimes we would meet with the rabbi; sometimes we would just scoot out after the closing hymn, "Adon Olam." Once a rabbi with an Eastern European accent had me read Hebrew aloud in his study, stopping me frequently to criticize my mixed-up pronunciation and hesitant decoding till I cried. My father lost his temper and nearly socked the old guy, and we left in a hurry. Mostly we decided these places weren't for us.

One Saturday morning in late August, we went to a sleek synagogue with beautifully landscaped grounds and a particularly well-heeled congregation. This was our first time in a Reform temple in DC. My father had been raised Orthodox and, although he rejected the strict ways of his father, preferred Conservative synagogues because at least they used Hebrew and sang prayers with traditional tunes. My birthday was coming up quickly, however, and he was beginning to think that I would be better off in a place where I could use English for most of the ceremony. I knew he hated the idea, and I didn't like it much myself, but I guess we were both ready to concede. Reform Judaism felt like a defeat for us both—it meant he hadn't educated me properly, and I hadn't become the *yeshiva bucher*, the scholar, he almost wanted me to be—but, after a year of fighting back from a heart attack, he was willing to make compromises if it would make us normal again. At least this is how I now imagine his thinking that day as we sat in this Modern American Temple, listening to the sermon and saying prayers mostly in English. Near the end of the service, the rabbi asked the congregation to rise for the Mourner's Kaddish, and the entire congregation began to recite the transliterated prayer in its original Aramaic. This was never the way any other congregations I knew had done the Kaddish—mourners always stood up while everyone else sat, and the sad ones read out the rhythmic words alone—but unconsciously I began to say the prayer along with everybody else. My father put his hand on my arm and said, "Hey, I'm not dead yet." I looked up at him in horror and embarrassment and sat down immediately. Two weeks and a day later, just after we had watched the *Gemini 5* astronauts splash down off the Bahamas, he died suddenly of a heart attack.

My father's death left us without a purpose. Throughout my childhood, his career and his orders determined where we would live and how long we would stay in a place. His ambitions for me defined my goals for school, and his curiosities drove us to the places we traveled on vacation. My mother always harbored her opinions and desires, and I think he never made decisions over her objections, but she largely gave herself over to his enthusiasms and dreams. She regarded his career as their common mission and his accomplishments as their collective triumph. Our Jewish life was defined by my father as well. He and my mother had constructed an idiosyncratic family culture in which we ate off separate plates for milk or meat meals and never ate pork or shellfish, but in Germany and Georgia we didn't buy kosher meat because none could be found within hours of our house. We celebrated Sabbath every Friday night and kept the holidays. It never would have occurred to us to ask for a Christmas tree or an Easter basket, but we were truly diasporic Jews. We knew little about how Jews lived in the enclaves of Cleveland, New York, Philadelphia, or Los Angeles. For my Cleveland cousins, most of their friends were Jews, and they attended a Hebrew day school. Rosh Hashanah and Chanukah and even Purim were actually school holidays for them. When my Reform cousins on my mother's side lived in Queens, they wore their Jewishness like a badge of urban identity, like being black or Italian. For us, however, being Jewish meant above all that we were unlike everybody else, save one or two stray families and an occasional GI. In the month before Christmas, any school I attended would be busy with holiday preparations I felt honor-bound to ignore. I remember one moment in fourth grade when the entire elementary school was arrayed on stage in rows to rehearse the final carol. I had refused to participate, so I sat in the audience and listened to all my friends and their brothers and sisters sing "Silent Night" to me alone. That Christmas Eve we drove down the snowy main road of the army post, and I looked at all the lights and realized nearly everyone around us was giving presents in honor of a god I didn't understand or accept. And now my father, who had kept us moving across the planet but anchored in his own insistent Jewish identity, could guide us no further.

But a different Judaism came rushing in to fill the void my father had left. My father's father and mother, my *zede* and *bubbi*, swept into our house as we were setting up for the seven days of mourning known as *shivah*. They were accompanied not only by my father's brother, Lou, and his family but also by strange Orthodox men brought in by distant

Goldblatt cousins we had barely met in DC. They came to mourn, a function my brother and I were clearly not considered qualified to perform, though they tolerated my mumbling the Mourner's Kaddish because I would turn thirteen five days after his death. My mother was invisible, and probably preferred to remain so rather than face them down. My father had left instructions that he was to be buried at Arlington, the national military cemetery in nearby Virginia, which holds the bodies of thousands of Jewish soldiers. But Zede insisted—no, he simply pronounced—that his son would be buried in an Orthodox cemetery and the army would have nothing to do with it. This was the Judaism my father had run away from, the one he could not prepare me for, but now his death invited all the stern commands and esoteric rituals into our lives.

Everyone, except Bubbi and Zede, ate from kosher deli platters that came wrapped in yellow cellophane. All the visitors talked in low tones, sitting on the miniature chairs provided by the funeral home because you are supposed to sit low to the ground during *shivah*. My mother's family and friends gathered round us and tried to set up a consoling mood for the mourning time. But no matter how much other people tried to comfort me, I found myself drawn to the Goldblatt side, to the side that shamed me for my lack of learning, my inarticulateness in the face of fervency and judgment. My father's parents ate only from food they had brought, on paper bags they spread out so that they wouldn't use my mother's plates or even commercial paper plates. The corned beef and pastrami came from Katz's Kosher Butcher, but no matter how kosher the caterer claimed to be, the meat might have touched cheese or a butter knife or some *treif* that a *goy*, a non-Jew, might have been eating in the shop, God forbid. The Orthodox mourners *davened* each afternoon and evening in our house that week, dipping and bowing in prayer, reading so fast in Hebrew that no one else could follow. All other visitors simply moved out of their way. I felt rejected and dismissed, confused about when to bow and when to stay still, when to sing aloud and when to remain silent. I wore my yarmulke like I was a guest in the House of the Lord, but they wore their little skullcaps like practiced professionals, like the recognized descendants of ancient *rebbes*. With every chanted word they uttered, I grew more determined that I would learn to pray like them, that I would earn the right to mourn my own father.

Two family members helped me emerge from this religious storm and find an entrance to the customs and texts that form Jewish literacy. The first was my mother's only sibling, Uncle Herb. I had always known my uncle as a quiet man, witty and kind in his home with Phyllis and his four kids, a salesman who followed his father into the export/import food business. Uncle Herb was very active in his Reform temple, and once they moved out of New York City to a small town on the Hudson, he became president of their congregation, but he was never a particularly religious man. Like my mother, he was primarily a person of this world: ethical and considered, skeptical of unexamined beliefs, loyal to family, and not inclined to judge quickly. He asked me to come to see him in his hotel room just before the funeral. We read the Mourner's Kaddish aloud together:

> *Mourner*: Magnified and sanctified be his great Name in the world which he hath created according to his will. May he establish his kingdom during your life and during your days, and during the life of all the house of Israel, even speedily and at a near time, and say ye, Amen.
>
> *Congregation and Mourner*: Let his great Name be blessed forever and to all eternity.
>
> *Mourner*: Blessed, praised and glorified, exalted, extolled and honored, magnified and lauded be the Name of the Holy One, blessed be he; though he be high above all the blessings and hymns, praises and consolations, which are uttered in the world; and say ye, Amen.
>
> May there be abundant peace from heaven, and life for us and all Israel; and say ye, Amen.
>
> He who maketh peace in his high places, may he make peace for us and for all Israel; and say ye, Amen.                                    (Hertz 399)

Then he asked me what I thought it meant. I had, in fact, never read the English before because I had always loved the sound of the Aramaic, a language closely related to Hebrew and heavily used in biblical and Talmudic literature. *"Yizgadal v'yiskadash shmai rabbaw"*—it felt so splendid in the mouth and conjured a stately procession of rabbis dressed in white, marching not toward a grave but toward a great eternal light. As with most Jewish prayers, the Kaddish in English seemed distant and dry, addressed to a God I could not reach. In other cases, I had ascribed my own private meanings to the convoluted and flowery

English in the translations I read idly during services, but this prayer had been almost entirely a matter of disembodied sound. I had, in fact, been afraid to read the English before because I had thought the Kaddish must mean something impossibly tragic, a secret message only mourners could hear. Now I was obligated to say the prayer every day for the next year and at least once a year for the rest of my life, joining those melancholy people who stood up at the end of services to say Kaddish alone. Herb was right to ask me what it meant, but I did not know how to answer him.

My uncle pointed out to me that the prayer never mentions death or the afterlife or pain. It did not refer to my father or anyone else who died. He showed me that the rabbi or cantor says almost the same prayer at other points in the service when mourning is not at all the purpose. Then he asked me to look more closely at the prayer. I began to see that it is primarily an elaborate, almost hyperbolic, praise song to a creator, an affirmation of creation, and a hope for future peace. He helped me think about the need to affirm life at this terrible juncture and to imagine a force behind life and death, "high above" the hymns and blessing "uttered in the world." I began to feel, if not comfort, at least a sense that I could imagine myself inside this prayer. His ideas, I later discovered, were not far from traditional readings of the prayer, but his words grew from the text we read together and the urgent need I had to hold myself upright in the midst of this bewildering religious onslaught. He didn't lecture me or harangue me with the language of God or how I ought to feel. He helped me see something larger in the words of a forbidding text and in a situation I could not control. It was my first lesson in reading poetry, and it was a consoling gift.

The second transforming conversation was more technical in character, but it also laid out a literacy path I could follow. The transformation began with gifts from my father's brother, Lou, although his long, rambling lectures to me were not the tutoring I needed at the time. He took me out to a Judaica shop and bought me my own *tallis*, or prayer shawl, and a daily prayer book. He bought me a set of *tefillin*, two small black leather boxes containing biblical texts written on parchment—one for the head and one for the arm, each with straps that need to be handled in a prescribed way—that one is supposed to wear during weekday morning prayer. I was grateful to my uncle for giving me what my father had not: the specialized equipment of prayer a thirteen-year-old is supposed to have as he or she joins the adult congregation. Lou also arranged to have me called up to sing the Hebrew blessing over the Torah before a reading on the Thursday following my father's death. The ceremony took place at a synagogue my father and I had settled on only the week before as a good possibility, a conservative shul with a sympathetic rabbi. This was a simple event, with only family and a small weekday gathering for morning prayer. My bar mitzvah—the bare minimum one should perform to achieve adult status in religious obligations—was over in a few minutes and a couple of mazel tovs.

When I received the gifts of *tefillin* and *tallis*, I was pleased and proud, but they also represented another challenge to my Jewishness. I had no idea how to put *tefillin* on, what to say, and when to say it. I didn't even know the proper way to drape the *tallis* over my shoulders. Uncle Lou assigned his son Bernie to teach me the techniques for prayer one afternoon before the bar mitzvah. Bernie, not quite a year older than I and more than a foot taller, had attended Cleveland's Hebrew Academy all his school life at that point. I admired his ease with Hebrew, with Torah and other revered texts, with the fine points of prayer, everything I did not know about the religion that had nonetheless marked me as different all my life. He and his brothers may have envied our secular life, but I could not see that at the time. He knew what I did not, and I needed to know enough to stand up to all those strangers in our house.

The poet Jerome Rothenberg edited a collection called *Technicians of the Sacred*, drawing on the shamans, priests, and holy men from a wide array of ancient traditions. Rothenberg's anthology attempts to recover religious texts for contemporary poetry, but most readers probably still see the strange holy words he collected as arcane, primitive, distant from the enlightened modern tradition. For all its centrality to Western thought, however, Judaism *is* arcane, even primitive, in its attempt to contain for a moment holiness that is otherwise not rendered in images and only tangentially connected to the daily suffering and joy of the human world. The Jewish God is not chummy or personal and may not even be characterized as paying attention to this world, despite all our troubles. For a thirteen-year-old boy, even one who has not lost his father in a strange new city, the technology of ritual can calm the sudden sense of the world as rudderless, impossibly complex, utterly arbitrary. Bernie gave me simple instructions on how to lay *tefillin* in the morning: one box on the forehead at the hairline, with a loop circling the head and straps hanging down the chest, the other box on the inner part of the upper left arm, pointing its texts to the heart, with straps wrapped seven times around the forearm and then wrapped in a pattern on the hand after the box on the head is in place and properly blessed. When wound correctly, the strap forms the Hebrew letters *shin, daled,* and *yod* on the hand, making the word *shadai,* a name for God that signifies one who created boundaries to the world. The instructions for laying *tefillin* are precise, and the procedure should not vary for the commandment to be fulfilled properly. I wanted to do everything as properly as possible. Bernie was patient, not condescending or patronizing, and in a couple of hours I had learned not only the basic steps but also what prayers I could say by myself and what I needed to say only in a *minyan,* a gathering of ten or more men and a Torah in the morning or evening.

I did not remember everything Bernie told me, but I followed his instructions the best I could most days for the next school year. Sometimes I went to *minyan* in the morning, and sometimes I lay *tefillin* by myself, not an encouraged practice because certain prayers shouldn't be said without a *minyan,* but many times I wanted to be alone. In the evenings I went to *minyan* in the synagogue up the street from the house we rented the year after Dad died. I felt it my duty to say Kaddish for my father, to prove that I could be the knowledgeable son I hadn't been before. As far as I remember, I never spoke to anyone at the *minyan,* and no one spoke to me. Usually there were only ten or fifteen men at any one time; most of them seemed very old, but some were probably middle-aged fathers on their way to or from work. My brother went with me a few times, but his anger at our Orthodox family was much greater than mine, and he soon stopped following me to shul. My mother, I found out much later, was furious at the synagogue because members there made no attempt to support me or even welcome our family to the congregation, even though she had joined so that I could attend Hebrew school. In fact, in her telling of the story, they were rude to her because no one quite knew what to do with a young widow and her children in their midst. She was never invited to join any synagogue functions, never invited to anyone's house. No one spoke to her except when she spoke first. But she held back her own feelings from me during that year because I had so dedicated myself to this path. She continued keeping a kosher kitchen, lighting candles on Friday nights, and celebrating holidays in our home long after I had stopped attending *minyan*. Much later she would say she kept kosher because of me, but the rituals were yet another way she found of keeping my father around us. She also secreted the family housekeeping money in my father's wallet, which she kept in the inside pocket of my father's uniform that hung in her closet till well after I left for college.

The year of mourning helped me through the transition to civilian life, but strict Jewish ritual couldn't sustain me for long because I made no lasting relationships in the process. I did make rather a fool of myself near the end of that year by volunteering to lead the youth service on a Saturday morning. I thought I knew the service well because of all my morning and evening prayer sessions. When I got up in front of thirty or forty kids and rabbis and teachers, however, I forgot words, blanked on tunes, misremembered the order of prayers, and generally made a mess of the service. I still couldn't read fluently, so when my memory gave out I couldn't easily refer to the prayer book. Like the time I botched the catching job on opening day of Little League three years before, I trusted my book learning and private repetitions but could not perform under pressure. People don't boo in synagogue, but I could feel their dismay and scorn. Despite my failures, I feel very little about the whole event in retrospect. I probably carried away no lasting shame because I knew so few people in the congregation. Except for one teacher in the Hebrew school, a thin little woman with a German accent and concentration camp numbers tattooed on her arm, I remember no one from that time. I made no friends in my Hebrew classes; I had been placed in a class with much younger kids because my language and religious background were not on grade level. I proved to myself that I could stick with religious study and prayer for that year, but when the year was over, I felt no attachment to the synagogue or formal Judaism. Nothing held me there except my will, and by ninth grade I had made friends in public school. Although many of these new friends were Jews—the neighborhood was predominantly Jewish—few were religious. By the following September, I had more or less slipped away from organized religion entirely.

Uncle Herb and Bernie gave me sustaining gifts. My mother's brother demonstrated an approach to meaning that is deeply embedded in context but careful in respect to text. The prayer he read with me could not have meant anything we wanted it to mean, and he carefully directed me to the words themselves (albeit English words translating an ancient language) for our discussion. But what we discussed had everything to do with the pain he and I were feeling, the gaping wound I would have to conceal as I stood up in the funeral and shivah services to mourn publicly. Meaning was borne up by love and born into it, but love was defined by a new meaning I was consciously constructing together with him. My mother later took this sustaining approach with me when I worked with her on my academic writing; it is crucial to my own teaching today.

I don't know where my mother and her brother learned to embrace literacy in this way. Neither of their parents went to college. My grandfather Max Kushner started work as a small child, the only healthy son in a large immigrant family from Lithuania, and built an export/import food business that actually made a little money during the Depression. But he never trusted anyone else, including his son, enough to expand his business beyond what he and a secretary could do. Max had little patience with other people's learning style and less respect for learning that had no practical value. Largely because of my grandfather's heavy demand for success, once my mother graduated high school at sixteen and left for college, she never returned home for a visit longer than a week till her own mother was in her seventies and dying of cancer. My grandmother Lillian was, as far as I could tell, a very kind soul who raised her children during the Depression and ordered domestic life for her overbearing husband. Wherever Herb and Selma got their attitudes, reading and writing mattered deeply to them, but this significance grew from specific human needs that literacy could satisfy within the web of relationships. They too were practical people, but ideas and emotions counted in their practical world.

Bernie's lesson was practical, but in a very different sense. First, he was my peer. Even though I looked up to him for his height and his specialized learning, he and I occupied the position of oldest son in our respective families. I knew there were things I knew that he did not. For one thing, I had always gone to school with girls. Even if I felt perfectly awkward around them, he had never even had a girl in his class till he managed to talk his father into letting him transfer to public high school as a junior. Yet I felt very much that he was training me in customs and techniques that I needed to know, letting me in on secret lore that would make me more prepared for an adult role. I was grateful to him, and his help solidified a bond I felt with him, but his brotherly tutelage also humanized the religious practices for me in a way that instruction from an august old rabbi would not have. I felt freer to modify and alter my practice as long as I paid attention to what others thought most essential. I never felt Bernie would disapprove of anything I did. I had plenty of other judgments to handle from my absent father and the image of my powerful little *zede* sitting in a straight-backed chair reading a very large book.

This sacred but technological approach to literacy taught me that one aspect of reading and writing—indeed, of all learning—involves just the brute work of maintaining a routine, following rituals even when I didn't quite know why, and allowing the meanings to become manifest in my life in inexpressible ways. Laying *tefillin* is one of the highest religious obligations in Orthodox practice, a mystical event each morning that binds head and heart to the divine presence, and yet it can also seem an obsessive repetition of meaningless motions involving leather boxes and straps and formulaic words. I wound the straps around my hand and arranged them on my head each day because they made me feel a part of a religion I associated with my father, even if he had run from this very form. I prayed to keep myself from feeling there was nothing to pray for.

I did not believe in God with any clarity, nor did I reject God because death had taken my father and deranged our lives. Neither blame nor logic offered me solace. Ritual did. My father and I had argued about God once at the dinner table. He had maintained that a religious Jew did not really have to believe in God at all because rituals and ethical commitments structured and motivated a good Jew's life. God, in his view, was a distant presence when it came to living righteously on Earth. I could not accept his argument at the time, couldn't even understand what he meant. Was it possible my grandfather with the black hat and long beard and tired eyes could pray as he did, keeping such strict religious laws, and yet not believe in God? But my year of attending *minyan* bore out what my father had insisted with such amusement at my outrage. Judaism was a matter of living the ethics of this world and fulfilling the *mitzvoth*, the laws and obligations of the Torah. God lay behind the words and deeds like warmth hides inside wool or wetness inside water. This is a literacy of action, both conscious and unconscious, that requires considerable devotion but rewards effort with an ineluctable sense of belonging. It could not last in my life in traditional form, but the habit of a literate routine larger than myself, one that ties me to others in a way I cannot fully express, this characterizes much about the way I write and read today.

The transition into a suburban school didn't start well. I began eighth grade only a week or so after my father died, and I hadn't even expected to attend that particular school because we'd planned to move to another neighborhood with my father. My future high school girlfriend Leah happened to be in my homeroom that year, and much later she told me a story about the first day, which I don't remember myself. I was sitting near the front as the teacher was calling all our names, and when he got to me he stopped and said, "Eli, I see you're new. Your records are mostly complete, but I don't have your father's occupation. What does he do for a living?" I burst into tears, something a boy should never do, especially on the first day in a new school. Certainly it wasn't his fault that nobody told him what had happened to our family. He treated me carefully the rest of the year, and I don't remember getting any flak from my fellow students. I do remember that later the same day I went to English class, and the boy sitting behind me was chuckling. I asked him what was so funny, and he told me he'd just seen a girl go into the boys' bathroom. We laughed together as the teacher started introductions. That guy became my first new friend.

I didn't know the etiquette, customs, or hidden knowledge of the suburbs. I never regained my place at the top of the class that I'd had in army schools and in fact never earned more than an A or two among the Bs and occasional Cs in high school. The kids in this school simply knew more about everything than I did, and I couldn't quite catch up. Junior high administrators started me in middle-level English classes but high-level science and math, I suppose because of my records in previous schools. But algebra turned into a disaster for me because my previous schools had been particularly poor in math. I was shocked in the early weeks to discover that there were numbers on the left side of zero. No one had ever mentioned the existence of negative numbers before! The whole concept frightened me because if I hadn't heard about number lines or absolute value, what else had my teachers neglected to tell me? Maybe they themselves hadn't known zero wasn't the beginning? Meanwhile, kids were making fun of me behind my back for my white socks and frumpy clothes, my military haircut and blocky glasses. I would come into science class, where I still felt some competence, to find a drawing of myself as an elephant or a hippopotamus or a frog, always wearing white socks and the wrong kind of shirt. In the end, the silly drawings probably helped me make friends because other kids in the class thought this treatment both juvenile and unfair, but at the time it mostly confused me. I would go home and tell my mother I needed new clothes, but she was as innocent of the codes as I was.

Kids in my eighth grade class were going to bar mitzvah parties, growing into the coed phase of suburban social expectations, while I joined a local Scout troop in an attempt to hold on to the boys' life I knew in the army. I arrived in Silver Spring as a Life Scout, only a few merit badges short of the highest rank of Eagle. At least this I knew how to do, and at first the Scout culture, which I had entered in Germany and pursued in Georgia and San Antonio when everything else seemed in disorder, felt familiar and comforting. I was among the older kids and held a higher rank than anybody else, so I began to be a leader in the troop. But without a dad, I didn't have much connection to the adults running the troop. I do remember one father, a writer for the *Washington Post*, who helped me on a campout once. I had just been named senior patrol leader and had the honor of camping by myself in a tent at the center of our site. We all played tackle football in the afternoon in a large cow pasture, and I had landed on my head during one big pileup. That night my head began to throb, and after midnight I went to the father's tent and told him I just couldn't stand the pain any longer. He was kindly, gave me some aspirin, and finally drove me home. The doctor said I had gotten a concussion in the game, but I felt I had let down my troop by not staying at my post.

The final break with Boy Scouts came when I finished all the badges necessary for Eagle. I phoned the scoutmaster to ask him what more I needed to do. We talked about my service project, and then he told me I needed a letter of recommendation from a minister. I said I was Jewish, and he said I could get a letter from my rabbi. But, I told him, I didn't have a rabbi because we didn't belong to a synagogue. This was the summer after I'd stopped going to the local shul, and I was feeling more and more unconnected to organized Judaism. The phone was silent for a moment. The scoutmaster finally said, "Son, you do believe in God, don't you?" I said that I guessed I was agnostic. I could tell this was not the answer he wanted to hear. He said, "You can't be an Eagle Scout if you don't believe in God. You'll need to write a letter testifying to your faith and get a letter from a rabbi to support you." I was devastated and frightened. Scouts had always been something, like baseball, that I could do with all the other kids, even if they were Christian. Now I was the wrong kind of Jewish, and if I couldn't prove my religious standing, I couldn't make this final rank.

My mother found a young Reform rabbi, newly arrived in town and not far out of rabbinical school, who agreed to talk to me about God and my beliefs. His parents and my mother's parents were friends; my mother had met him once when she was in college and he was a little boy. This rabbi invited me to his house, and we sat in his study. I liked his casual manner and his willingness to let me talk, even if I didn't know much about Judaism and didn't love my experience with synagogues. We talked for well over an hour, and by the end I felt I could say to the Scouts that I believed in God without falsifying my beliefs. He made me feel that my doubts and questions were well within the range of traditional Jewish thought and that Judaism didn't require a ringing and steadfast testimony to faith the way many Christians understood it. He ended up writing a beautiful letter of support to go along with my short statement to the Board of Review in my troop. But then, once I had finished the final service project required for the rank, the scoutmaster called to tell me that I had been turned down for Eagle because my project was not sufficiently large. No one had suggested before that the set of flowerbeds I spent all of August putting into my school's quadrangle did not fulfill the rank's requirements. I took this as a verdict on my crisis of faith and decided I could live with having been denied Eagle Scout because leaders in the troop thought I didn't believe in God sufficiently.

I was beginning to integrate into the new civilian and secular world. I stopped going to minyan after my eighth grade year, and I ended my years in the Scouts the fall of ninth grade. My political polarities were changing too, as the news came in about Vietnam. The army had conferred a service medal on my father after his death, and a general handed the box to me at the ceremony. He told me he'd help me apply to West Point if I ever decided to become an officer, and I entertained that idea as I entered into civilian life. Thus I came to Silver Spring a committed supporter of the army and a staunch anti-Communist. After all, I had visited East Berlin and knew how bad the Communists were, though in truth I had very little evidence to support my adamant positions. My friends from that time still remind me that I argued in the Current Events Club after school for the so-called domino theory in Southeast Asia—that if the United States didn't take a stand in Vietnam, then Cambodia, Thailand, and eventually India would fall to the Communists. This marked me as conservative compared to many of my new friends, some of whom were reading columns in the *Post* that actually questioned the government's judgment in Southeast Asia.

By ninth grade, my resolve to defend the military was wavering. I had become president of the Current Events Club but also a circumspect dove. When a boy named Henry in my class got into trouble—mostly with his mother, who was president of the PTA at the time—for selling Mao's *Little Red Book*, filled with memorable revolutionary quotations, I bought one of the first copies from him and proposed that we discuss the book in Current Events Club, which precipitated a sequence of events that landed Henry and Mao in the county paper and the *Post*. I imagined myself having terrible fights with my father about the need to pull out of Vietnam, but on the other hand, I hoped that he would have returned from the fighting and agreed with my friends and me that this was a wrongheaded war. He had wanted to go to Vietnam in the very early stages to help wounded soldiers avoid disfigurement. I wondered what he would have seen in that bloody mess we saw over dinner every night on TV. I worried that I was betraying him, but my mother seemed to be on the side of the growing peace movement. I wouldn't have told her so at the time, but she gave me the courage to listen to those becoming more and more critical of the government.

In tenth grade, I wanted to define myself as I entered Montgomery Blair High School, where my sophomore class included more than seven hundred students. I tried out for wrestling, the only sport that gave a small guy a chance to compete with others his size. For two years, I trained with a fervor more obsessive than spiritual. The arcane language of moves and feints, the rituals of the locker room, and the elaborate customs surrounding "pulling" weight all bound us to each other in a brotherhood of self-inflicted pain. My first year, I started the season at a slight 108 pounds, having lost my childhood chubbiness in what passed for a growth spurt. I wrestled on the varsity because I could make weight at 96 pounds and still beat the one other guy who could also make that weight. We worked out in a heated practice room cranked up above ninety degrees, often wearing rubber suits over our full sweat clothes, doing endless push-ups and leg lifts in preparation for drills on take-downs and switches and rolls. Our two-hour practices culminated once a week in scrimmage matches that would determine the varsity lineup for the next match. At night, those of us holding or cutting weight allowed ourselves a little meat and vegetables, monitoring our calorie intake like models before a beauty pageant. This was ritual stripped of any pretension of mysticism, but boys will find meaning even among spit rags, sweat-drenched tights, and discarded headgear. I certainly did, even if that meaning made me slack-jawed with the loneliness my father had left in me. We admired the quick and the strong, derided the weak as "fish" or worse, and mostly kept our worries to ourselves. After a match, for one glorious day, we could eat ice cream.

I appreciated the camaraderie because the collection of guys, mostly working-class and only a few on the academic track, reminded me of kids I knew in the army. Every guy had a story, a myth that grew up around his behavior or bearing. Tommy, for instance, was a captain of the team. He wrestled at 115, down from about 135 pounds the rest of the year, and he would lovingly describe to us his rituals for eating so that tiny portions seemed bigger. We all admired him—especially us smaller guys—because of his quickness and incredible stamina, his winning record, and his knowing half-smile as he pranced on the mat to meet an opponent. He joined the navy after graduation, a year ahead of me, but was given a medical discharge later because he'd damaged his kidneys losing weight. Another older teammate, Fran, who was a star in football and had good grades, went to the Naval Academy, and I imagine he served in Vietnam. I don't know what happened to Bonner, who would turn to me as we dressed for a match and ask if I thought it would affect his strength that he screwed his girl the night before. One especially mythic character, a black/Asian guy who quit the team and graduated before I arrived but had a reputation for brilliant moves, came back once to hang with us. Later we heard he'd sped through business school and become a stockbroker out West, working in an office by day and living in a cave in the Rockies by night. Despite the pain of sweating off that last pound to make weight, I loved being one among this band of characters, my hedge against the suburban scene that was fast becoming my world.

In my school life, I worked my way into upper-track courses, particularly in English, and the kids in these classes had come to accept me as one of them. I had never been around so many peers who felt confident in school, who cared about their grades, and who came from families where both parents went to college. They talked about college themselves, but they also talked about politics—especially the war that was threatening all of us draftable boys. My friends and I protested the war with increasing vehemence from 1967 till 1970, when we graduated, but we didn't notice who in our own grade was headed to the service and who was slated for college and automatic draft deferments. We questioned school hall passes and dress codes and smoking bans, but we didn't ask why some got expelled and others got scholastic honors. We asked why our teachers went on strike for better wages and why we read old books when new books were coming out all the time, but we didn't ask why black kids just across the line in DC had no books at all. We didn't ask why in our school—with perhaps 15 percent of the population African American—few black kids placed into upper-track classes. We accepted that girls could excel in science (I lived in terror of Mrs. Abramson, the fierce chemistry teacher who brooked no fools, and most of the leading science students in my grade were female), but we didn't notice that all the doctors and scientists on TV were men. In fact, I had never heard of a female doctor among my father's colleagues and remembered only a single woman officer.

Like all of my peers, I saw what I saw and missed what disappeared behind our privileges.

My academic friends had little to do with sports and few of them went to games or matches, but they found me a curiosity, one of their own in the jock camp. I didn't tell them I wasn't comfortable enclosed in the high-track world, that I enjoyed having friends among wrestlers and the occasional football player who wrestled on the off-season. I even got to know some of the basketball players, who showered with us at the end of winter practices, their long, tall bodies—mostly African American in contrast to our mostly white team—such a contrast to us squat fellows built close to the ground. We busted on them about how easy their practices were, how wind sprints were their toughest challenge and even those were run in a cool seventy degrees. They took it with great humor, knowing the loudest of us couldn't dribble a ball and sprint at the same time. When the basketball team won the state championship and the national anthem came on over the loud-speaker at the University of Maryland gym, I was moved to tears just as I had been on still evenings in Germany when taps was played and the flag came down. My friends in the antiwar movement and those who worked on the literary magazine wouldn't have understood why I cried. I hardly knew myself.

My mother attended one of my early matches and never came to another. I was winning, but that didn't mattered to her. I had lost all that weight and was probably irritable and withdrawn at home, and I'm sure she expected me to be injured any moment. She never much cared for sports, and I'm sure for her a wrestling match just looked like two underfed boys straining to tear each other's heads off. She probably couldn't accept that I wanted to be an athlete—a little too Christian and middle American for her taste—and saw little value in my spending time sweating, lifting, and running, especially when I didn't seem any happier for it. Still, she never told me I couldn't stay on the team, even when our family doctor declared I was the only case of malnutrition he'd ever seen in his practice. I knew she disapproved, but I had to wrestle for reasons I couldn't explain to her or myself. She let me go along and focused her attention on my academic work. My grades weren't what they had been in elementary school, but she never hinted that my grade point average worried her. She was interested in something inside or underneath the academics, not the shiny surface of school, and she transmitted her attitude to me with a calm love that sometimes unnerved me, sometimes infuriated me, but kept me steady nonetheless. She cared most about consistent attention to the task at hand and a deep ambition for intellectual engagement in the service of social need. She was a much more effective coach than I ever encountered in any sport. She was, in fact, my best writing teacher.

My mother made an agreement with me in high school. She was an excellent typist, and she offered to type exactly what I wrote out longhand for any paper. However, she reserved the right to read as she typed and critique my drafts. Every element of grammar, perspective, analysis, and rhetorical style fell under her critical eye. She would hand me back a draft with little check marks in the margins, and we would go through the entire paper line by line. She never rewrote anything, although she would sometimes show me how a sentence could be less repetitive or worded more economically. Mostly she would identify the conceptual or argumentative difficulties I was getting myself into. She challenged broad assertions and demanded evidence for every point. She taught grammar not by rule but by effect, indicating the confusion a particular error could cause. She taught me parallel structure, sentence variation, how to modulate tone in an argument, when to use an apt unusual word and when to choose simplicity. She was crafty about what readers expected and brilliant at mining a quote for its essence, but she never lectured or preached abstract principles. She led me to discoveries through sharp questioning and considered any claim I made that sounded remotely promising. Above all, she took my ideas seriously and held me responsible for what I said I thought.

Her criticism might have seemed brutal to an outsider, but I never doubted her respect for me. Sometimes we would work together till two in the morning; I would scribble inserts and notes in response to her critique, and she would type and retype through three or four drafts when I had hoped one would do. She would sit at the kitchen table and read what I'd written, chewing on her thumb and stopping now and then to make her little marks. While my siblings slept, I would busy myself with a *Time* article or reread *New Yorker* cartoons in the bathroom, nervously waiting for her verdict, knowing that she wouldn't let that point in the third paragraph pass for an adequate counterargument. I'm not sure why I didn't storm off and type the damn things myself, but I think her close attention comforted me. Our sessions were intimate but not personal, absorbing but not smothering, political but not public. In short, these conversations about writing offered a teenage boy a relatively safe way to remain connected to his widowed mother. She was teaching me to think but not what to think. Her approval meant more to me than approval from even my favorite teachers; I wanted so much to write a paper that would simply wipe away all her frowns and worries. I knew I had revised successfully when I came back for her critique and her nostrils were flaring over a barely concealed smile.

About this time, I began to have teachers in English who challenged me by opening up a complex literary world that contained familiar quandaries in strange terrain. Mr. Ganz, a big man who would occasionally go on crash diets consisting exclusively of eggs and steak, taught the standard tenth grade fare of *Lord of the Flies* and *Grapes of Wrath* with great compassion and a talent for reading aloud. While I was slowly performing my way out of upper-level math courses, Mr. Ganz was recommending me for the English high track of Mrs. Miller's eleventh grade American literature class. Mrs. Miller seemed old and frightening, though I expect she was merely in her late forties. She constantly played with her big bead necklaces while she talked, lecturing as though she were in direct spiritual contact with the dead author at hand. She had us read a rigorous curriculum from the Puritans to Arthur Miller, with a lingering unit on Faulkner, about whom she had written the MA thesis that sat prominently on her desk. Occasionally she would seem to recognize that she had wandered too far across the room from her thesis, and she would fly back to it and lay her hand on the bound volume for solace and strength. She once dramatized to us her struggles with writing her opus: in one corner of the room she sat scribbling by herself, then she stomped over to another corner to expatiate on her burning ideas to her unblinking husband, and when he simply told her to go write what she'd said, she stomped back to her writing desk and scribbled again.

Through the literary magazine I met the elder of English at Blair High School, Mrs. Wubnig. If Mrs. Miller's histrionics challenged us to engage in the difficulties of American prose, Mrs. Wubnig's calmer but fiercer intelligence modeled for us an inquiring life among texts. More regal than her colleague, she initiated upper-track English students in tenth grade, when I was not yet judged to belong among the smart set, and each year she named all her honor sophomores by the characters she assigned them to play in their reading of the *Iliad*. She was not convinced about me—after all, I hadn't received a Greek name from her, I engaged in sports and politics, and I sometimes misspelled or misused words—but she approved my election to editor of the literary magazine in my senior year, after I had resigned from the wrestling team. She allowed me into her senior AP English class, where we read *Macbeth* and Dostoyevsky and, most important for me, Kafka. My inability to follow the logic of "electron filling" in Mrs. Abramson's eleventh grade chemistry class marked the end of my school science career, and my failure to grasp the definition of a "function" discouraged me from trigonometry and graphing, but English teachers accepted me among the chosen, even if I wasn't one of the chosen of the chosen. Mrs. Johnson let me take her drama class and write plays instead of act as my main contribution. My history teacher, Mrs. Ellowitz, recognized I was bored with the usual textbook and gave me an independent study on economic and social theory. For the first time in my school life since Mr. Irvine, teachers' personalities mattered to me almost as much as the personalities of my friends.

Indeed, my friends were the most vital reason for going to school. I was driven by a need to know people and be known by them. Except for a girl I was sweet on in tenth grade, who left suddenly for Virginia, and two sisters, close friends who lived down the street but moved with great sorrow to Pittsburgh in our senior year, nearly all the kids I knew when I entered high school remained until graduation. No one dropped out, no one died, no one moved away. Most of my friends had known other students since elementary school. People not only stayed in one place in this neighborhood but also regarded the arrival or departure of a student as an unusual event. They never quite got over the one kid who moved to Maryland from Muncie, Indiana, nicknaming him Muncie till the day we graduated. I loved having friends for more than a year, and yet I was haunted by the idea that because no one knew my past, no one could know me; my acceptance in this social network was at best a happy fantasy that could end in a moment. I hadn't earned my place by birth or longevity or exceptional talent. Perhaps that was why I felt so compelled to make every friend I could and start ambitious projects that brought together people of different backgrounds, races, and classes.

My brother joined the national antiwar movement, hitchhiking to meetings with Trotskyites and student radicals when he was twelve. Not much later he started smoking and then began experimenting with drugs. I thought he was very cool in a way I could never be—after all, he could grow a ponytail while my hair just curled wildly around my head—still, we didn't have much in common at the time. My sister was still the precious little girl of my father's vision—her room and nearly everything in it was pink—but I knew she missed her daddy in a way that passed consciousness. Sometimes she would cry that she missed a boy named "Danny" from kindergarten, and even in my unsophisticated state I knew she was calling for her father. My mother had started a career in the federal Health, Education, and Welfare Department (what is now Health and Human Services) and came home every night with stories of some hope and more frustration, especially once the Nixon administration came in with its hostility toward health programs started by the Democrats. I recognized, through my teenage haze, that she lived with a terrifying loneliness that dwarfed my own.

I felt responsible for my mother and siblings but could do very little for them. I ran from unspoken and imagined obligations by plunging into intense activity. Most of these commitments involved writing, looking outward and inward. My outward and public writing life developed through student politics. In the spring of 1969, my junior year, an older student named Mark Stein called me at home. Mark was president of the student government in my high school as well as the president of the state student association. I barely knew him through a tutoring program I started for the school's honor society, but he had somehow decided that I should run for the presidency of the Montgomery County student government. One of Mark's conservative rivals at another school had put up a novice with his political perspective for the office, and Mark needed a junior liberal candidate to oppose him. Mark and his faculty advisor, Mr. Michaelson, known affectionately by everyone as Mr. Mike, gave me a two-week crash course in the politics of the county school system, the issues that activists fought over, and the allies and enemies in the organization. I wore a coat and tie to a meeting with student representatives from all the county's high schools, shook hands and smiled, made a speech that felt like I was talking into a vacuum cleaner, and garnered polite applause. My few jokes made no sense because I didn't know the audience, while my opponent stuck to his script and presented a stolid but dependable persona. I lost by a few votes.

This whirlwind election initiated me into a world of school, county, state, and national student politics that was intoxicating and absorbing. Montgomery County released a policy statement in August 1969 called "Student Involvement in the Educational Process" that opened the door to far more student engagement than ever before in program development and school policies. The following academic year, therefore, was an incredibly productive time for students to propose changes in student life issues, offer suggestions for pilot programs, and voice objections to outmoded curricula. Sparked by a block of innovative proposals written by a single high school student, a senior named Chuck Kiefer, a number of us joined together to pass progressive legislation for the county student government to present to the school board. At Mark's urging, I also chaired a statewide committee focused on the issue of race relations in school, promoting what was then called "Black Studies." I never won a student government election, but I got a reputation for being a good student politician, probably mostly for my enthusiasm. After a state convention where I delivered a report on race-related courses, I was quoted in the *Baltimore Sun* as saying, "I really love this. I don't know when I'll be able to do it again unless I go into politics" ("Politics"). I suppose I was contemplating a career in politics because I was fascinated by the complexity of crafting legislation and the intrigue of parliamentary maneuvering, all for the sake of good causes but often perpetuated by their own heady momentum. My mother had written about race relations in her master's thesis in 1949, and for the first time I could see why such a study might matter. I felt I could actually do something about problems that were causing the cities to burn. I can't say I knew much about the reforms I advocated so fervently—I had not, for instance, actually visited areas of DC destroyed in the April 1968 riots, though 1,200 buildings burned not ten miles from my house—but I felt I was on the right side.

At that time, a more radical contingent of students was challenging the system from the outside. Norman Solomon, now a well-known progressive commentator and media critic, was then a Blair High School student with a big head of Jewish hair and a signature army jacket. Norman caused a tremendous stir in 1967 or early 1968 with the publication of a scathing critique of the county school system. He testified in front of the school board and demonstrated the schools' effect on students by squashing tomatoes in his fists at the board's witness desk. I admired Norman tremendously, though he was older enough that I saw him only at meetings and never actually met him. I marveled at the impact his radical position had on the system. His work was probably a major impetus for the county's new policy on student involvement, and most of the legislation from student government in the following years represented a fleshed-out and domesticated version of ideas Norman had originally raised. Because of Norman, more moderate students were granted the right to testify before the school board with recommendations for reform.

Left-leaning kids in our school established the Student Organizing Committee (SOC) and began questioning all kinds of pedagogical practices, calling for larger blocks of time for classes, more politically engaged courses, and of course an end to the war. Many of my friends joined SOC, but I couldn't bring myself to leave the more sanctioned politics of student government. I continued to raise issues within the system and to be influenced by those who stood outside. Unlike most parents of the time, my mother wouldn't have objected to my taking a more oppositional stance—she never stopped Aaron when he took up radical politics at a much earlier age—but perhaps my father's army devotion to duty held me inside the system, "fighting the Establishment from within," as some called it. I wanted to be more revolutionary in 1969, but I wasn't convinced that agitating was any more effective than legislating. I figured we needed both, and I felt more comfortable (guilty, but not ashamed) standing up on the Left and yet still in the system. My father might have approved of my hope to position myself IN the system but not exactly OF it.

At the same time I was pursuing politics with a fury at school, I led a regular suburban high school life. My friends knew me as a rather sunny boy—always willing to jump into another project, always ready to talk to a friend about personal problems or political turmoil. When we weren't arguing about politics, my more conservative friend Jeremy and I spent hours poring over the school phone book, discussing girls we wanted to date but were afraid to call. Some friends were apparently smoking pot, but I managed not to notice; if I had known what they were doing, I probably would have been too scared to try it myself. I went out on dates to movies like *Easy Rider* and *Butch Cassidy and the Sundance Kid*. I even saw *Barbarella* with Jeremy and our gruff friend Earl on a night we all wore our high school letter jackets to the risqué show. My family and I watched *Star Trek* and the *Smothers Brothers Comedy Hour* before they were canceled, *Laugh-In* and *Mission: Impossible*, even an occasional *Ed Sullivan Show* on Sunday night. Friends threw serious parties where we talked about art and war and relationships or danced to the Four Tops and the Temptations and the drum solo of "In-A-Gadda-Da-Vida." I remember my first girlfriend, Cindy, singing "Dona, Dona" and strumming guitar at one of her house parties.

Away from my high school routine, however, my inward struggles grew with greater fury. My mother knew that I took long walks alone at night and fought hard to hold back constant waves of despair. She finally took me to a therapist after a wrestling practice when I couldn't stop crying and had to leave before my teammates noticed. The therapist—I'll call him Dr. Kaufman—was a classic psychoanalyst of considerable reputation in the city. His office was dark, one wall fully lined with books, his desk decorated with arcane figurines straight out of Freud's Vienna. He was a baldheaded older Jewish man with a tic in his right eye; he smoked a cigar through our sessions and sometimes fell asleep as I lay on the couch and he sat in his easy chair behind me. He seldom said more than "What d'ya figure?" and wouldn't respond to questions. I gathered from reading Freud on my own that an analyst was supposed to remain silent and that I should talk about my dreams and my childhood. Sometimes I would drift into dream myself during a session, thinking that speaking directly out of my unconscious would somehow reveal the secret of my condition.

Kaufman never asked me how I felt about my father dying or my mother carrying the weight of the family by herself. He remained mute on the subject of girls, family problems, and concerns about college. I left his office each week lonelier than when I arrived. I took two buses to get to Kaufman's office once a week (more sessions at the holidays and summers, fewer during wrestling season) for most of my high school years, but I managed to keep my friends from knowing about my therapy. Seeing Kaufman seemed shameful and best kept private. My secret psychoanalysis would have been great comedy—his snoring as the soundtrack to my somnolent monologues—if it hadn't been such a wasted opportunity. Here was a place I could have mourned, without a Hebrew test or risk of public exposure. He might have been an older man I could confide in, but instead every session he impersonated the absent, inaccessible father. In fact, literacy again became a requirement for this mockery of mourning because I had to undertake a research project just to clarify what I was supposed to do in Kaufman's sessions, why his office was furnished as it was, even why he smoked a cigar. My mother realized he was doing me no good but could think of no alternative. When Kaufman called my mother to keep me from going away to school after I graduated because he "couldn't vouch for my safety," she finally told him off. A few years later, he called to ask her on a date, and she hung up on him. She didn't share any of this with me till I was in my thirties. For both of us, it was a great relief to be done with Kaufman.

I started writing for myself around 1967, my first year of high school. I wrote a verse of a song after I kissed a girl on a date for the first time, but that journal has disappeared. I do still have a notebook I kept for Mr. Ganz in the spring of 1968. I don't know where he came up with the assignment. It wasn't common in the school to require a journal, but he may have been following a progressive teaching trend of the time. The entries in my journal are mostly about death and too-clever conceits framed in vaguely Shakespearean language—

> Death is but a sleeping life
> For those who are beloved
> But if you die
> From memory's eye
> Then death . . . is Death

—or teenage science fiction about life on Earth being a training ground for the children of a wiser culture, with death as the graduation point for a soul that has learned its proper lessons and can go on for higher education. Ganz's written comments are spare and mostly pure support ("good—Real good!") but also sometimes truly personal. After an entry about how the place where I least felt like crying was at the graveside of my father, Ganz wrote in the margin: "I have somewhat the same problem. When I go now, I usually go alone. At first I thought that people expected me to do a particular thing and this made me more uneasy. Alone I can do whatever I wish—read, think, remember, etc.—and make the 'visit' more natural." I find his note so touching now. Rather than talk directly about his own loss or try to pry into mine, he simply wrote in solidarity, as one who also visited a loved one's grave. I don't remember ever having a personal conversation with him, but I did feel that he cared to understand me, and in a very understated way he encouraged me to write. I don't know that he saw me as a potential writer, but he certainly recognized I was pretty raw inside. His end comment on that early section of the journal reads: "Eli—I appreciate very much your sincerity and honesty. This has all been a great help to me. I hope that this journal affords you some therapy." I don't believe he was being condescending by presenting the journal as a way I could help HIM to understand me. I suspect that, like many young writers, I did not want my work thought of as therapy but hoped to have my little notes appreciated for their stunning insights and imaginative leaps. Writers in the beginning often seek legitimacy for their feelings, and literary recognition appears to confer legitimacy better than therapy does. Given my experience with therapy at the time, I would not have been anxious for another dose of that medicine. But I knew Ganz meant well, and I continue to feel grateful for his kindness.

The journal went on into April, when there is a poem in response to Martin Luther King's assassination:

> And then a fiery spark appears
> A bullet or a man
> The people wake from conscious sleep
> The Dreams are gone, the truth comes out
> Depression, riot, war.

In June, I jotted down another poem, for Bobby Kennedy's assassination. No mention in spring of 1968 of the student protests in Paris or Madrid or Columbia University, nothing about the Black Panthers or the Prague Spring. Ganz's last comment was probably in late April, and after that I was writing for myself. The entries that summer get breathless and uncontained about my frustrations with my mother and my own teenage unhappiness, but only a few entries could be called personal. Increasingly, my entries include observations about the police and bus riders, little drawings of fanciful people and everyday objects, as well as notes for student activities. One entry, titled derisively "An Official Scouting Assignment," lists five reasons why people believe in God—mostly cast in an anthropological tone—and four arguments against belief in a supreme deity. A few brief ideas and longer sketches for poems, stories, and plays appear; two of these became pieces I published in the school magazine. The last entries are notes from the early days of eleventh grade chemistry and Mrs. Miller's impassioned lecture on *Paradise Lost* to begin junior English. I seem not to have kept a journal again till the first year of college, when I started a regular habit that has continued for over forty years, but perhaps in making these first entries I was finally beginning to mourn my own way.

## 3

## Into the Daedalean Dreamscape

MR. GANZ WAS THE high school defensive line football coach. Despite his lineman size, he was a gentle man who loved the literature he taught us in tenth grade English. During a teachers' strike, he and the quarterback coach (also an English teacher) held a class for their students in a recreation center down in the park. They handed out the words to songs by Bob Dylan and Paul Simon, played us the songs, and then asked us to consider the texts as poetry. This was a bit of transparent "relevance," but I admired Mr. Ganz enough to go along with subjecting our music to school scrutiny. After all, the class was off school property and the picket line rendered the proceedings unofficial, almost secret. We started with Dylan's "It's Alright, Ma (I'm Only Bleeding)":

> Darkness at the break of noon
> Shadows even the silver spoon
> The handmade blade, the child's balloon
> Eclipses both the sun and moon
> To understand you know too soon
> There is no sense in trying

Mr. Ganz led us from "born with a silver spoon in his mouth" into a landscape of privilege and apocalypse. I didn't want Dylan songs to have defined meanings, and I would have resisted, but here was a possible way to think about words without shutting them up in my father's surgical logic or my mother's sensible compassion. Poetry could mean by what it did not say or by what was supplied by the readers or could be generated new on the spot. It could be mysterious, even inexplicable, yet not as closed-lipped as a Hebrew text with no translation. Later we marked the strong and weak stresses in Simon's "The Dangling Conversation": "And I only kiss your shadow, / I cannot feel your hand." Suddenly the songs I'd listened to over and over in my darkened bedroom had structure, a spine of stress and release, a rhythmic edge even without the music.

In my journal for Ganz, I wrote a few short, vaguely surrealistic stories. I sent a piece about an eye in a Dali landscape to the school literary magazine and had it promptly rejected, but submitting my work for publication stirred me as much as it terrified me. I joined the staff of the magazine the next year and began to witness how others read submitted work: writing could be performance and experience for readers rather than expression for a private self. I wrote a choreographed dramatic poem about an Adam with no Eve, and this was published in the magazine. In my senior year, I wrote a Theater of the Absurd play about race and gender relations on a bus, and it was staged before a school audience. As I sat in the auditorium waiting for the curtain to go up, I began cursing in a very loud whisper out of fear that the entire crowd would stand up in disgust and walk out. In front of me, a boy with his arm around his girlfriend turned and told me to shut up, that there were females present. The play ended and they called for the author to bow, and I felt vindicated, freed, guilty for my little triumph.

Even though I was the editor of the literary magazine my senior year, I never felt literary enough. Others knew about Cezanne and Kandinsky, had read T. S. Eliot and Dylan Thomas, could make allusions to Christian rituals or English kings. They wrote denser, more mysterious poems while mine seemed muddy with politics and my own dread. Invariably I found myself smoothing over arguments and making sure the younger editors felt included, and then I would get angry at myself for being dutiful like my mother rather than eccentric like my friends. Henry, for example, the originator of the kerfuffle over Mao in junior high, continued to be a leader among us for his intellectual curiosity and independent reading habits. A baby-faced boy with tortoiseshell frames around quizzical eyes—often with one eyebrow raised by something innocent I'd said—Henry could be intimidating as well as amusing on paper. He sent me a long letter using Freud and Faulkner to analyze a dream he'd had in which a "woman gave a luxurious dinner party, replete with a marvelous and original cream sauce. Then some Fullabrush-type priests came to the door and put little Eucharistic croutons for everyone in the cream sauce." Amy wrote brief poems about distorted images and fate, and Tammy composed an angry elegy she read at our first Moratorium service against the Vietnam War in 1969. Almost every poem Ellie submitted we published; he was clever, used spaces and line breaks inventively, and alluded to e. e. cummings, the Kama Sutra, Zen, and the Catholic mass. Ana, a Cuban American girl who edited the art section of the magazine, painted expressive lines with a careless gesture. One day she took me through a gallery downtown, stationed me in front of one canvas, and commanded me to look at the PAINT rather than blather on about what the "picture" represented. In comparison to all of them, I felt clumsy, overserious, naive. I was an immigrant from a khaki country, where colors carried only heraldic meaning, awe attached to bombs, and wonder distracted from the mission. The junior editors liked me because I was kind to them, and the seniors were my friends for reasons I didn't quite understand, but I considered myself undereducated and a bit obtuse compared to those who'd been in good civilian school all their lives. I was ashamed that my greatest contribution to our literary efforts seemed to be keeping a rambunctious staff on task without factional warfare.

The arts drew me, but I couldn't help but be pulled into student politics as well. I hated domesticating the passionate call for Revolution within a language that principals and board members could accept from dutiful, college-bound students. The radical politics of Norman Solomon and Student Alliance kept calling to me, mocking my good-boy positions. I helped organize a march against the War during one of the Moratorium days—six hundred students walked out of the school and down 16th Street to the Capitol—but all the while I feared someone would smash a window or throw a rock at the police. I never felt radical enough but couldn't take more extreme action, whatever that might be. Once I was invited to a meeting in a house somewhere in the heart of a wealthy suburb. The speaker—a white, college-aged guy with a goatee—harangued a handful of white high schoolers to join the White Panthers and "subjugate yourselves to the Black Panther Party." His rap appealed to me, but I didn't see how the White Panthers would help the black student leaders I had met from the District. They needed schoolbooks, their buildings were falling down, their friends were dropping out. Sure, I wanted to respond to the riots in DC, but I didn't see how my following this goatee would change anything. And he scared me.

In my senior year, I didn't go out for wrestling. I was sick of cutting weight; the hunger made me want to bite wallpaper. I'd run a friend up against a locker the previous year for the crime of plucking a pen out of my writing hand when I hadn't eaten for twenty-four hours. Lifting weights in my basement had been a clandestine pleasure, but I could never make up for my height with extra bench presses. Still, the practices, the holds, the heat stayed with me. I remember reading Kafka's "A Hunger Artist" to my brother as we rode on the train to visit our grandparents in New York City. He fell asleep, but I felt for the first time I had truly entered into one of the books we were reading in school. Kafka wrote about the meaningless extremes that haunted me, passion in the face of institutional indifference. I don't know if I consciously recognized him as Jewish, but the strange world Kafka described felt far more familiar than Faulkner's Yoknapatawpha County. Part of me felt I had betrayed my teammates by walking away from wrestling, but writing represented a more urgent struggle for me.

I shut off in a private preserve the anxieties about my father's death and my own right to survive him. Kaufman policed that preserve, though his somnolent psychoanalysis never fully dominated what it sought to contain. Writing grew to rival analysis, to be both the terrain I needed to map and the act of cartography itself. Already I had developed a split in my life. On one side I wished to close the door and write, a desire I followed but feared as selfish, unproductive, dangerous. On the other, I needed to be involved with politics, social issues, and people, a commitment I accepted but doubted because it led me to be too public, optimistic, wordy. Despite my wish to be a brooding intellectual, I couldn't turn away from a lively conversation or an ambitious social project, and I talked myself silly when I knew I should be reading and writing silently. When I walked alone at night through the suburban neighborhood where we lived, my activities all seemed frenetic and beside the point. These neat brick and siding homes on winding drives, what did they amount to? What did my nicely sanctioned student government maneuvers do to stop the War or end racism, as our buttons called for? My literary friends were reading French, and I was writing committee reports. Was I not dedicated enough to stand apart and write poems?

This doubt about my intellectual commitment intensified during the college application process. I went with my mother to visit various eastern colleges, the ones my friends in the advanced placement courses were applying to. I fell in love with Wesleyan because I saw it as a utopia: small, intense, politically engaged. On the application I wrote:

> I believe that the individual should work on and study the things that interest him most while constantly thinking of ways to use his skills and interests to benefit his community. I think that at the same time the community should not discourage or look down on activities just because it is not interested in such activities. . . . Each person can contribute to the campus community, but the campus community should also contribute to the person.

College was to be a place where I could pursue public action, and in exchange I would be supported in my writing even if that private, selfish act seemed shameful to others—or to myself. If the school were prestigious enough, then its reputation would consecrate my literary ambitions. Moreover, a college campus seemed a richer version of the army posts I had known, where you could bowl for a quarter a game and watch a movie for fifteen cents. College had none of the guns or marching orders so anathema to the generation and social class I had adopted as my own since my father died. I told Wesleyan that I wanted to go into writing, politics, or teaching (in that order) and that the sense of community I had felt on a visit there made it my first choice. I ended my application with this plea: "Please believe that what I have said is not (if you'll excuse the expression) bull, that I really want to go to Wesleyan and that I really believe I can make my best contribution there." The begging tone worried my mother, but I thought sincerity would win the day.

Wesleyan rejected me, as did all the other prestigious schools I applied to. A few safety schools accepted me, perfectly fine schools, but I didn't want to go to any of them. They were too close to home or too large, but most of all they did not have the reputations that would validate my longings. My high school class had been filled with overachievers—including many of my friends—who were going to places with names that justified themselves; my grades and SATs had been just enough less impressive that I didn't make the cut. The four years of learning how to be a civilian fell away, and I felt the same sense of exclusion, the same verdict of social and intellectual incompetence, as I had when I entered the suburban system and kids laughed at my white socks, army crew cut, and insufficient math. I was devastated by the thought that I had played the "well-rounded student" game with all the sincerity and verve of my middle-class peers, but I'd been turned away like a buck private barred from the Officers' Club. The disaffected attitude of late 1960s radicalism hadn't prepared me for rejection by prestigious schools.

Soon after the college rejections, two friends told me they had received letters from a midwestern liberal arts college they had turned down for better offers. Beloit College still had openings and asked successful applicants to tell their friends about the school. Beloit was small and far from home; I decided to visit and flew out to see the campus by myself. The school set up a stay for me in the dorm room of a fellow who was away fighting a court battle after burning his draft card, and I thought that was noble on the radical scale. The campus was four blocks long; the buildings had ivy on them. I walked through the empty campus (students were on spring break) feeling finally free to make this decision rather than wait for the judgment of distant arbiters of intellectual value. The admissions officer, a comfortable big man with a brown mustache, assured me I'd be accepted immediately. The college offered an unusual twist to its program that sounded like the school my mother had attended in the 1940s, Antioch College. First-year students went three full semesters—through the summer—and then arranged their academic terms, vacations, and a required work term off-campus during the middle years of school. It gave me choices about when and where to study, and it was far from my mother. The fact that it wasn't Brown or Yale or even Wesleyan began to appeal to me—screw them if they couldn't love me—and within a week I had signed on to attend Beloit College.

Near the end of my senior year, I asked out a girl I had long admired but never expected to date. To my surprise, she accepted an invitation to a movie (I think it was *Gone with the Wind*, rereleased in American theaters around that time). I sat with my arm around her shoulder until the blood completely drained from my fingers. There had been a major demonstration that day in Washington, and we heard that the National Guard was called out to control the protesters. Sara turned out to be far more radical than I ever knew. She had never helped organize marches and had never dressed in anything more outrageous than a yellow Peters jacket, but her politics turned out to be somewhere between Black Panther Bobby Seal and Columbia radical Mark Rudd. After the movie, we sat in a little park built over the Silver Spring, for which our town was named. We were talking about race and revolution, and I was thinking about trying to kiss her, when suddenly we heard a rustle in the bushes. As if a Russian film director had cued him to burst on the scene, a tall, sandy-haired boy stumbled out of the shrubbery and fell on his knees at the spring. We recognized him as James, the newly elected student government president. James unknotted a red bandanna from around his neck and dipped it into the water. His face was smudged and his jeans and T-shirt torn; he looked like he'd been fighting Cossacks. We called to him and he came over to our bench. He recounted a street fight with guardsmen downtown, the crowd throwing back tear gas canisters and running from personnel carriers. When James left, Sara and I sat for a while longer, embarrassed we had been at the movies when the Revolution began and wondering if everything now would fall to pieces. I drove her home and we kissed, but I knew by that time she had an older boyfriend in the Movement. After all, I had a girlfriend myself I liked just fine, and I was leaving for college soon. I don't believe I ever talked to her alone again.

I went off to college determined to do nothing but literary projects. I thought the frantic activity of my high school years had branded me "not serious." Perhaps a person just couldn't be engaged in both political and literary work; I needed to be quieter and more selfish. Beloit had assigned us to read Hermann Hesse's *Siddhartha*, as well as *The Autobiography of Malcolm X*, over the summer for our Underclass Commons Course (UCC), a writing and reading seminar required of all entering students. In both books, the title heroes seek individual wisdom that leads eventually to a greater commitment to communal needs. Both emphasized to me that I needed to focus inward before I could act in the world again. I was struck in Hesse's text that Siddhartha enters upon his worldly phase only after attaining interior mastery: "I can think, I can wait, I can fast" (56). At the point he articulates this formula, he also recites his first poem and immediately wins his first kiss from a woman. I promised myself that no one would mistake me for a jock, a politician, or an activist in this new phase of my life. The big demonstrations were over even though the War was not. Riots and assassinations had turned politics into a Cubist canvas washed in blood. Drugs and sex had replaced politics as the currency of hip. I didn't need more analysis; I needed more art. I would become a poet and face the world through words. I would leave political change for people who wanted to yell and organize.

Starting college in the fall of 1970, I thought I might major in psychology or English or classics. A major seemed incidental to my desire to write. I signed up for an introductory creative writing course, a class I hoped would give me some guidance, though I was sure that I would have to take this path alone. Early in September, I wrote my brother: "As for me, I'm really enjoying it here. Tonight my creative writing class is going to meet at the professor's home so we can in his words 'study writing while we slowly get drunk together.' He said he was kidding hurriedly but it will be an interesting event no matter what happens." Indeed, we sat around that night in a circle in Dr. Sanderson's living room and drank white wine from a large round Almaden bottle, my first drink with an adult when we didn't say a *bruchah* beforehand. As the semester went on, I tried to control my enthusiasm in letters, separating myself from my family while still anxious to tell them of the changes I was undergoing. I started off a letter dated September 23 with the insulting lead "Family: I have nothing in particular to say to you." However, within a page I had slipped into this account:

> The real reason I'm writing is because of the enclosed poem. I was assigned a narrative poem of 16–20 lines for Creative Writing. I'm really happy with what I have written. . . . After finishing the poem . . . I was so stoned on creativity that all I could do was joke and smile, mostly smile. Once that evening I was sitting in a friend's room listening to James Taylor . . . and I thought of the poem, and I thought of how I had made cookies earlier that evening with some girls from my [English] class, and the happiness I felt took over all of my body.

The letter was as open as I could be with my family—particularly my mother—and I doubt I ever sent a poem home again. Soon after, I became far tighter-lipped and higher-handed about writing, but this letter suggests that making poems was associated for me then with growing autonomous, leaving behind the sense and logic as well as the loneliness of my mother's world. I could have sex, get stoned, be happy staring into a girl's eyes or at my own poem. The visceral feeling I describe—even in that early time—represents what I later came to call the poem-life, the imaginative ground accessible through the operations of art in the medium of language.

Mr. Sanderson told us one afternoon that John Berryman would be reading that night at the student union. He told us something about Berryman's career, and that Berryman had been drunk most of the time since he'd arrived on campus, but that we would hear some powerful poetry if we attended the reading. My roommate Joel and I arrived late and had to stand at the end of a long, crowded hall as Berryman took the stage. Decidedly drunk, sounding like a slowed-down phonograph, he read what he called "theballpoim," a poem about a little boy who loses a ball in the harbor, which ends:

> People will take balls,
> Balls will be lost always, little boy,
> And no one buys a ball back. Money is external,
> He is learning, well behind his desperate eyes,
> The epistemology of loss, how to stand up
> Knowing what every man must one day know
> And most know many days, how to stand up

What transfixed me about that poem or the others he read that night? My reading of the poem now—though I'm warier of the drunken bathos, the male codes, and the fascination with death than I was at eighteen—still leads me to see the poet negotiating a provisional place for the self or selves caught within the stern message of Fathers and religious tradition that equates knowledge with exile from the Garden. That negotiation continued, for Berryman, through the long trail of splintering selfhood in *The Dream Songs* and presumably failed sometime before he threw himself from a Minneapolis bridge into the Mississippi. But if I had to point to specific instances of language in "The Ball Poem" that may have reached me on that dark November evening, they would be the flatness of "no one buys a ball back" and the quiet syntactic derangement of "And most know many days." The terror in those phrases echoes Berryman's frightening digression that night when he defended Hemingway's suicide by saying, "He was trying to make the best prose he could make." More than any nameable emotion, what overcame me was the very fact that one could do such work in the line and the sentence, with an ear tuned to inflection and a willingness to inflect however one damn well needed to. Berryman obliterated the nurturing of Mr. Ganz, the drama of Mrs. Miller, and the fierceness of Mrs. Wubnig. I hadn't known language could mean so much to a man.

In my freshman seminar, I encountered another text that stamped itself on my emotional life. Martin Buber came up on our syllabus midway through the semester, after Hesse and Malcolm X and James Joyce's *Portrait of the Artist as a Young Man.* By that time, I had discovered the dubious joys of drink, and one Sunday morning I settled down in an empty study room with my copy of *I and Thou,* a blank pad of paper, and a stern hangover. I had not yet learned to mark up textbooks, having been warned by my mother and all of my elementary teachers never to write in a book, but I identified one passage that shined through my morning-after fog. This was the early passage that begins "I consider a tree" (7), in which the disembodied voice of the philosopher names various ways one could know the physical being of a tree and never leave off seeing it as an object. Then Buber observes, in a rabbinical tone, another level of encounter: "It can, however, also come about, if I have both will and grace, that in considering the tree I become bound up in relation to it" (7). I spent most of the morning and much of the afternoon composing and erasing and rewriting the first paragraph of a paper due the next day, trying to name but failing to articulate Buber's distinction between I-It and I-Thou knowing.

I must have eked out a short paper that I hated, for it is nowhere in my files. If the paper disappeared, however, the tree did not. I found Buber's language deeply attractive even as I found his metaphysic almost embarrassingly familiar. Here was a philosophy not built on Christian sacrifice but on Jewish ethics reimagined in a spiritual key. For Buber, I-Thou knowing does not rule out experience in the world but prizes most the relation between beings bound in a mutual gaze of recognition. Joel and I adapted and critiqued Buber, and the humanist psychology of Viktor Frankl and Erich Fromm, on our long walks around the city and along farm roads. Buber also became a shared topic with our new friend Sylvie, who lived across the quadrangle in the women's dorm. We would light shabbas candles with Sylvie and her roommate, Cleo. We both feared Sylvie's version of Buber as too loving and domesticated, but we were fascinated by her earnestness, comforted by her uncompromising warmth. At the same time, Joel was also drawn to Cleo's non-Jewish wonder at our muddled brand of intellectual bravado and psychosexual clowning.

In the summer term, I took a course called The Daedalean Dreamscape, taught by a fierce Texan writer/teacher in the English department named Dr. Ray, who called students by their last names and set every student's remark in the context of tennis or Nabokov. I never much understood what the course was about—we read *Lolita* and *Pale Fire*, Durrell's *Alexandria Quartet*, and Eliot's *Four Quartets*, talking always about labyrinths, mirrors, time—and I was never a favorite in a classroom built on a hierarchy of favorites. Each week, we submitted a journal entry to the class. If Dr. Ray thought your comment smart, it got appended (with a gloss by him) to a growing document held at the reserve desk for us to read the next week. If your entry wasn't deemed worthy that week, you got it back with a short note about its failures and potentials. I didn't idolize the man as others did, but I worked hard at not being intimidated by him. Besides, I was going to be a poet, and Dr. Ray really only cared about fiction and tennis. At midterm, I submitted to him the beginning of a novel based on a dream about evolving lizards and a prison escape on a vast, flat plane, all narrated by an old frog. Dr. Ray mostly criticized my shoddy spelling and grammar as undercutting any chance at irony. Still, the class journal and the manuscript due at the end of the semester were my first glimpses of professional competition in American literary life.

Dr. Ray's wife, also Dr. Ray and also Texan, was extremely bookish but easily as intense as her husband. She taught my freshman humanities seminar where I met Hesse and company. While the male Dr. Ray's distinguishing characteristic was a bald head, which he rubbed thoughtfully when somebody's comment invited us back into the labyrinth, his wife's prominent features were enormous black glasses, dark eyebrows, and long, straight brown hair. She was as small-framed as he was physically imposing, but she seemed the more powerful intellect. At first, I thought her strict manner off-putting; I described her to my brother as being "adept at bringing college right down to the high school level." But after she wrote on my first assignment that she accepted me as a serious writing student, I began to pay attention to her. She decided she would educate me properly, independent of the class curriculum, and set out for me a series of three explications, the first of which was on a perfect little poem by Yeats called "The Fish":

> Although you hide in the ebb and flow
> Of the pale tide when the moon has set,
> The people of coming days will know
> About the casting out of my net,
> And how you have leaped times out of mind
> Over the little silver cords,
> And think that you were hard and unkind,
> And blame you with many bitter words. (56)

She asked me to identify "not only stanza pattern, metre, rhyme and other sound devices but also diction, syntax, devices of rhythm which are beyond metre. Rhetoric. With each device, try to think what the effect of it is. So you will not just be saying 'Aha, alliteration!' but will say 'alliteration which does such and such.'" Her assignment was quintessentially New Critical, and in fact Drs. Ray and Ray had written a textbook in which students were urged to use different colored pens to mark up a poem or a prose passage for various sound patterns and rhetorical devices. Under their system, the page became a many-colored web that proved how complex a language machine could be. She forced me further and further into "The Fish" until I gave up on her quest for a verifiable teleology in the poem, but along the way I learned how a poem can be parsed and prodded and what a poet could weave together. I never did get past the impression that critics must show themselves always a step cleverer than the poet, which I thought indecent. The poem slipped through my cords, but I couldn't blame Yeats or the poem or Dr. Ray for that.

All my attempts to submit to expert training left me feeling I could not be a poet in school. Yeats's poem remained impervious to my dissections, and my own poems, peopled (if at all) by an occasional Eliot character ("Women staring at the hall lightbulbs that / stare all night at them"), became mostly concerned with a balance between rhythmic experiment and flat, adolescent statements about death set in vaguely exotic scenes:

Sadly, thinking of death,
the Hopi girl
Weaves the heavy sack.
She is unafraid of the old or
Infant body that must fit
The heavy weave.
The smell of cotton
Beneath her fingernails
Is the remembered smell
Her husband wakes to.
He thinks this now, as he sits
On the wooden ladder
Near their open door.

I knew nothing of Hopis, or weaving, or cotton, but I loved the collocation of actions distanced in time—the weaver working and thinking,
the husband meditating alone—while death replaced sex as a more
seemly (and safer) topic for a young poet to explore aloud. I liked the
regular iambic rhythm made bearable by a truncated line and the occasional anapest. I exalted when I could get spondees to fall right ("At
the whispered smell / Of long dried sweat"), but I burned with a sense
that nothing I wrote could stop the ordinariness I felt, could earn me
a place outside the usual order of college classes and dorm food. My
work seemed empty and unaccomplished, and I kept a razor blade on
the windowsill next to my desk to remind me that this work was serious and involved the greatest risks. I didn't know how a poet should
proceed to educate himself.

I cannot find, in journals or draft material or personal letters, any
indication of the very real events of my life at that time. I had fallen in
love with Tracy that winter, made love for the first time, sustained my
first real heartbreak when she wouldn't see me anymore. I hitchhiked
cross-country for the first time with Joel. Someone on our dorm floor
took bad acid and permanently damaged his brain. My poems were
turned down by the literary supplement to the college newspaper, but
the large and pompous editor assured me snidely that I was "better than
Robert Bly." My friends and I watched *Wild Strawberries*, *Zorba the
Greek*, and *Last Year at Marienbad* in the student union and trooped

back to our rooms to listen to Muddy Waters, Howling Wolf, and Otis Spann. We drank bourbon and heard our lovelorn friend Sam sing his latest blues tribute to "Arabesque of Albuquerque." I read Dylan Thomas aloud during late-night arguments with Joel about whether it was better to be a poetic genius and die young or to be a respectable nobody and live long. None of this appeared in the writing I did then, though I wrote a film script, stories, poems, an occasional journal entry, and many letters home. In short, I never allowed the characters and drama of my waking life to enter my writing life in identifiable ways. I had always been told by writing teachers to "write what you know," but that advice struck me as banal and appalling. I didn't know much of anything, and I hated what I regarded as the ordinariness in the life around me. The collection I turned into the male Dr. Ray at the end of the summer term of 1971 was entitled "Scetches [*sic*] and Notes for Dreams of the Real World," and the remove from lived experience announced by that title was mapped by the muted poems contained there. He didn't much care for my poems, and he despised my errors.

What was I afraid of? Certainly the fear that I might have no imagination or intelligence or spirit for this enterprise of poetry, which, after all, seemed to be practiced only by men trained at Harvard or Yale and steeped in the Christian tradition of revelation and transubstantiation. Buber moved me, but could a minor Jewish philosopher, with his gray beard and dark rabbinic eyes, stand up to Christ's theologians? Certainly I feared I wouldn't be the genius my father expected me to be. I feared my mass of sexual desires might overwhelm my good intentions—the old werewolf fear from childhood—and drive any chance for love away. Had I not taken my father's place in the family, as Dr. Kaufman might have pointed out if he'd broken his analytical silence? Below everything else, I was afraid to encounter my father's death, which had so dismantled my world that I could neither grow beyond the loss nor operate without it. Would my writing defeat these fears or merely paper them over? Was I fooling myself with heaps of words on my desk late at night, or would my assemblages someday read as legitimate poems to someone else? Would writing justify a life that, after all, amounted otherwise to very little?

My friends and I listened to the Grateful Dead and The Band, drank red wine, and ate ice cream stolen from the dorm cafeteria. During a

Wisconsin snowstorm, Steve, my neighbor in the next room, and I pulled an all-nighter for our Russian literature class: he wrote on Alyosha in Dostoyevsky's *The Brothers Karamazov* and I on Bazarov, the nihilist revolutionary in Turgenev's *Fathers and Sons*. Tracy introduced me not only to love but also to her favorite architect, Paolo Soleri, and his city/building Arcosanti. Together we watched her favorite movie, Truffaut's *Stolen Kisses*. Joel and I walked more miles late at night, discussing Holocaust dreams, city planning, and Bach. Anne taught us all how to drink vodka and smoke cigars and dragged us to see Todd Browning's *Freaks*, where the well-meaning midgets and odd-shaped sideshow artists adopt the scheming "normal" woman into their circle with the chant:

> One of us
> One of us
> She is now
> One of us!

Stopping at George Webb's Diner after I smoked pot for the first time, my friend Chas and I watched the twin clocks on the wall to see if they really, really told the same time, and then he solemnly wrote down the lines

> Hydrogen Bombs via
> a telephone endgame
> becomes a deeply buried
> cheezburger

and had me date the poem and promise to keep it in my files.

In a poem I wrote at the end of my first year at Beloit, I unconsciously conjured a picture of my state at that time:

> I know I see my mouth unfettered, but
> Hung with alabaster ornaments ready to
> Drop and break into the guilty pieces that
> Will cut all little feet.

This fear of speaking, fear that writing would legitimate feelings I could not bear, competed with a tremendous need to put words together in surprising ways. I wanted to be known as a writer, wanted the intensity

I felt to mean something beyond adolescent pain or fodder for analysis. I remember sitting at my desk in front of a blank page late at night, wanting to grasp the air or reach out beyond my window and drag a poem into words. In fact, one poem speaks of an "old stone miner" who "cuts / the air into the blocks that fall," which was my sense of the poet's job, and the constant demand to fashion more poems: "The vicious air above the sea swirls, / It moils uncut." The poems from that time are mostly scenes rendered in simple, slightly rhythmic language, often containing only a few characters frozen as if in a photograph: the Hopi girl and her husband, Hebe and Hercules after they have been banished from Olympus, mice playing in clothes abandoned in the woods, a dying old man passing on a family legend to his son and daughter.

I was studying Latin, translating the *Aeneid* in an independent course with the only full-time Latin professor at Beloit, a popular teacher so busy that I often had to talk with him while he stood in the doorway of his office, one foot in the hall, his cheek laid against the doorjamb while I read him my latest translation. I hoped that the further back I reached in Western literature the more I would be able to discover what a poem was and how I could make one. English seemed too easy, too obvious a choice to study. I decided I needed to study Greek, but the classics department was too small at the college, and so I began to think about transferring, finding my way back into one of those eastern colleges that had rejected me before. I was clumsy and unlearned. I needed training along the old apprentice model, but I wanted no part of fathers who might tell me what to do. I wanted to sit anonymously in lectures by famous professors on the history of poetry, on Plato and Aristotle and Longinus and Philo, on the anthropology of spirit. I was making up the making of poetry out of my own small reading, and my poems were too slight for anyone else to notice.

The reading began to save me and pull me forward near the end of my year at Beloit. That Daedalean summer I read too much Eliot. He casts what poet Kenneth Koch calls a "baleful influence" on young poets (Koch says the same of Yeats and Auden in his poem "Fresh Air"), and I was no exception. *Four Quartets* plunged me into the mysticism of "Garlic and sapphires in the mud / Clot the bedded axle tree" and riddles of negation and stasis:

At the still point of the turning world. Neither flesh nor fleshless;
Neither from nor towards; at the still point, there the dance is,
But neither arrest nor movement. And do not call it fixity,
Where past and future are gathered. Neither
   movement from nor towards,
Neither ascent nor decline. Except for the point, the still point,
There would be no dance, and there is only the dance.    (15–16)

I could not then glimpse the High Church in Eliot's celestial imagery, the stern white Western traditionalist hiding behind the selfless and timeless axle tree. Nor did I know enough even to recognize Yeats in that last line about the dance. Eliot's poetry only brought me to write abstractions and sonorous rhythms, though I did learn from him to listen closely for rhyme and near rhyme. And Eliot led me to Pound's *ABC of Reading*, the book that began my independent education as a poet.

One of our roommates, who had spent nearly the entire spring alone in his room reading poetry and meditating, dropped out of school in May—a result of too many drugs and too little sense of why his courses mattered. Mike left me his poetry collection and a note telling me to carry on my writing. We soon began to get religious letters from him, and he had converted to fundamentalist Christianity by the end of the summer. His pleadings to Joel and me to follow Jesus didn't register with two Jewish boys still torn between *kashruth* and *schickses*, but Mike's poetry collection proved invaluable to me. Among the books he left me were a selected William Blake, Don L. Lee's *Don't Cry Scream*, Robert Creeley's *For Love*, Robert Hayden's *Words in the Mourning Time*, Denise Levertov's *O Taste and See*, and the *ABC of Reading*. Lee (later Haki Madhubuti) and Hayden introduced me, respectively, to the rage and patience in African American poetry. I had already somehow stumbled on Martin Duberman's history of Black Mountain College, and that tale of a school reinventing education built upon the arts and literature lit me up. I loved hearing about the writers around the big figure of Charles Olson—Creeley, Levertov, and Robert Duncan among others—deeply committed to writing as an art but also an outlaw bunch crashing cars into trees, making Happenings with John Cage and Merce Cunningham, erecting the geodesic dome with Buckminster Fuller. M. C. Richards centered her pots, Anni Albers wove, and her husband, Josef, taught his strict color theory; Willem de Kooning and Franz Kline rode in on large abstract canvases from New York. And all the time, everyone talked. I imagine Creeley writing of this time in his well-known poem "I know a man":

> shall we &
> why not, buy a goddamn big car,
>
> drive, he sd, for
> christ's sake, look
> out where yr going. (38)

This was a utopia I could build for myself if I chased them all, into that darkness, urged on by Pound's harangue to read as if it mattered more than death.

I had a very dim sense of the poetry tradition. Pound left no doubt on this point: I was ignorant. But I knew I wanted to be a part of "the vicious air above the sea swirls" I had written about in my own poem. I had no big car, but it certainly was time to drive. I decided to leave school and head to New England to find a manual job and a little room in which to write and read. An acquaintance told me her family would put me up in Amherst if I wanted to look for a job there. I told Beloit I was off to a work term in September. My draft number was low, and my draft board would have snapped me up in a second if I had left school officially. But I didn't hesitate to hide behind Beloit's work requirement if it kept me out of Vietnam. Marches and protests still had not stopped the War, and Nixon was in the White House, but I was going to rocky Massachusetts to read Blake and write my poems.

## 4

# Following Williams

I ARRIVED ON THE Cornell campus in the fall of 1972. They let me in as a transfer after Harvard rejected me and both Yale and Amherst discouraged me from even applying. I decided that an Ivy with an ag school and a reputation for labor relations was more my kind of university anyway. I carried my backpack, a duffle bag—more books than clothes—and an attitude. Hadn't I worked at a print shop in Amherst and a museum in San Francisco and hitchhiked across the country since I left Beloit? I intended to study the origins of poetry with Cornell's best professors and then wade back into the world to write. The gorges, the meandering roads, the gardens, the tree plantation would be my main companions and true classrooms. I didn't need anybody if I had places to walk, a library, a desk, and a brilliant lecture now and then to attend. I would be inside the great university but not a part of it, neither cheerleader nor activist nor athlete but a poet on the edge, reading my way into the tradition but bound to write outside of it.

Cornell assigned me to an old house on Stewart Avenue full of male transfer students, most of them engineers. This was an experiment for the university because transfers had not, apparently, been successfully integrated into campus life before, and so a quasi-fraternity to give us ready-made camaraderie seemed a promising idea. Nearly as soon as we met each other, the news spread that a transfer student had committed suicide a day or two before by jumping into one of Ithaca's seductive gorges. That set a dismal opening note for the house, and we barely smiled at each other as we settled in. Secretly, I honored the death as a sign that Cornell, after all, was a serious place, a place where learning could be dangerous. Of course I wanted to laugh, to have friends, but I could do that anywhere; every moment of college needed to give me the background I lacked, the command of literature, art, and history that I craved. I had been reading on my own for a year and knew just enough to recognize how painfully little I knew. Eliot had said one could not write past the age of thirty without a sense of history. Pound proclaimed in *Guide to Kulchur* that "the history of a culture is the history of ideas going into action" (44), and in nearly every essay he emphasized what a "man" did in the masculine work of poetry and criticism. For instance, he praised Thomas Hardy: "No thoughtful writer can read this book of Hardy's without throwing his own work (in imagination) into the test-tube and hunting it for fustian, for the foolish word, for the word upholstered" (*Kulchur* 286–87). I took Pound's tough ban on soft or elaborate language to heart. By that time, I already knew that Eliot and Pound had been fascist sympathizers, and I'd turned away from Eliot's highbrow show of erudition, but I couldn't deny the magnetism of Pound's imperious tone and dropkick opinions. History mattered, not in the sense of kings and wars but of what people had written and written against. I wanted to prove I could be as serious and learned as they. I would know my history so that I could keep my poetry new. I would make poems from material so lean and un-fussy that no one could tear them down for a hundred years. That was what Pound (and later Louis Zukofsky) called the "test of poetry." Language could stand against death and change if lines were constructed with the right combination of passion and craft.

I met my two roommates in our big room on the third floor. Both were studying engineering. Miles had transferred from a military academy and made his bed so tautly you could bounce a quarter on it. At night he slept only on top of the cover with an extra blanket he stowed each morning, a trick he had learned to pass 7:00 A.M. inspections. Sam came from Long Island and was mostly miserable studying calculus, statics, and dynamics. He fell behind in his studies and caught up only in the one liberal arts course he liked. We were an odd trio, often not talking for hours, but we were friendly enough. Sam joked that when I studied, I was the "picture of concentration," which only made me annoyed with myself that I was pleased to appear so. According to a letter I wrote home early in the first semester, on my birthday I hardly spoke to them at all while they told each other stories of fights they'd had or seen; I sat there "looking knowing and making them feel very uncomfortable," but I couldn't leave the room because "I enjoyed listening to them talk." Once we turned off the light and got into bed, they sang "Happy Birthday" to me in the dark. I wrote to my sister:

"All this comes from taking myself too seriously and I begin to do that immediately after I renounce it. . . . After the most serious time I feel very free, as if I really do have a long life and plenty of time to do whatever I want." I had just turned twenty, but most days I felt I had no time and too much to accomplish.

Reading and writing were my stays against death, but in school my passion for words seemed to exclude friendship. I wanted my studying to matter, wanted my choice to write poems to be as solid in the world as building a dam or driving a truck, and other students weren't going to help me with the task. I drew a strict line between school life at Cornell and what I felt was the more real adult world I had lived in the year before. I developed wary relationships with two other transfers, Don and Pru, both of whom had idiosyncrasies that kept them at odds with the usual undergraduates. Don was a lifelong city boy bound to learn farming in the ag school after a dissipated period as a photographer in London. Pru majored in biology, never wore shoes till the snow fell, and traveled the campus with her Great Pyrenees dog by her side and a cockatiel on her shoulder. We treated each other carefully too, hanging out occasionally, but often deciding we needed to get back to work instead.

Few others had stepped out of the school stream, at least not that I could tell. This was a point of pride for me, though I'd been a non-student hardly a year. Even my draft board hadn't registered the change, but I felt the time away set me apart. I'd sketched hippie crowds on Sundays in Golden Gate Park and hauled trash to the town dump in Belchertown, Massachusetts, in a company truck. I'd heard Allen Ginsberg read in San Francisco and fallen in love in Boston. I wore my experience like I wore my hair, uncut and uncombed. Outside of school, I had met people who were just living their lives and didn't need art to justify their existence. In Amherst, I worked alongside typesetters with burn scars on their forearms from the huge Linotype machines that sometimes spat hot lead, a vet who ran the folding machines and cursed blue ink when a job would jam, and two old master printers who still hand-set their own cold type and produced wedding invitations and business cards on letterpress machines. Amid the symphony of letterpresses inking and pressing in rhythm, the giant offset presses' chug, the cutter machine's basso thunk, and the high snap of folded pamphlets hitting their guides, I moved through the shop picking up trash, gathering jobs for delivery, and wheeling new loads of paper. I'd overhear the workplace preoccupations and gossip from everybody. The women in the assembly room took me in and showed me how to collate more efficiently when we had a big job to get done. They put aside for me a copy of a cookbook we produced for a UMass home economics class because they thought I needed to know how to cook for myself.

Nobody at Hamilton Newell Printers could quite understand what I was doing there if I had already started college, except for Dave, the layout artist in the front office, who befriended me and invited me out to his farm. He had moved from Cleveland with his wife and kids, as well as two other couples, to live on the land and get away from city life. They kept goats and a garden, and they were converting the barn into a studio and music space. I lived not far from the job in a rooming house owned by a John Birch Society guy who was taking in young men, he told us, in case a revolution came and he needed protection. Dave's farm in the country was my respite, a place where people who valued the arts accepted me as somebody trying to make something for no money. We drank wine and smoked pot and listened to Crosby, Stills, Nash, and Young. It all seemed better than fine, as long as I didn't pay attention to the lonely ache I always felt. Occasionally I would hitch-hike to Boston to visit Sue, a friend from high school who was going to Radcliffe. There I met her best friend, Corinne, and fell in love with her and Harvard and the city. I tried to transfer to Harvard and was rejected. I felt like Jude the Obscure, the self-made scholar prowling on the margins of Oxford in the Thomas Hardy novel I was reading. Corinne was a sophomore engaged to be married to a senior already accepted into law school. The moment seemed painful and sweet, the love right but misaligned, my ambitions encompassing me and yet unattached to a story I could not make legible to anyone else.

The people I met in Amherst functioned quite untouched by the closed academic system of papers and testing, and this was for me a liberating way to live. I loved being on my own, reading only because I needed to fill a gap in my picture of poetry, an art so far from anything my family had known, so distant from the comfortable but alien sub-urbs I had recently left behind. I carried Blake with me from Beloit; Blake's commentators led me to Keats, his poems and letters, and the great biography by Walter Jackson Bate. The Bate biography recounts in loving detail Keats's process of composing poems and highlights Keats as a self-disciplinarian at the edge of the English Romantics' circle. I went with Corinne to a class where Bate was lecturing, but the real professor seemed pedestrian compared to the intimate narrator of his book. I was working my way through an anthology of mid-1950s American poetry that my Beloit roommate left me. I must have found William Carlos Williams in that anthology, staring out like a hawk from a photograph. I had heard his name from Pound's essays and began to seek out his poems. I didn't know where all these modernist words were coming from, but I hunted for more in the Amherst College library and in the bookstores in Cambridge, piecing together some narrative thread about Eliot and EP and WCW, but also about Hilda Doolittle (H. D.), Wallace Stevens, Marianne Moore—those who left the United States and those who stayed behind to make American poetry. I read Williams's autobiography and then his fictional autobiography, *A Voyage to Pagany*, recognizing his twin desires to travel with the bohemians and yet stay home with the working folks who formed the substance of the country.

I began to form a myth for myself from the Romantics and Modernists: the poet—hovering between social classes and at the edge of a literary scene invented by its participants—writing as hard as he can and earning a living at skilled manual jobs, especially printing. Through a friend I did give a "poetry" class to a group of kindergarteners in an experimental school, playing music for the kids and asking them to draw to the rhythms, but teaching seemed too simple for the arcane ideas I wanted to explore. Medicine, the day job for both Keats and Williams, briefly occurred to me as an alternative occupation one day while I was cleaning out garbage cans at the press, but I soon ruled out doctoring as too scientific, too time-consuming, and too close to my father's career. No, on the whole I thought I would be a printer by day and a poet/scholar on my own time.

People at work didn't know about my life in poetry, my poem-life. I could share their complaints on the job, about bosses, the weather, and even sometimes the Vietnam War. Occasionally I might have a conversation with someone at Dave's farm about Art. I got excited and, depending on what I had been drinking, even declamatory. When I visited Boston, I would talk to Corinne about poetry because she was studying history and literature and knew much more about the coherent story they told in her classes and critical books. But mostly poetry was my personal gig alongside other people's gigs, and that felt just fine. Someday maybe people would know about me, but for now I had work to do and not much yet to show for it. As Bob Dylan sang, "But I'll know my song well / before I start singing" ("A Hard Rain's A-Gonna Fall"), or as Keats noted to himself, "Half done is once begun." I would go to a reading at a local school—for instance, a wonderful full-throated recitation by Russian poet Andrei Voznesensky at Smith College—and return home to my room revived, full of undifferentiated energy. A reading would open up the skies, challenge the world I was building for myself, and remind me that poets were living and moving through the world. I would look at the beautiful undergraduate women and dream of meeting one, but I felt safe in my private mission and not so lonely I needed to break my solitary practice. If I was lucky, readings would be on a Tuesday. I drove the company car those nights because I picked up camera-ready copy for the *Mt. Holyoke Choragus* newspaper every Wednesday morning. In the morning, I'd glide through the western Massachusetts fog, thinking about the sounds of the night before and the poems I could write. For all my dreaming, I felt remarkably common. I was one guy earning a paycheck along with the others at Hamilton Newell.

And then there was San Francisco.

I left Amherst in December and returned home to my mother's house in Silver Spring. My old roommate Joel had left Beloit that fall as well and was working the overnight shift in a lab analyzing the urine of GIs returning from Vietnam for evidence of drug use. He was reading Alan Watts and other mystics, taking acid and talking to his *bubbi*. In spare moments, he tried to get us both jobs as far away from his family's house as possible. We had a friend who was doing his Beloit work term as an experimental patient at the National Institutes of Health, where doctors fed him, gave him colds and flu for them to cure, and provided him with free long distance phone service, a rare perk. Joel used the phone in our friend's room to call San Francisco looking for work. He didn't have much luck, but he managed to find us volunteer jobs. Mine was at the California Academy of Sciences, in the exhibits department, and his was with the Sierra Club. We figured we'd pick up part-time work in a restaurant or bookstore once we got there. Joel just had to leave town. I guessed I was ready for an adventure, and Joel was my best friend. My mother gave me the family's old Pontiac Tempest station wagon, and we gathered a strange collection of riders from a DC college ride board and prepared to set off. Two nights before we left, I had a panic attack about what would happen to me in California, how I might be changed like a werewolf in horrifying ways, lose my mind, never come back. The next day, a psychiatrist friend of my family's talked to me about the trauma of my father's death—he had been at my father's side when they tried to administer oxygen to Dad on our apartment floor that Sunday morning—and told me I could make my own way, that in fact I HAD to make my own way, despite the "kick in the head" I'd received. I carried his stark encouragement with me as I pulled away from home with five other people and all our packs and duffels overloading a station wagon headed west.

We broke down in Amarillo, Texas, in the middle of the night and had to send most of our riders on ahead by bus. One rider stayed around. Lloyd was an African American guy who knew songs and poems by Gil Scott-Heron and the Last Poets by heart. He chanted us "The Revolution Will Not Be Televised" for hours as we drove. When we were stranded in Amarillo, he went off by himself and met up with us later for the rest of the ride. Joel and I walked and talked through the streets and ended up in the public library for much of the few days we spent waiting for the crankshaft to be replaced. We stayed in a flophouse you could rent by the night or the hour. I was reading Norman Mailer's *Armies of the Night* at the time. Through Mailer's long, funny political rant about trying to levitate the Pentagon in protest against the Vietnam War, I learned about Robert Lowell and Denise Levertov. I found Lowell's *Notebook* in the Amarillo library and insulated myself for a time from Texas. When we got back on the road again, our spirits were tempered, but we were more determined to get there. Lloyd was more subdued, even a bit needy. We stopped in Los Angeles and searched around South Central for Lloyd's sister but never found her. We finally dropped a forlorn Lloyd off at a strange corner and drove on up the coast.

Within a week, the car's transmission died on the San Francisco hills, and we sold it for a hundred dollars to a Divisadero car dealer.

We spent New Year's Eve in Schlomo Carlbach's House of Love and Prayer, a new age, makeshift Chasidic center where Joel's brother had a friend studying Talmud. Someone in the kitchen rapped to me about macrobiotics, and I had no idea what she was talking about—having never knowingly met a vegetarian and never eaten brown rice—but I knew we were no longer on the East Coast. We found a studio apartment in Haight-Ashbury. By 1972, the neighborhood was no longer the bright center of alternate consciousness. It was a pretty seedy area for drugged-out leftover hippies and gay communes looking to Stonewall for inspiration. I began working at the museum as an assistant to the taxidermist and sculptor, picking up pay in the evenings at the sculptor's basement studio, baking plastic aquarium furniture in a pizza oven and pouring plaster frogs to sell at the museum shop. Joel soon found a job working with autistic kids in a group home about an hour and a half north of the city, and I kept the Haight apartment by myself till I moved in with some Beloit friends in Bernal Heights. Joel's leaving was difficult for both of us, but we had to find our own way, and his was definitely not in the city. I wanted to go to readings and bookstores and maybe even meet some poets in San Francisco, and once again I felt I needed to do this by myself.

The friends I moved in with welcomed me but kept to themselves. The landlords' cats tended to urinate on my sleeping bag, but otherwise we all got along well enough. I learned to eat vegetables and granola and yogurt; we bought food in common from a co-op. I smoked pot with them in the evenings until I realized it made me impossibly morose and unable to read or think, and then I declined more often than not. The Beloit friends introduced me to the cooperative school where one of them worked, and there I saw free school philosophy at work for the first time. I met a married woman with a beautiful little girl in the school. This older woman drew me into a brief, confusing, and not totally platonic relationship based on our mutual love of art. I could not entirely walk away until she took me to a lecture by the rising star of the human potential movement, Werner Erhard, and I realized that his ripening cult and a head-trip affair with a married woman were too much California for me. All the while I was writing Corinne furious and funny letters about what I was seeing, who I was meeting, what I was reading. I walked for hours in Golden Gate Park, stopping in this shaded corner or on top of that sandy hill to jot down cryptic little notes in marbled cover composition books that I've now lost. I could not yet call myself a poet, but I wanted so much to be one and had no idea how I could turn these disjointed lines and disembodied observations into a thing others would recognize as lasting verse.

I went to every reading I could find and followed up on names I heard by reading these new poets in the main public library or digging up their books in the used bookstores across the Bay in Berkeley. One unforgettable event was a reading at the Longshoremen's Union Hall, a benefit for Cesar Chavez's organizing effort for farmworkers, where Lawrence Ferlinghetti, Philip Whalen, Robert Creeley, Robert Duncan, and Allen Ginsberg all read to an audience of three or four hundred people. In between the headliner poets were younger, revolutionary poets from black, Asian, and Latino communities. Ferlinghetti started off, the thin little proper gentleman, troubadour of underwear and ironic exclamation. Whalen, then a burly logger of a man and not yet the Buddhist monk he was soon to become, charged up the audience when he barked and crooned Beat lines like

> We kill each other quite artistically
> Exquisite tortures, exorbitant crimes
> Think of the glass flowers in the Peabody Museum
> I am limited insofar as huge areas of my brain
> Dissolved in Hitler soap-vats
> Dispersed as radiant poison over Japan                    (220)

and stopped in the middle to take a long pull from a jug of wine. Creeley read in his hesitant, riveting, self-scrutinizing voice. When a drunken heckler interrupted him, Creeley fixed his one good eye on the character and muttered something—an incantation, a gentle threat—that shut the man up. Duncan came in late and swept through the audience in a magnificent cape, reading his mystical poems to the universe. And Ginsberg ended with wide-mouthed poems and a long version of a Blake song, accompanying himself on the harmonium backed up by a young, beautiful long-haired man strumming a guitar.

I assumed that studying poetry at Cornell would be a grueling academic test, like starting wrestling season all over, but this time with books and interpretations rather than weights and moves. The passionate and funky months in San Francisco lay behind me; this was the ivy-covered East where they wouldn't care about West Coast yawps and my inner probings. I knew no one, and no one knew what I carried with me. I hardly knew myself, but I figured the poetry I had lived could not be translated into classrooms or papers. Before the semester began, I went to the best-known poet at the school, A. R. Ammons, to ask him if he'd advise me in an independent major focused on Western poetry—including Latin, Greek, and German, the languages I proposed to study. Archie, as his students called him, was a sly North Carolinian for all his folksy expressions, but he didn't laugh at my pretensions. He simply allowed that he probably wasn't the best person to work with me but that my project sounded ambitious. He asked what I had been reading, and when I mentioned Pound and Williams, he agreed that Williams made the way for us all but thought Pound's rhythms were not as interesting as they seemed at first. I didn't know then that Archie had, in fact, driven Williams around the New Jersey countryside in his car after Williams's debilitating strokes, but I was impressed that Ammons could question Pound in so matter-of-fact a way. Maybe he was right—I'd studied Pound's rhythms closely, but perhaps they paled over time. Ammons's remark may have been the single most important gift he gave me as a teacher. He helped loosen Pound's grip on my poetics and opened me to Williams and much that followed from him. It would be years before I could finally say good-bye to Pound—in grad school I published an essay on gender in *The Cantos* that served as my valediction both to Pound and to literary criticism—but I needed to untangle his voice from the carping judgments of my Orthodox relatives. The anti-Semite and the Jews both challenged me to seek knowledge as the price for my ambitions.

I was heartened by Ammons's honest and casual tone, but I still thought I needed to earn the right to call myself a poet with a great deal more learning than I possessed. I signed up to be a classics major, studying third year Latin and first semester Greek. I took Great Moments in German Literature, too, and a course on Romantic poets, which I loved most of all. I would stop outside the undergraduate library after hours of study and try to envision Blake's angels burning in the beautiful rounded tree standing by the path that led down to my house. But no matter how hard I studied, I really wasn't much of a language student. The fine points of declension and conjugation escaped me while I sought for curious words and the wider historical picture I lacked. Still, I willed myself to be a scholar. I proudly announced to the chair of my department after a month or two that I wanted to apply for a Rhodes scholarship to study classics. He looked puzzled and asked how much Latin and Greek I had. When I told him, he sat back and said in a kind voice: "Mr. Goldblatt, a freshman in classics at Oxford has at least ten years of Latin and six of Greek." I dropped Greek and decided I would settle for a reading knowledge of Catullus and Goethe.

I imagined my return to college as something between a medieval test of strength and character for knighthood and St. Jerome's hermit sojourn in the desert. But I liked people too much, and my desire to write generated more joy than the ascetic life would allow. As committed as I felt to searching out the roots of poetry, I wanted to live with other poets, to be one among artists and thinkers in a scene like the ones I'd witnessed in San Francisco and read about in pre–World War I London or New York. I wanted to talk and laugh, to listen to strange stories and sad adventures, to drink and shed tears. At night, I listened to blues on my little Panasonic turntable, and I imagined poetry cast in the hard language of imagism, charged with the wide-ranging fervor of Black Mountain poets Creeley, Duncan, Olson, and Levertov, gathered into the singular voice of Muddy Waters or Jimmy Reed and suffused with the wise sorrow of Mississippi John Hurt. I laughed for an hour after I wrote a short poem about my brother wearing suspenders, and I tried for the immediacy I found in Catullus in an imitative lyric that year:

> Licinius, I knew better company.
> I remember low pines there
> over pumice grass and wind.
> We watched once the peddler leaves
> bite yellow and red, prize circlets
> at the branches.
> We imagined, mailing houses wonder
> what becomes cliffs, or the plain
> to make her visible.
> We knew skies and did not

think them leather. And now
we have before us this blind woman.
She laughs to show no teeth!
And I have a hole in my pocket.
My friend, you know, there is no luck.

It had an academic feel to it—a young man's nostalgia, a lesser version of Yeats's early verse—but I was proud of the rhythmic contrast between the spondees in "did not / think them leather" and anapests of "And I have a hole in my pocket." I thought I was writing something close to real poetry, and I wanted to read my poem to somebody. Perhaps learning alone would not get me closer to being a poet.

I began to visit the weekly open reading series at the College of Arts and Science coffee shop, known as the Temple of Zeus for the Greek statuary that stood on a wide shelf above the tables. Ammons and other poetry professors used to attend; sometimes there would be fifteen or more readers, both graduates and undergraduates. It got to be quite a show sometimes, when students left over from the radical days read long, funny political manifestos and graduates wrote about farm life after the days of the war on the War. This was the beginning of women's consciousness-raising, and young women were writing poems influenced by Sylvia Plath, Anne Sexton, and Adrienne Rich. Some were publicly contemplating suicide. Few experimental poets read, and they showed the influence of the New York School led by Frank O'Hara, Kenneth Koch, and John Ashbery. I started attending, of course, to see if my work was better or worse than other poets', but soon I realized I was spending more time finding fault than listening to the poems. Once I began to listen, I recognized that some poets in fact were quite good while others were boring, sentimental, or rude. Finally, I decided that I had no right to criticize anybody else if I didn't have the courage to read my own poems. The day I signed up to read, I feared the entire audience would stand up as one and walk out upon hearing my first few lines. To my amazement, my two poems dissolved into air so fast I barely remembered reading them; suddenly people were clapping politely and I was sitting back down. No one threw stink bombs or called me names. As the weeks went on, I began to see around campus other regular readers. I made some nodding acquaintances and even drank coffee with a few of them. I still felt it my job to write alone, but the readings indicated that others—some my own age and with no more obvious preparation than I—were out there writing alongside me.

I continued to see Corinne in Cambridge through that year. She had broken off her engagement with the law student, and my occasional hitchhiking trips into Boston were a great release from the cage I had built myself. Corinne taught me how to study literature. When she had a paper to write, she went to the library and took out a stack of books on her subject. She didn't read every word, but she gleaned ideas and quotes from the critics. It never occurred to me until then that you could take out a book and not read the whole thing. I thought somehow it was cheating not to read everything an author had to say in a book or to claim you knew a critic's position by reading only a few pages. On one visit I made to Cambridge, she was working on Hart Crane, a poet I loved reading when I lived in San Francisco. I had even read some criticism on him, but Corinne's research was far more extensive. She actually wanted to know what he was saying in a poem like "Voyages." I had never been concerned with meaning when I read lines like these in the second section over and over again:

> O minstrel galleons of Carib fire,
> Bequeath us to no earthly shore until
> Is answered in the vortex of our grave
> The seal's wide spindrift gaze toward paradise. (36)

It sounded so fine, why would you ask what it meant? She taught me that one could actually seek the main verb in Crane's sentence, or question what would happen once the seal's gaze "is answered." We had a wonderful few days tramping through her paper, making meals in the dorm kitchen at Currier House on the Radcliffe campus. When she wanted to work alone, I would walk for hours with my friend Ken who lived in the dorm next door, talking about Watergate and Nixon's reelection, the Munich attacks on Israeli athletes and the Vietnamization of the War, or whether poetry or philosophy meant anything in a time of slaughter and public dishonesty.

But Corinne had more important lessons to teach me than careful literary analysis. My relationship with her was rocky at times, and the night before I left Cambridge was always difficult. I didn't know how couples actually talked to each other when they disagreed; I had never witnessed such a scene at home. At times, I felt too young and stupid to have an adult relationship with a smart woman who actually wanted something from me besides a hitchhiking story, a disquisition on art, or sex. She wanted an emotional honesty that I couldn't comprehend, let alone produce. For all the challenges I felt personally, the tension across gender lines was mounting all around us. In November 1971, soon after I'd met Corinne and before I'd gone to Cornell, she and our mutual friend Sue invited me to meet them in New Haven where they were attending a conference called "Economic Perspectives on Women," a gathering they had heard about through the Cambridge Women's Center, where they sometimes volunteered. Men couldn't attend any of the sessions, of course, but I did sneak in the back of the room during the closing, which involved mostly hopeful and angry speeches bolstered by music and an incredible feeling of sisterhood in the room. I had never experienced anything like it, and the power of the women together scared me more than I wanted to admit.

To see how little a young man like me mattered in this gathering, or how much Corinne and Sue drew strength from the other women, shook my settled gender place as the oldest son of a widowed mother, though I could not have recognized that at the time. I could see that men had shut women out of powerful positions, but I couldn't yet imagine how enormous the task would be to change the normal arrangements. I returned to my job at Hamilton Newell after the conference and didn't even notice the gender division between the women in low-wage jobs collating and binding while the men on the shop floor got paid more to run the machines. Still, the conference—and heated conversations about gender with Corinne and Sue afterward—did begin to penetrate my male armor. Their calls for equality made sense most when I thought about my mother and her struggles with the nearly all-male health bureaucracy in Washington.

Producing actual papers for my classes was terribly difficult for me. I remember spending all weekend in a carrel of the library writing and rewriting the first paragraph of a paper on Shelley's "Mont Blanc." I had such large feelings about the poem, but I could not say anything intelligible in the analytic language of the classroom. I admired my teacher, Dr. Parker, immensely; he was exactly the sort of brilliant professor in the front of the room whom I had come to Cornell to find. But I couldn't produce discussions of the poetry like his lectures: incisive about the argument of the poem, steeped in the history and philosophy of the time, tempered by current critical debates. I wrote an inarticulate appreciation of Wordsworth's "Yew-Trees," full of earnest but perplexing sentences like "There is an entire expression of opposed and separating thoughts moving within a single presence." Dr. Parker handled me kindly, despite my occasional spelling errors and convoluted prose, but he remarked: "If I understand what you've argued in this paper, the interpretation seems to me an extravagant one, though building on an understandable intuition that in the description of the trees there is some correspondence to language that might be used to describe the activity of the mind. . . . You have some sharp things to say, but on the whole the paper is uneven." The B was a gift, I imagine, for the sake of my obvious desire to commune with the poem.

On Halloween of 1972, I was invited to a party at the Telluride House, a coed living community for highly motivated academic students. To myself, I sneered at it as a fraternity for smart people, but I was attracted as well as repelled by the clubbiness I sensed in the Telluride residents I'd met. Somebody in my Romantic poetry class invited me, and I was pleased that she would want me there but wary of being rejected. It felt like eighth grade all over again, but I dressed in what I could find for a costume and showed up at the appointed time. I was a bit early, but food was out and people were starting to appear in elaborate costumes that seemed tied to inside jokes among housemates. I got more nervous and drank some wine or doctored punch, and when someone handed me a joint, I smoked along with everyone else despite my penchant for dismal thoughts when I got stoned. I knew a few people vaguely, but no one much noticed me until a small group asked me to join them in a room upstairs. The costumed characters kept growing more and more arrogant and disdainful in my mind, and in the little room I realized this was a collection of English majors. Some I recognized from readings at the Temple of Zeus. One of them looked at me and pointedly asked in front of the group if I considered myself a poet. By this time, I was almost completely unable to speak. In that heady paranoia with which marijuana can burnish a soiree, I imagined these intellectual stars exchanging glances and chuckling to themselves. I managed to answer in a few words, but I could feel myself spiraling down and did not want to share my mood with this proud and self-referential crowd.

I left the party and stumbled down the hill to my home among the engineers. Stopping at a food truck in front of our house, I tried to order a "fruit pie" but mangled my pronunciation so badly that the vendor said, "Buddy, I think it's time for bed." I felt an intense shame and imagined my mother's frown spread across the cloudy Ithaca night. I could not be what I wanted to be. I was neither smart nor clever enough. I came from the wrong background, went to the wrong schools, and read the wrong books. Or I read the right ones the wrong way. I couldn't make myself understood, my emotions and ideas remained petty, and my poems amounted to little fire and no heat. I needed people too much, could not detach from them enough. I got up the stairs and into my bed but fell asleep fantasizing that my roommates had called the asylum to send a crew to tie me up and haul me away. A "nervous breakdown" would free me from all my ambitious plans and release me from obligations I had set myself to learn German and Latin, master the history of poetry, win the Yale Younger Poets prize before I turned twenty-two, and still be the hitchhiking printer who owed nothing to Telluride House and professors of criticism.

That winter break, my brother and I met in New York City for a week to paint my grandparents' apartment. My mother's parents, Max and Lillian Kushner, had lived in Morningside Heights ever since I was old enough to remember visiting them; I had been beaten up on the playground in front of their building when I was eight. The collocation of Harlem housing projects across the street and Grandpa's high-rise complex, with its small businessmen, Columbia professors, and retired schoolteachers, was what I thought of as the City—plus *My Fair Lady* or *Camelot* and the dinosaurs at the Museum of Natural History—but now I was reading Frank O'Hara and wandering through the streets as if inside one of his "I do this I do that" (163) poems:

> If I rest for a moment near The Equestrian
> pausing for a liver sausage sandwich in the Mayflower Shoppe,
> that angel seems to be leading the horse into Bergdorf's
> and I am naked as a table cloth, my nerves humming.      (91)

O'Hara was like Catullus, undyingly sexy and unnerved, a sensual soldier for verse. I tried to get New Yorkers to meet my eyes and noticed
peculiar little inscriptions on buildings. I visited Gotham Book Mart
in the Diamond District, seeking poetry among the Orthodox jewel
dealers. Above the door of the bookstore hung a metal cutout sign that
read "Wise Men Fish Here," and inside, poets like Marianne Moore and
W. H. Auden had once searched for books as I was doing.

Aaron had managed to graduate high school a year early and started
working for an old black painter named Quincy, who would mutter
while they worked: "I gotta get outta the paintin' business." They soon
parted ways, but now Aaron had moved to western Massachusetts,
to live in a cabin in the woods and apprentice with a carpenter friend
of the family. His path and mine lay far apart, but we shared an army
childhood, and the scar from Dad's death bound us together. We had
great fun painting all day and drinking our grandfather's whiskey each
night. We drank well, but we drank carefully, never actually finishing
any of the bottles. Though he didn't touch liquor, and he pitied anyone
who did, Grandpa knew what bottles had come from which business
associate and would have noticed if his liquor cabinet emptied out. He
didn't much approve of either of us in those days. I talked too much
about art and didn't want to become a doctor like my father. Aaron
wore his hair like a hippie and worked with his hands instead of going
to college. But my grandparents had moved elsewhere for the dura-
tion of our painting stint, so we had the run of the apartment where,
as kids, we'd played war in the halls. I didn't feel so anxious around
Aaron, didn't have to prove I was this or that to him, and he didn't give
a damn about what I was reading. We were beginning to be friends
again after years apart.

By the spring, I started drinking beer with poets I'd met at the Royal
Palm, the Collegetown bar that arts and science students frequented.
Only at the point I had a few friends among the poets did I begin
to realize I could choose not to be a banished creature in my own
invented forest. I didn't need to be a monk for poetry. But as I became
more comfortable in this new, more social life, the contradictions of
my chosen path seemed harder to ignore. What would I do for a living, majoring in classics? Increasingly, I didn't want to be a professor.
Professors seemed too far away from the lives of people I'd met hitch-

hiking—the waterbed salesman headed to Arizona, the former sergeant who'd been court-martialed in Panama for bigamy, the mysterious young man driving to an unnameable doom in the Nevada desert, the grizzled old truck driver in Massachusetts who propositioned me just before he let me off—and professors certainly knew even less about the daily routine of production at a place like Hamilton Newell Printing. I wanted my poem-life to be anchored in the day-to-day that was not informed primarily by the literary, no matter how driven I felt to immerse myself in the tradition. I admired poets like Kenneth Rexroth, who knew classical philosophy and Asian poetries but had no academic degree, hiked the Coastal Range, and worked in leftist politics. Kenneth Patchen stayed in college only a year and wrote, despite years of pain from a spinal injury, achingly of love but also of his father's life in the steel mills. Gary Snyder, Philip Whalen, and Lew Welch had all been rangers in West Coast forests and made poems with a muscular Zen spirit and challenging Beat rhythms. And what about black poets like Langston Hughes and Amiri Baraka and Gwendolyn Brooks? They didn't make their livings interpreting other poets. What could I do that would allow me time to write and also experience life outside classrooms and research institutions? Teaching kids never occurred to me, and Cornell afforded no chance to learn a trade. For a week that semester, while I was struggling to translate Petronius and Thomas Mann for my classes, I contemplated becoming a lawyer. I wanted to learn the literature for my own purposes, but I wasn't a good enough language student to make German or Latin my life, and my literary criticism too easily fell into tautology and idiosyncrasy. Still, a career in law seemed dismal and unappetizing; only Wallace Stevens, among the poets I'd read, had been trained in law. I gave up the idea soon after I saw my mother that spring break. She looked at me with something very near horror when I told her I might study law, and I was hard-pressed to argue with any enthusiasm for torts and taxes as my trade.

Then one night in March, I took a walk through a snowstorm in Ithaca. I walked past large houses and empty stretches of forest, stopping every once in a while to watch the snow erase the road. I thought about what mattered to me, what I was good at, what I did when I wasn't forcing myself to act selfish or unattached. I found myself dwelling on stories from my friend Sue, a premed at Harvard, about working at a women's health center and at Brigham and Women's Hospital, witnessing tubal ligations and making sure that surgeons didn't sterilize poor women who still wanted to remain fertile despite multiple births. I began to imagine myself caring for sick children in the projects, driving from place to place and delivering babies, or ministering to fevered patients during an epidemic. William Carlos Williams delivered thousands of babies and still wrote poetry at every opportunity, typing a poem between consultations or jotting down lines as he drove:

> The supreme importance
> of this nameless spectacle
>
> sped me by them
> without a word—
>
> Why bother where I went?
> for I went spinning on the
>
> four wheels of my car
> along the wet road until
>
> I saw a girl with one leg
> over the rail of a balcony     (*Collected Earlier Poems* 258–59)

Williams was seeing the world and bringing its words into his poems, or inventing a world in his poems out of which the outside world could take its shape in the mind. I loved the immediacy of that girl striking her careless pose both on the balcony and in the poem called "The Right of Way." The wet road perhaps slyly echoed Pound's "In a Station of the Metro": "The apparition of these faces in the crowd; / Petals on a wet, black bough" (*Personae* 109). But for Williams, people weren't "apparitions," not ghosts from Dante, but live beings populating a world the poet/doctor moved through on his rounds.

I didn't think I should decide my own life based on one poet I admired—that would be cheap and softheaded—but if Williams could be a doctor and a poet, why couldn't I? I'm sure I thought of my father that night, but I didn't dwell on him. He was so different from me. He had been a natural at science while I nearly failed high school chemistry. He knew nothing about art except Picasso because he was famous and the Soyer brothers because they were Russian Jews. I knew next to nothing about my father, but I refused to be an artless technician. He had always wanted to perform surgery on the mouth, and he didn't mind joining the military to do it. I would use medicine in an entirely different way: to help poor people and hunker down with them in times of disease and death. Williams would be my spirit guide, my talisman against the onslaught of mere fact, a poet who wrote well and yet also saved lives. I would go to medical school and prove that I could do math like my father after all, balance chemical equations and appreciate the periodic table, discourse on acid-base balance in the blood and anatomy of the hand, but I would continue my growth as a poet, studying on my own and attending readings whenever I could. My brother was learning the trades of carpentry and house painting. I would learn doctoring as my trade and write my poems free from English majors.

As soon as my decision was made, my literature classes became a pleasure again. I changed my major from classics to classical civilization, a lighter requirement for which I needed only a few more courses. That loosened up my fall schedule so that I could take a writing seminar with Ammons alongside biology, chemistry, and physics courses for the pre-med track. But the pleasure I gained in my arts courses didn't particularly translate into higher grades. The spring ended with a weeklong orgy of studying for my classical art final—drawing the statues, the buildings, the bridge arches—just because I loved the forms and the history of styles and the act of drawing. I didn't do well on the exam, however. I aced the identification questions, but my essays were so enamored of the works that I couldn't manage to say anything ABOUT them. My decision to study science seemed to have freed me to appreciate the art, in the old-fashioned use of that term "appreciate," but with little motivation to analyze or categorize. I thought myself unburdened of critical debates I did not choose to enter. Art would be a part of my particular poem-life, but I could draw my own conclusions, independent of academics. I was in fact giving up one system of arrogance for another, embracing the illusory freedom of the self-taught American individual, but at the time I felt I had solved a great riddle and defeated my own monster.

I ran into a similar contradiction in my Shakespeare seminar. I set myself a modest task for my final paper: to propose a theory of tragedy based on Othello, Macbeth, Hamlet, and Lear. Using critical language from Northrop Frye, Aristotle, and Longinus, I worked for two weeks reviewing every scene, tracking the rise and fall of action and hero, charting the intensity of language, identifying the moments of sublime catharsis. At two in the morning the day the paper was due, I had a horrifying revelation as I was typing the last pages of the longest essay I'd ever written: all I had done was tell the plot of each play. My grand theory amounted to nothing more than pointing to the text and saying, "Don't you see?!" I was appalled, but I had recognized my folly too late to start again. I admired Professor States, an eminent Shakespearean who seemed to know every critic personally and could wring out the nuances from the briefest scenes, but who also would deliver whole speeches from memory in the style of this or that famous actor. I finished typing the paper, slept a couple of hours, and dragged myself into Dr. States's office as if turning myself into the police. I knocked on his door and heard a flurry of papers, throat clearing, and a muffled "Yes, yes. Come in." I felt I had interrupted something unseemly, but when I opened the door I found the professor alone, staring at his typewriter with papers piled everywhere. I mustered my courage and said: "Professor States, I'm turning in a paper I've worked on very hard, but I recognized only late last night that it's nothing but a thirty-page tautology." He looked at me, looked down at his typewriter, looked back at me, and said, "We're all involved in tautology, Mr. Goldblatt." I received an A- in the course, a grade I always felt reflected his benign solidarity with me at that moment more than any hidden virtue in my self-absorbed prose.

My mother was baffled by my decision, but I made a passionate plea for the rightness of a medical career, and she made no more objections. My grandfather was overjoyed, but I tried hard to convince myself that he misunderstood what I intended to do and that his approval did not mean I'd merely made an expedient choice. Of course, it's one thing to decide to go to medical school and an entirely different enterprise to prepare, apply, and be accepted. I had no idea how to be a premed and knew practically no one who studied science except the engineers with whom I shared a house. They weren't much help for course selection, as few took biology and only the one chemical engineer from Montana actually liked chemistry. He had once lectured me, while we were playing pool, about the Three Laws of Thermodynamics: (1) you can't win, (2) you can't break even, and (3) you can't get out of the game. I realized years later that he was right in his cowboy way, and I remembered his swagger when I began teaching sciences a few years later and wanted to make chemistry seem a little less serious. But I needed a kindly ally, an advisor who could help me choose my courses and make science seem less foreign and unsympathetic, less my father's world and more my own.

Chemistry was a particular puzzle for me. I was not afraid of biology, and physics class had a new hands-on format that sounded fun and would fulfill the premed requirements in the catalog, but I was afraid of the more challenging version of first semester chemistry. I went to the professor teaching the higher level to ask if I really had to take his course for medical school. He was a young, tall, dark-haired, fast-talking character who appeared uncomfortable speaking to an undergraduate needing advice. "I'm not going to recommend a course for you," he said. "We have a policy here at Cornell. We let the student hang himself." I knew he expected premeds to take the harder course, but his answer made me even less inclined to do what he considered right. I wandered around till I found the professor who taught the alternative course, the one they informally designated for "poets." I resented the implication that poets couldn't learn science, but I wanted to meet the teacher anyway. I talked to Dr. Hoffman for a half hour, and he told me he'd be happy to have me in his course but thought that, on the whole, medical schools preferred the other. I appreciated his honesty and thanked him. Despite wanting to study with Dr. Hoffman because he seemed sympathetic and interested in me as a student, I signed up for the other course. I learned in this exchange that I would have to make decisions on my own, that in science the level mattered more than the teacher. The humanity of a science teacher could only be a bonus; the primary goal remained assimilating the content well enough to use it at the next level. My biology class would have six hundred people enrolled, and my chemistry class had at least three hundred, but there would be no need of interpretation or debate. The instructors would present, and I would take notes, read the book, study for the tests, and try to earn better grades than the next person. If I wanted to go to medical school, I needed to prove I could learn science the way science was taught.

I also needed to demonstrate that I was interested in medicine. In fact, I needed to find out for myself if I had the stomach for sick people and bloody wounds, doctors and nurses, hospital cafeteria food, and long hours under fluorescent lights. This wasn't a theoretical shift of position or a subtle alteration of style. To be a doctor, you had to become a doctor, and that would require a radical reinvention: how I spent my time, with whom I passed much of the day, what I thought about once the day was done. I began to volunteer at the Tompkins County Hospital emergency room in the spring and continued at the Mt. Auburn Hospital in Cambridge, Massachusetts, where I lived with Corinne that summer. Entering through hospital glass doors, this time with the idea of belonging there for work rather than visiting my father or having my tonsils removed, I felt the uneasiness of moving out of the life I'd imagined in libraries and bookstores and into a life not yet my own. My father had gained authority for what he could do more than for the rank he held. And what he knew came not only from books but also from encountering every permutation of complaint, disorder, and injury. I remembered the coffin-shaped box in our living room when my father was preparing his cases for board certification, his pictures of mangled faces and charred thighs and the astounding improvements after surgery. Aaron and I especially stared at the little babies with mouths like tent flaps that became well-formed lips over months under my father's care. Could I face these fearful asymmetries with his bravery and good humor?

The first time I saw a doctor click a bone back into place—the forearm of a teenager who had fallen during track practice—I watched calmly, began to feel shaky, and made it back to my volunteer's stool just as my head went light and I nearly passed out. I overheard another doctor consulting with a carpenter who had fallen backward off a ladder and damaged the nerves that passed through his elbows. I saw the carpenter's face and the face of his wife as the doctor told them he might never use his hands for work again. At midsummer, they brought into Mt. Auburn a ten-year-old boy wrapped in a foil thermal blanket, his face scratched but calm, dead after a train hit him when he and his friends were playing on the tracks. I could not call them cases, because I had neither a doctor's data nor his white coat to distance them from me. As hard as they were to face, I felt I belonged in the emergency room, a witness to what they and their families confronted. Perhaps I could help someone someday, but at the very least I wanted to know how families lived and died, what might improve their lives. I loved poems and poets, Marianne Moore's "imaginary garden with real toads" (31) and H. D.'s "Rose, harsh rose, / marred and with stint of petals" (Doolittle 5), but I didn't want my work or my life to be a scholarly exercise built on clever experiment and learned allusion, a competition for the coolest and least attached demeanor.

Living with Corinne and her friends that summer in a rented house off the Radcliffe campus, I stopped writing poetry altogether for nearly a month, thinking perhaps I could be free of the burden of having to write, of having to maintain an internal life that at times felt so isolating. But despite the emergency room at night and my day job at a wallpaper warehouse in South Boston—where I memorized pattern numbers to store fancy and plain rolls among miles of bins—and the realization that I must wipe the bathtub after a shower and put the toilet seat down after a pee if I wanted to live with women, writing wouldn't go away. I composed a long, rambling poem on a walk one evening and came home and wrote it down at the kitchen table on a large paper bag because I hadn't even bought a new journal or made a place in our room for writing. It felt so damned good to write; leaves cast shadows again and conversations suddenly filled with verbs. I needed experiences outside the library, no matter how horrifying, but I needed the poetry as well. Perhaps I was more like Williams than I was like my father, even while I grew to know my father better as I walked the hospital corridors. In any case, if I continued on this path, I'd have to make my own way in an era unlike anything either of them had experienced. The Vietnam War looked like it would finally end, and the hated Henry Kissinger had won the Nobel Peace Prize. Watergate unraveled before us every day on TV, stiff men with droning voices masking the utter depravity of their schemes. The 1960s were receding, and a cynical dryness in public life seemed to be taking its place.

## 5

# Dry Creek Road

THE ROAD TO MEDICAL school from Dr. Parker's Romantic poetry class led through the vineyards of Northern California. After I decided in a snowstorm to go to medical school, to make science my public career while pursuing poetry as my personal work, I spent my senior year taking premed courses but also openly declaring myself a poet. I read regularly at weekly readings in the Temple of Zeus coffee shop, hung out with the poets at the Royal Palm bar, and went down to Ithaca House Press once a week to print a page of whatever poetry book we were publishing at the time. I wasn't much of a printer, and no one seemed to be able to teach me about how to run the letterpress in the basement, but I don't think I was any worse than the other young poets in the collective. We did manage to accept, print, and bind some pretty good books, even if they sustained an ink blotch or an upside-down *e* on the pages now and then. I'd go down each Friday, print for a few hours, and then go upstairs to the apartment of my friend and mentor David McAleavey, where we would eat whatever he had cooked and drink a bottle of cheap scotch I had brought, ending the evening with a game of chess that I invariably lost. We talked about Modernism and the New York poets, about avant-garde music and jazz, and about our own poems. He had already published one poetry collection and was working on a capacious series of poems I admired. He was writing a dissertation on the poetry of George Oppen. I soon came to love Oppen's taut and raw poems, so enigmatic and yet so direct, charged with a consciousness about language that is profoundly social but seldom explicitly political. That Oppen and many of his fellow Objectivists were Jewish hardly mattered to me at the time, but their aesthetics and ethics resonated for me in a way few other movements had ever done. David never questioned me about medical school, and as far as I remember, we seldom talked about the years to come, though he must have been thinking about academic positions for the following year. He treated me like a younger equal, and I tried to earn that respect. Once when we were fairly drunk, I asked him if he thought, from reading my poems, that I had talent. He replied that he could never tell someone yes or no about talent because talent wasn't the issue; the important thing was to keep doing the work despite all the reasons to stop that the world throws before us. Only I could determine my own ability to keep writing.

I took a poetry seminar from Archie Ammons that fall. It was a special course, held in a building reserved for rarified study and honored guests, and he let in only a dozen advanced undergraduates. Most of us knew one another from the Temple of Zeus readings, but a few people were entirely new to us all. Archie wasn't a critical teacher— "Very fine poem, Miss B," he would rumble, "take the week off"—but he had a comforting presence that made risk possible. He presided over an incredible gathering of serious writers with a variety of poetic allegiances—to feminism, the New York School, and Wallace Stevens, among others—but our growing fondness for each other softened any competitiveness. A few of us took the craft as our life's work, and at least four of us published a volume or more of poetry after college. At the time, there was no campus literary magazine, and some of us joined with a couple of Cornell grad students to collect poems written by undergrads and grads in a publication called *The First Anthology*, using monies from a fund Archie had access to that year. I also had my first poem accepted in a national literary magazine, albeit one sponsored by the English department at Cornell, and felt for the first time that my poems had some weight, some ability to survive on their own. I worked through the science courses, wrote poems that others accepted as real, and had friends who did not think my ambitions strange or unworthy.

One of the poetry students I hadn't known before was Sandra, a slender young woman from Long Island who wrote spare but vibrant poems about the natural world. Sandra turned out to be an accomplished science student, an entomologist in the agriculture school, and she idolized Nabokov for his writing and his knowledge of butterflies. She spoke little in the seminar because she knew so much less about literature or feminism than the leading poets in the class, Julie and Wendy, who were passionate readers of Sylvia Plath and Anne Sexton and could intimidate with the urgency and wit of their poetry. When Sandra found out I was taking premed courses, she opened up to me, and by the end of that semester we were deeply involved in a relation-ship that lasted more than a year and carried us very far afield. After our first night together, Sandra brought me to her lab and showed me hissing African cockroaches; she was a fascinating mix of passion-ate brilliance and studied innocence, a scientist with a penchant for personal mythology. I read her love poems by Catullus and felt both knowledgeable and needed. In the spring, I spent more and more time with Sandra, pulling away from my other friends, sometimes quite thoughtlessly cutting them off. I finished the basic premed courses and continued to write, but now in a different sort of isolation, one defined by an intense love affair that let in very little outside light. By the summer, I was studying organic chemistry eight hours a day and living with Sandra in a tiny apartment on a steep Ithaca hill, stealing time to write but reading nothing new.

Sandra went off to entomology graduate school in Riverside, Cali-fornia, that fall, and I stayed behind to study comparative zoology and biochemistry, apply to medical school, and take one last writing seminar with the grand old man of the department, Baxter Hathaway. Baxter had started the creative writing graduate program, and he'd seen the rise of the writing industry in his many years at Cornell. He had more emphysema than lung by that time, but he would sit patiently and listen to us, often not commenting more than once or twice in a two-and-a-half-hour session once a week. At the last class meeting, he summed up in his longest speech of the term, wheezing through a disquisition that ended with this lingering farewell question: "I admired . . . all your poems this semester . . . but I keep wondering . . . what do twenty-one-year-olds . . . really have to say?" My peers were outraged, but I thought his point well-taken. What did we know? What were we trying to accomplish? Were we willing to face up to our lack of experi-ence and our excess self-importance? I missed Sandra fiercely that fall, but I regarded the pain as part of my emotional training. My brother was traveling with friends in South America at the time, sending letters from the road in Ecuador, Peru, and Bolivia. I envied him his freedom and his willingness to take chances, but it was like the old days when he liked green pepper and I liked carrots. His adventure was happening in the outside world while mine would come through science and the body. Committed to my new life plan, I convinced myself that Baxter's criticism didn't really apply to me. My career choice would require me to assimilate much over the next years. I'd have to find out for what and for whom I wrote, or my choice would crush me.

After a torrent of letters exchanged through the fall, Sandra and I reunited at the winter break in Ithaca. We set off in my red VW Beetle for her California home late in December. On New Year's Eve, we stayed in a cheap hotel off the highway in New Mexico, with winds howling and the night hostile to lovers who were really strangers to each other. An ecstatic beginning had lent our relationship an adult patina, but the sustaining armature of college was now gone. Once we arrived in Riverside, I began looking for work but could find nothing. I went out dutifully every day and applied for jobs one after another in the classified ads. It never occurred to me to look for a job in an office, despite my degree. All I wanted was to labor with my hands, work in a print shop, or fill orders for a shipping department. At one warehouse they wanted somebody to unload oranges, but the foreman took one look at me and said, "Sorry, but we want a guy with more meat in his jeans." I came home each night steeped in my own incompetence but trying to appear brave for my brilliant girlfriend. Sandra was one of the only females in a lab of science cowboys who probably thought she could do better than an unemployed poet. Was I a boy wanting to be a man or a man fearing he would always be a boy? On Valentine's Day, a holy occasion in Sandra's calendar, I managed to get a one-day gig hosing down a huge motel parking lot so that I could bring her roses and take her out to dinner, but the solution couldn't last. Finally I got hired on at a temp agency, which sent me to a cosmetics factory at the edge of town. There I worked for the next couple of months, measuring out ingredients for liquid makeup we mixed in vats two stories tall. The foreman was a handsome Chicano that all the women on the line admired. He spent every lunch break with the prettiest one, though he had a wife and kids at home. I felt nearly invisible, filling the beakers and weighing the drums, while the foreman got to run up the ladder and pour the precious oils into the tank, girls on the line watching him climb. Once, the bosses had me grinding pigment and adding fragrance to lipstick wax in the composition room, and it took me more than a week to wash the shades of red from my arms and the stink from my hands. Another time, a chemist from the East came to develop a new and improved cold cream, but he couldn't get the formula right. The goop kept congealing in the man-sized vat where we mixed it. Three times I had to climb inside the tank and scoop out the greasy stuff with a dipper. I don't know what they did with fifty-five-gallon drums of botched cold cream once I wheeled them off the factory floor.

I remember straining to block out the radio and shoptalk while I read a few pages of Paul Valéry's essays on poetics at lunch behind the loading dock:

> Now, this work, these researches, these struggles of the poet against the stringent conditions I had set myself—and whose indirect importance so few people grasp—were never, I must say, wasted efforts. I made those hours of labor and tension yield everything they could possibly contain. The art of poetry is, happily, not an exact one. At every instant insurmountable problems confront one. A nothing—and a beautiful poem is shipwrecked, achievement compromised, the charm broken. The poet's brain is a sea bottom on which many hulls repose.     (154)

My "stringent conditions" were to appear just like every other worker but to carry on my "researches" surreptitiously, in a part of my psyche that would flow alongside experience like an underground stream beneath a road. Sandra, meanwhile, was ever more drawn into the culture of evolutionary science, occupied by the question of how a gene that causes an ant to give his life for the colony can simultaneously pass the gene on to the next generation. She became increasingly frustrated with my introspection and ambivalence about medical school and our lives together. I would come home exhausted, smelling like a discount drugstore, only to be caught in a storm at home I could not comprehend or magically transmute with a Catullus poem. I tried to shut out work and worries when I sat down to write at the little card table set up in the otherwise conventional living room of our Southern California garden apartment, but occasionally my journal contains carefully dated self-conscious entries I had written after a fight. We tore at each other and loved each other by turns. I wrote endless lines that started off as vaguely threatening couplets—"Lovers are the champions of the world / And the sun burns hot against their skin"—but eventually recombined them into forty-five quatrains of seemingly random urgencies:

Lovers are the champions of the world
Political in so far as at large
Once home, wire all that to the beach
Transformed every day over the din.

I began drafting a verse play called *A Poet's Comedy*, about a traveling poet who recites poems of excess emotion for a fee to impromptu audiences. Sandra's parents visited, a friend from the Ammons seminar stopped through town with her boyfriend—we had been roommates that fall while I was waiting to join Sandra in California—and sometimes our relationship seemed nearly normal, almost adult. The day I got into Case Western Reserve University's medical school in Cleveland, Sandra and I spiraled into another crisis because I could not bring myself to ask her to come with me. I could hardly think of going there myself. Emotions cycled from high to low and back, but mostly everything ran together in a terrifying inner scream. I pretended to keep my impulses in pristine little boxes, frozen in lines of verse that—as Ezra Pound would say—could not cohere.

And then suddenly my old college friend Joel visited from Northern California. He had gathered how miserable I was from phone calls, and he came down to talk. After only a day, he invited me—or, grudgingly, Sandra and me—to come up to his little house on Preston Vineyards in Healdsburg, at the end of West Dry Creek Road in the Sonoma Valley. Much to Sandra's disapproval, I went up with him to visit the grape ranch, secured an offer of a job in the field, and came back to Riverside. I can't tell exactly the order in which these events occurred because, despite all the upheaval, I wrote very little in my journal about daily life that spring, preferring to draft carefully abstracted verse and an occasional discourse on art, punctuated rarely with a truncated or florid statement about the relationship. Sandra surprised me one night at her colleague's dinner party by abruptly announcing that she was withdrawing from the graduate program. Suddenly we were on our way north in my VW, pulling a tiny U-Haul trailer filled with furniture and books. In the back seat rode her cat and the two goslings that Sandra insisted on buying for the trip to the country. We arrived and started work, the goslings died of cold in the Northern California spring, and our relationship crazed like a windshield smashed by a hammer. Our Beloit friend Sylvie, with her great sympathetic spirit, came to visit Joel and me from San Diego, but Sandra saw her only as another one of my friends arrayed against her. Sandra took my journal while I was at work and wrote on all the blank pages, accusing me of betraying our love. I couldn't bear the emotional strain anymore. Within a month of our arrival in Healdsburg, I flew with her back to her parents, dropped her and her cat off with them in a New York City parking lot, and forced myself to walk away.

During a short respite at my mother's house, my mother told me as kindly as she could that I was not allowed to fall apart. I would just have to pull myself through this emotional mess; she needed me whole. I had never heard her speak to me with such cold desperation, but it was a merciful message. Soon I was back at the end of Dry Creek Road, planting rootstocks and tying vines to trellis wire, alternately crying uncontrollably and laughing at the freedom I felt. Joel was usually somewhere else on the ranch, cultivating between vines with the old gray and red tractor, hiding the occasional posts he tore out when his turns went too wide. The Mexican guys I worked beside stared at me with amazement and sympathy, puzzled by my outbursts but perfectly willing to accept me as one of the crew. They were all undocumented, leading a much harder life than Joel and I were. After all, we lived in a two-room cabin right on the property, with a functioning kitchen, toilet, and shower and a wood-burning stove for chilly nights. They lived five or eight men to a shack down the road, ate rice and beans if they could get them, sent most of their money home, and could be captured by immigration agents anytime, day or night. Once a man disappeared on a Thursday. The rest of the crew said he'd been caught by "La Migra" and shipped back to Tijuana. By the following Monday, he was back digging holes with the rest of us, his barking laugh echoing across the field. I tried to pick up Spanish from these generous men working so hard around me. For the first time, I wanted to know a language not for poetry or religion but because other people were speaking and I wanted to join the conversation.

I set up a little writing room in a shed behind our cabin. Wooden loading skiffs on dirt served as a floor, and a plank wall stood between the zinfandels and me. I wrote on an old trestle table just big enough for a rented typewriter and an open journal. Joel was trying at the time to transform himself into a concert pianist, though he had trained far more in Hebrew than music as a kid. He rented an upright piano for the house, but he saved his serious practice for the grand piano in the Episcopal church in town. We would get up at four thirty and make coffee in grim silence, and he would drive off to Healdsburg while I went out to the shed to work on my verse play or finish a lyric about a nearby peak:

> you're scattered
> over the valley.
> walnut trees black green
>
> against a white sky—
> I walk down from Bradford Mt.
> the earth whistles its discords—
>
> snakes & slugs of delight,
> the creek switch-backs,
> insistent honeysuckle
>
> blossoms on stone
> a hidden cicada, a horse's
> bones drying now near
>
> half a year in the sun
> beneath the blind trees.

Joel would return at six thirty, we'd heat up some beans from the night before and maybe fry some eggs. After breakfast, we'd report to the foreman, Paul, for work by seven thirty. We worked till noon, fell asleep over sandwiches for lunch, and went back to work till five or six. Before dark, Joel would water his patch of strawberries that wouldn't fruit till next year, and we'd drink a beer or pour a jelly jar of local red wine. Sometimes we'd go out to a bar in the college town of Cotati, but mostly we hung around reading and listening to music, talking and watching the beautiful valley and its miles of grapes and plums go dark under another night of stars.

Joel told great stories about the characters he'd met in Healdsburg, like the last of the original Italians who brought grapes to Sonoma, an old man who talked funny and made great sense. I described the consolation

Carlos from Michoacán offered me when I was crying in the field. Carlos, the elder of the crew, looked eighty but must have been forty-five. He communicated his concern in our shared language of nouns and gestures, but his kindness came through when I needed it most. Joel had discovered Charles Ives—a modernist composer strikingly parallel to poet Wallace Stevens—and was rapturous over Ives's mixture of American popular and classical art music, with its jerky syncopations, discords and unisons, and memorable but ghoulish heroes, as in "The Circus Band":

> Where is the lady all in pink?
> Last year she waved at me I think,
> Can she have died? Can! that! rot!
> She is passing but she sees me not.

On the weekends, Joel practiced in the cabin on the upright that sounded pretty decent, considering he once got so frustrated with his playing that he flipped the damn thing on its back and Paul had to come with the tractor to hoist it up again. Once or twice we'd drive down to Berkeley to look at the used bookstores and the college girls, but Dry Creek seemed to offer the healing we both needed for our wandering Jewish souls.

We idolized the foreman, Paul Bernier. Paul could fix anything on the ranch with a wrench and a screwdriver and an old beer can. He was less than ten years older than we were, but he was far more experienced and confident. He'd served in the navy, traveled the country and the world on his motorcycle, and put in time at a few other vineyards before coming to work for Lou Preston, who'd bought the ranch a year or two before. You knew Paul was mad by curses that thundered the length of the ranch, and his refrain "I wish somebody around here would PAY ATTENTION!" sent us searching back through our chores for any little details we'd forgotten to do or a machine we'd left running accidentally. Once Paul asked me to burn some stacks of old prune-drying racks that were cluttering the lot next to the barn. I worked all morning to forklift them carefully into the field away from everything and set the stacks on fire, one at a time. Before I went to lunch, I checked the burned stacks twice to make sure the embers were out. But as I started walking slowly back to work after lunch, I saw smoke rising from the field and heard Paul bellow. I ran as fast as I could, imagining the worst, but what I found was worse than I'd imagined. The whole field was on fire, and the flames were moving dangerously close to the barn with its tractors and rigging and a tank of diesel fuel. Paul and Lou were running around with extinguishers trying to put out the blaze, and suddenly a fire engine from Geyserville came racing down Dry Creek Road and stopped across the creek bed. Firemen tramped toward the fire with hoses. The fire was out in an hour, but I felt stupid and guilty. Paul didn't help me either—didn't yell, didn't say a word. He just shook his head and walked away to his house on the other side of the barn.

As Paul asked me to do more tasks around the ranch—irrigating the plums or unclogging a Rain Bird sprinkler head that had gotten a stray pit in its nozzle—I appreciated his wisdom and his yearning for a ranch of his own. He told us that he wanted a vineyard where he would use no chemicals and have a steady crew that worked with him every year. He wanted a woman who could, as he put it, "share this natural trip with me." It was the first time I'd ever heard of farming without oil, without fertilizer, without pesticides, and it seemed impossibly noble. He sent me out one day to fix a leak in a buried irrigation pipe under the new Fumé Blanc vines. I dug and dug until I found the source of the leak, but I couldn't quite get the pipe cut and patched properly. I was halfway back to the barn to get Paul to give me a hand—really, I wanted him to do it for me—when I realized that all Paul would do was figure it out for himself and work till he got it right. I could do that myself. So I turned around and made myself figure out a way to patch the pipe. Damned if I didn't fix it. Paul had taught me a lesson without even showing up. We felt it a great wrong committed against Paul when men and big trucks from a large winery rolled in one morning in midsummer to take over supervision of the vineyard after Lou had signed a contract to sell them his grapes. Lou seemed less admirable to us than Paul, even though Lou was pursuing his own brave project to build an independent winery down at the end of the valley. Instead of a baseball cap or a straw cowboy hat, Lou wore a beret when he cultivated. He wasn't the rough-hewn worker we wanted to be. All we could see then was that Lou had the money but Paul, Carlos, Josefat, Hilario, and the rest of us did the work.

Summer was coming to an end, and I would have to pack up for medical school. I seemed to be closing off a major portion of my life, cutting myself off from the intellectual freedom I had finally begun to feel at the vineyard. In the five years since I started college, I had finished scores of poems in hundreds of drafts; completed a verse play; written long, mostly readable letters to family and friends; and filled journals and sketchbooks with notes, lines, and drawings. I'd read a lot of poets, in no particular order but with a slowly flickering sense of history. I was just beginning to understand how to handle a sentence with care but not reverence, how to shape a line in accent and sound—what Charles Olson calls the "breath" in a poem—and excavate an image from half-remembered dream. The poems were still clumsy, not as solid as I'd hoped. I dimly envisioned my poetics: a mix of direct address and estranged discourse, vatic secular prayers that could stop traffic and make buildings sway. I had perhaps fifteen poems I thought could hold up under multiple readings. Would I leave my writing life behind in this exquisite valley? I dreamed of social gatherings where everyone was drinking coffee but the restaurant refused to serve me. It was against the law, they had run out, or the group rose up and declared I couldn't have coffee. I awoke each time desolate and angry with myself. Coffee was poems, passionate talk, the drink in the Temple of Zeus. Could I continue to have an intellectual life, a poem-life in medical school? Was I selling myself out for security? Was I too cowardly to keep working at the ranch and write as I had been doing? I asked Paul what he thought about my taking a year off and staying at the ranch. He looked at me like I'd asked him to set the tractor on fire. "A year OFF? A 'year off' from what? Look, Eli, either go to medical school or stay here, but don't pretend that Healdsburg is off and Cleveland is on. It's all your life." As usual, Paul saw through me.

Joel was returning to school at Sonoma State to study music, and so I prepared to move on, too. To celebrate the end of summer and my departure, we bought a keg of beer, dug a pit outside our house, and roasted a leg of a deer Paul had found newly killed on the side of the road. The Mexican crew came by after work, and we ate and drank ourselves silly, professing our brotherhood forever.

My father's
parents, Gisella
and Menachem
Goldblatt

My mother's parents,
Max and Lillian
Kushner

Dr. Harry Goldblatt as a captain
at Ft. Sam Houston, Texas, 1960

Selma, Aaron, me, Sharon, and Harry—the Goldblatts—in our living room
in Texas, 1961

Me (*left*) with Aaron and a monkey at Bertram Mills Circus in London, 1962

Aaron (*left*) and me in front of our mother's house in Columbia, Maryland, 1979

On the houseboat in Maine, 1977

Temple of the Sun, Palenque, Mexico, 1979. Drawing by author.

National Cathedral in Managua, Nicaragua, 1980. Drawing by author.

Marketplace in Masaya, Nicaragua, 1980. Drawing by author.

Bluefields, Nicaragua, 1980. Drawing by author.

6

# White Coat

ON THE FIRST DAY of medical school in September 1975, I felt myself moving through an anxiety dream like the ones I'd had all summer. I was in the wrong classroom, didn't know what textbooks my unnamed professors required, and couldn't remember how I got there. We were all milling around in hallways that would presumably become familiar, looking at our classmates sideways, wondering who might become our lifelong friends. Some people were surely a good deal older than I, but most looked fresh from undergraduate school. I must have appeared pretty young myself, with my scruffy half-beard, flannel shirt, and khaki work pants. I still wanted to carry a bit of the vineyard with me. My classmates dressed casually but neatly, no noticeable hippies but no business types either. Case Western Reserve had a reputation for accepting unusual students for at least a portion of the class. When my father attended med school at Case, after completing dental school and a couple of years in Israel, they called people like him with odd career paths the "queer ducks." That was probably the category under which I had gotten in myself. My science grades had been decent but not stellar, my science board scores merely good, but my general knowledge scores were high, and I'd sent them a sheaf of poems that apparently didn't hurt. I hoped that at least a few of my new classmates were not pure science heads. On that opening day, everyone must have been as nervous as I, but I could feel only my own sense of disjunction and doubt. The faces around me seemed flinty and uninviting. Now that this faraway career choice had hardened into a reality of lecture schedules and lab assignments, I had to accept that the School of Medicine and the University Hospital were my new home, med student my new identity. I would be a short white coat for the next four years.

I did speak to two of my new classmates that first day. Tommy was a small, intense Italian guy from New York City. He spoke in quick bursts that seemed almost inarticulate because his words were so guarded;

like all of us, he had something to prove. Saul had been an undergraduate at Case Western and was merely moving to a new building for school, but he seemed a little dazed and disoriented by how much the stakes had changed in the few months since he'd graduated. Saul was an earnest, soft-spoken Jewish guy, son of Holocaust survivors who had made a modest living with a retail store in Cleveland, and he was contemplating a PhD in biochemistry along with his MD. I remember standing on the street in the September sunlight, joking with them about how we could go into a department store and order a living room full of furniture based on our medical student ID cards, but we were all disconcerted by the responsibilities, family expectations, and shifting social positions that we had only just begun to glimpse after a few hours as future doctors. We didn't even own white coats yet. I walked home to my newly rented, barely furnished apartment. How had I returned to Cleveland, my birthplace and my father's hometown?

Coming back to Cleveland seemed eerily predestined. I had been born there in my father's second year of medical school and had often visited my cousins in Cleveland Heights whenever my family's transfers permitted. The Levs, dear friends of the family who had gone to high school with my father, lived only a few blocks from my cousins' house. Zede had died years before, but Bubbi had only recently left for Israel when I arrived. All the cousins were now in college or beyond, and my uncle had followed his mother after a painful split with his family over a business deal gone spectacularly wrong. My aunt, whom I had always loved, remained in the family house, and at first she invited me to live there in one of the many empty rooms. I needed to have my own place, but I did stay with her when I first arrived while I waited for my apartment to be ready. One afternoon in August, when I was wandering through my cousins' rooms, remembering our sleepovers and secret conversations, I came across a long paper written by my cousin Danny. Danny had been a religion major, and this was his analysis of the Book of Jonah, recounting the travails of the biblical prophet swallowed by "a great fish." I sat down among Danny's books and dived into the paper like a lost man. Danny wrote well and with conviction, but his words affected me most because he was writing about me. Jonah had been called by the voice of the Lord Himself to proclaim against the city of Nineveh, but instead he had run away. He nearly drowned himself and his fellow passengers when he slept at the bottom of the ship while God set a tempest on the sea. And then, after spending three days and nights in the belly of the fish, Jonah embraced his mission and successfully turned Nineveh from wickedness, but he grew despondent when God did not smite the city as He had promised. Jonah's second struggle with God, therefore, required that he learn the depths of mercy. When I finished Danny's paper, I was nearly in tears, but I could not cry; I felt a great terror about the game I was playing with my life. I, too, was running from a calling. But was poetry my calling and medical school my whale, or was medicine my calling and poetry the big Christian fish that had swallowed me? And for whom should I show mercy? For the Mexican migrant workers, who had no health care or decent housing? Or for me, who might be betraying myself in this new career? I couldn't turn back now, no matter how I pitied myself. Two years ago, I'd committed myself to make my living with medicine and my life in poetry. I needed to see if I could carry out my plan.

Aaron visited me just before the semester began, and his visit provoked my first complete poem in my new city. He had dropped out of Beloit College himself, where he went for a year even more tentatively than I had, and was now studying in a ceramics program in rural North Carolina. Whether he was doing carpentry, or working on a farm, or traveling in Bolivia, or making pots, Aaron always seemed more in his body and in his life than I. Maybe I spent too much time in my mind, but his work always reminded me that we had a shared legacy from our father, who, for all his training, had worked with his hands. We also shared Dad's death, as I wrote in that poem:

> by a father's blessing we know death
> where it stands for the nothing behind
> a glass of bourbon, an elegant job of mechanics,
> an incorruptible joke, flowing down
> like a good god's grace

We both felt the painful blessing for the depth it gave our lives and the negative space around mundane joys we could recognize as meaningful rituals. My sister was growing up more introspective, like me. However, as my mother's only companion, Sharon seemed lonelier than either Aaron or I had ever been. My little sister was suddenly finishing high school, thinking about college but not very happy, for reasons I couldn't fix. I could do nothing about the loneliness my mother and sister lived with; even a degree in medicine couldn't fill their empty spaces.

Case had a novel pedagogical system. I knew from my mother's stories that the school had instituted its radical approach just as my father was entering in 1951, and my course of study would be similar at least in spirit to his. The unit of study was not the course, and there were no midterms or quizzes or even prescribed textbooks. There were, in fact, no grades. The whole entering class, some 170 of us, gathered in one big lecture hall all morning for lectures in interdisciplinary units that progressed through the fall from cell biology to metabolism and then in the spring from cardiovascular, pulmonary, and renal function to tissue injury and mechanisms of infection. Thus, the liver was our home till Christmas. Indeed, one of our professors referred to the liver and the "periphery," meaning everything else in the body. We studied a few diseases that revealed metabolic pathways, diabetes particularly but also sickle-cell anemia, obesity, and gout. We could choose from an array of textbooks to supplement the lecture notes that instructors gave us each class. No one actually said this explicitly, but whatever book explained the topic well for us could serve, just as long as the lectures made sense and we passed the day-long exam at the end of the unit. Exams were pass-fail. As long as you scored above a certain percentage, your anonymous test wasn't "identified," and you could go on to the next unit. If you were identified, we were told, they helped you catch up. Other students would never know if you failed an exam unless you told people or you failed so many exams they asked you to leave.

Mornings were devoted to classes, some afternoons to clinical electives, and each of us was assigned to a pregnant woman in the first week of the semester. I would follow my "patient" through all her prenatal visits, be present at the birth, give the baby the first shots, and follow the family into the subsequent year of pediatric care. This was the aspect of the curriculum we most looked forward to and most feared for its reality. Any other family health problems our "patient" wanted to share with her student doctor might be part of the experience as well. We were to be historians and advocates but not physicians as we learned along with these women about pregnancy, childbirth, and infant development.

Meanwhile, most of our time during the week was devoted to independent study wherever we chose to hole up. Except for clinic appointments or elective classes, I studied from one o'clock till ten in the library, with an hour off for dinner. The system was humane, rooted in medical practice from the opening day, but unavoidably it was suffused with an unspoken pressure to study every second. The careless student might miss an obscure detail that could save someone's life later on. Most of us were still afraid someone might figure out we weren't really all that good and ask us to leave, and we had no perspective on the endless sea of information with which medical training confronts the novice. I allowed myself an occasional look at the nursing students studying nearby—flirting with female classmates could get complicated, and they were drowning like the men—but otherwise there was no room for personal time. As it was, I got up at five to write in my journal or draft a poem for an hour before I showered, dressed, ate, and walked down to class. At night, I tried to read poetry, but I often nodded off before I'd managed more than a page or two. I kept the *New York Review of Books* in my kitchen for breakfast reading, the *New York Times Book Review* in my bathroom (the articles were shorter), and poetry or philosophy in my living room. Science books remained strictly by the door. Only writing, sleeping, and dreaming were permitted in the bedroom. I was lonely as hell but managed for the first few months not to notice.

I had an initial friend in a classmate I'll call Carl. He was a little older than I, but like me he had been interested in literature in school and worked in other jobs before deciding he would go to medical school. He'd driven a cab in New York City, worked as an aide in a psychiatric hospital, and found great pleasure teaching children with severe learning disabilities in Boston. Like me, he was coming off a very painful romantic breakup. In his case, the relationship had been a good one, but he hadn't felt ready to ask her to follow him to Cleveland. He too identified with the music and politics of the 1960s, and so I could share my misgivings with him about the class distinctions between doctors and other people. He shared a house with a radical nursing student, a community organizer, and a social work student; they later became my friends when I could spare a moment to have dinner there on a weekend. Carl and I studied at a distance so that we would not distract each other with social conversation, but we ate dinner together, and often he drove me home after the library closed. But our talk was always highly controlled, truncated by self-discipline. Carl worried that the intense pressures in our program required such sharp focus that sharing too much would open a flood of emotion he couldn't control. He had a rule that if I asked more than two questions in morning lecture, especially if the questions were even slightly critical of the medical system, he would move his seat and not talk to me for a day or two. I understood his fear and used it to monitor myself. We were like hunkered-down soldiers in foxholes, afraid to show our heads, but sometimes the level of constraint rose to intolerable repression.

The circumstances required buddies, even if we didn't have the psychic space to be actual friends. Carl introduced me to another member of our class, Peter, and the three of us, along with Saul and Tommy from my first day, often ate together in the hospital cafeteria. Peter told funny stories about how he had been singled out to go to medical school by his Jewish family early on. His dear grandmother's dying words were, "Peter, I can die happy because I know you are going to be a doctor." Saul was the serious one, accepting our socialization without question. Tommy and Carl had New York in common. Our camaraderie eased the tense days, and Peter's jokes about his family's expectations gave me the perspective to accept my grandfather's maniacal investment in me as the replacement for his lost son-in-law. The dinner hour in the cafeteria was often the one moment in the day when I felt I could become accustomed to life as a doctor. After all, I'd lost my first tooth in a hospital cafeteria. My father must have had dinners like these with his colleagues when he studied at Case. Medicine could be my home, too.

But early on, I began to develop a reputation for being critical of the medical establishment. In our first week, even before we met the pregnant woman we had been assigned to follow, the instructors scheduled each of us to be videotaped interviewing a mock patient, to introduce us to the challenge of meeting and interacting with real people. All we knew was that this patient had just been diagnosed with diabetes, and we were to represent ourselves as student doctors who would help the patient through the initial stages of accommodating to the disease. We'd had perhaps one introductory lecture on diabetes, but in fact I knew little about its course or outcomes. I walked into the interview room in my new white coat, determined to be as helpful and sympathetic as possible. After the initial greeting, the actor told me she was worried about losing her hands or feet to the disease. I hurried to assure her that nothing like that would happen to her. Then I went on to explain that my function was to be an advocate, someone who could protect her "against the doctors." When the interview was over, I thought I'd done a terrific job, but the supervising physician came in ready to tear my head off. What did I know about this disease to assure her nothing frightening would happen? And who did I think I was, setting myself up against my colleagues and teachers? Was I in medical school or not? I realized that I was not play-acting, even in a mock situation, and that the issues both patients and doctors faced were terribly serious. I did see myself as aligned against a medical industry that seemed faceless and heartless, but once I put on my white coat, I was implicated also and couldn't easily distance myself. I had no right to project my ambivalence on people who just needed help. I resented the scolding and avoided that doctor for months afterward when I saw him in the hallways, but I had to admit he was right about my performance. He made me sit through the videotape of my interview, and what I saw on the screen was a cocky young student trying to show how enlightened he was without the slightest recognition of the other person's anxiety. A pretty humbling way to start a career.

I promised myself I would do better when I met my own patient. In fact, real life was far kinder to me than mock drama. A few days after the diabetes interview, I was introduced to Rose, an African American woman early in her pregnancy. She was a couple of years younger than I and married. Her husband worked in an industrial furniture factory, and she had no other children. We got along splendidly from the first, but I tried hard not to take anything for granted and asked her often to tell me if I was missing important information. Particularly because I knew so little about what she was going through, I began to realize that my main job was to listen closely to her and help voice her concerns to the attending physicians. Listening would be my answer to that brash young man in the mock interview, and listening would be the only function of value I could offer Rose. Writing had always been about my words, my ideas, my clever sentences; I judged myself by my words' effect on others or assumed that they simply didn't understand the quality of my contribution. Now, as with my Mexican friends in the vineyard, language was about what other people had to say and how I could respond honestly and usefully to them.

If my aunt initially welcomed me back to Cleveland, the Lev family converted the message into a weekly event. They had a shabbas dinner every Friday night at their house, and I was always invited. Because their four daughters were living their lives elsewhere, Shirley and Bob entertained a large extended family who lived within a few miles and came together every week. A shabbas with the Levs was a pleasure I allowed myself only occasionally, but I needed their warmth and unlimited acceptance more than I could admit. The roast chicken, overdone vegetables, kasha and bows, wine and challah were most welcome—a reminder of home, although my family seldom had so many people on a Friday after my father died, and Shirley's cooking outshone my mother's. Bob sat at the head of the table with his kind smile, hardly talking at all except to prompt someone else to tell a story or describe an accomplishment. I didn't know the complex relationships and family stories very well when I arrived, but I soon learned enough to follow the conversation.

One crisis in the family was that a little girl of one of the cousins, call her Celia, developed a very large hemangioma under her chin soon after birth. A hemangioma on the skin is a concentration of blood vessels, a common benign tumor in infants that can be found anywhere but is most often on a baby's head or neck. This one was particularly large, the size of an angry red baseball when Celia was still only a few weeks old. My mother had developed a hemangioma in a similar place when she was a baby, and she always carried a considerable scar under her chin that fascinated me as a child, although few people could see it by the way she held her head. The condition isn't life-threatening, but this hemangioma was large enough to be a serious problem for Celia. It bothered the child and could easily get infected. The family worried about the trauma of a girl growing up with such a growth on her face, and they and the doctors agreed it needed to be reduced and eventually removed through surgery.

Luckily for me, Celia and her family were being treated at the University Hospital, only a short walk from the library where I studied. A baby's health seemed to me a legitimate reason to leave my books for an hour or two during the evening, and I would stroll over to her ward on nights when Celia was staying over to look in on the baby, talk to the family, and learn what I could about Celia's condition from the doctors. I became close to Samuel and Martha, the worried parents, and this became a spot of human connection I could find in my day of cell biology and biochemical pathways. Celia got excellent care, and very soon the hemangioma began to shrink, a little at a time. I did nothing but show up, but the family was grateful to me as if I'd helped in her care. Through the ordeal that fall, I grew closer still to the extended Lev family, and whatever I did to help Celia and her parents, I gained immensely from the warmth of their love at a time when I felt cast out of my own dreams.

I felt particularly young next to the doctors who roamed the clinics and wards, but both they and their patients justified our unceasing study. The classroom science was interesting enough—the depth to which one could know about a disease process and yet be relatively ineffective against it amazed me—and I found that with a regular study routine, the endless pathways and tiny complex structures formed themselves into more or less comprehensible units. Even in that first year, however, medical school wasn't really about the classroom. We had to invest our library and lab time in order to earn the privilege of learning about other people's lives in minute detail and of holding a front seat on the drama when disease disrupted a person's ordinary patterns and expectations. It was in that drama that we were meant to form our identities as doctors. Sometimes this led to a clash of expectations, as when a classmate asked me snidely one day in clinic if I intended to be a "country doctor" because I never wore a tie with my white coat. But largely we supported one another in our excitement about entering the clinical phase of our training; after all, it was why most of us wanted to be doctors in the first place. All these lives around us seemed incredibly precious, and their urgencies gave our lives more substance and value.

I felt the infusion of energy from clinic work like everyone else, but I also felt the illusion of our vicarious role as caretakers in training. Early in the first semester, a group of us went on a field trip with our preceptor, a physician who met with us on Thursday mornings to address difficult human questions about the practice of medicine. He took us to a nursing home, where we met with people who had been afflicted with terrible and rare metabolic disorders that had made regular life impossible. One woman, I remember, sat in a wheelchair in the sun while we walked by. She had a condition known as Wilson's disease, an extremely rare disorder in which the body does not rid itself of the tiny amounts of copper we ingest with food but instead stores the excess metal inappropriately in the liver, brain, and other organs. She had been a vibrant and promising young woman when suddenly her mental and physical health started to deteriorate inexplicably; by the time doctors diagnosed her properly and put her on a copper-free diet, her body had already sustained irreversible damage. She was hunched and misshapen and could not speak to us, but as we walked by, splendid in our white coats and well-groomed confidence, she laughed uncontrollably. I felt somehow she was telling us that our sensible world of scientific answers masked a much more precarious existence in which one could be a strapping young lady one minute and a crone the next.

The more I learned about this unseen world of threats to well-being, the more I tried to put aside my vacillations about medical school and focus instead on the work I had to do everyday to help Rose, Celia, and others I might meet in practice. Sometime in late September I wrote in my journal:

> Yesterday I remembered the little phrase by someone, perhaps Stephen Spender or someone he quoted, about the artist having the luck of seeing a miracle everyday. It was freeing to remember that that was a real experience & is. The miraculous occurs so often & with such contiguity with disappointments & short sells that the possibility of it fades in my mind, even though the fact of it never can.

The obscurity in my personal writing shouldn't hide the impulse here to see what a rare vantage point I had at the time. I saw people in great pain—a clinically obese woman who had been raped by her father, a young man who had just weathered a sickle-cell crisis, diabetics challenged by late-stage vascular complications—but I also saw people devoted to addressing these ills, trying to relieve pain and alleviate suffering. I could be one of those who helped, despite my reservations.

In that first month, I took a brief elective independent study following Dr. Smith, a senior obstetrician on staff who was going back for a second specialization in psychiatry. I had at first chosen to work with Dr. Smith because I thought I might become an obstetrician—after all,

William Carlos Williams delivered babies—but I became fascinated by the mental disorders associated with pregnancy. Dr. Smith introduced me to a young woman with hyperemesis gravidarum, a condition of pregnancy involving persistent and dangerous vomiting that goes beyond any normal morning sickness and into the territory of eating disorder. In 1975, few people were talking about anorexia or bulimia in the general public, but I recognized this complex of syndromes relating to food intake from my wrestling days, when I could stand in front of a mirror and see myself as fat even though my doctor had pronounced me malnourished. Eating disorders seemed bizarre yet familiar, ridiculous in a land of overflowing supermarkets and yet perfectly understandable as the mind's struggle for autonomy. But psychiatry didn't seem to help me understand this withdrawn African American woman who showed little affect and no energy in her pinched face, and I could not accept the psychoanalytic explanation in some of the articles Dr. Smith gave me. My questioning didn't endear me to the doctor, and one day in his office, he looked at me sharply and said, "Eli, what is wrong with you?!" I had apparently let my ambivalence show too much. I decided after the elective that men should just stay out of obstetrics until more woman doctors had reimagined the profession (this was the year before Adrienne Rich challenged the male obstetrical world with *Of Woman Born*, but feminist critiques were beginning to percolate among the medical students who would listen). This experience did leave me with a lingering desire to go into psychiatry, if for no other reason than to make some sense of the battle between those who wanted to treat inexplicable disorders with talk and those who wanted to use drugs as their primary therapeutic tools. After my own terrible experience with psychoanalysis, psychiatry frightened me, but the idea would not go away. At least analysis dealt with the mental side of suffering, but was talk enough?

Near the end of October, we took our first big examination. We all expanded our study times and neglected other duties, afraid that our good student instincts would betray us and we would fail the test. On the exam day, we spread out among the labs and small classrooms, answering hundreds of multiple-choice questions for hours. We staggered out of the exam rooms mostly relieved, and a group of us decided that we would go out to dinner together that night to celebrate, even though we wouldn't know the results for a day or two. Someone found an inexpensive Greek restaurant not far from the school, and ten or twelve of us showed up that night, including Carl and Tommy as well as men and women who sat near us in lecture but whom I didn't know. We ate and drank, and for the first time since we'd arrived, we dropped our guard in a group and shared how we'd gotten there and admitted our fears about medical school. I remember listening to a classmate I'd always avoided, a loud Jewish guy who always wore his shirt open to show a gold *chai* pendant on his hairy chest, telling me that he had always wanted to be a doctor, and not just for the money. He loved the science in a way I did not, but the experience of following a pregnant patient was drawing him into the human side of the profession. I realized that I needed to be less judgmental, that not everybody had to do this work for my reasons. We were all trying to do something we weren't sure we could do. I didn't reveal much, nor did Carl (if, in fact, he was there at all; could he have begged off to play his guitar by himself?), but I decided it was OK to like these people; they were my colleagues and could be my friends. A part of me held back, the righteous poet who complained he'd be better off reading at home or the political activist who pointed out we were spending more money in an evening than Carlos would see in a month. Would I be playing golf and taking gifts from drug company reps soon because my rich colleagues were doing so? But we'd just taken our first medical school exam, and I had to let myself feel relief for one night. The retsina went down so smoothly, and I needed to get drunk among friends.

Around this time, my high school girlfriend came to visit me. Leah and I had enjoyed a low-key, comfortable relationship in our senior year that had mellowed into a solid friendship in the years since. We hadn't kept in close touch, but we were always happy to see one another when we did meet at holiday parties in Silver Spring, and we exchanged letters occasionally. She had made an effort to stop by Cleveland on her way back east from Oregon, and she arrived just after my exam but before I had sunk into my hermetically sealed routine again. We went out to dinner at a cheap Chinese place near my house and then to see *The King of Hearts* at a movie theater that had played the movie for months. At dinner I was amazed by how much I didn't know about her growth in the previous five years. She'd been smart but tentative in high school, always doing well but never trusting that she was as capable as our more illustrious peers. She'd actually convinced her friends that she wasn't ambitious, though I always thought she had much more to contribute in class than she usually said. Now she told a story of her growing love for archaeology, about how she became a site manager and a leader in her department. She was beginning a PhD program in anthropology, and she seemed to me to have a clear professional direction for her life. As she spoke, I envied the crispness of her passion, the way her old reticence had transformed into self-assurance and determination in the methodical world of gridded digs and sifted dirt. I told her about my sojourn on the vineyard and how I was settling in: the study routines, lectures and labs, OB visits with Rose, poems I was writing in the morning. She listened but didn't say much till after the Alan Bates movie about crazy people saving a village.

The film had been playing so long, and the weather was so miserably wet, that we were the only people in the theater that night. When the show ended, we ran to my car in the rain and sat there talking. Water descended in sheets, heavier than anything I'd seen in years, and Leah asked me why I was in medical school. I gave her my best stock answer about how I wanted to help people, how I didn't want to make my living teaching a subject I loved as much as poetry, how I could do so much more politically as a doctor than as a teacher or a printer. She let me have my say and then asked again: "I know all that. But why are you in medical school?" I went into an explanation that had to do with finding my father, challenging my poetry with the actual suffering of people I met in the hospital, encountering types I'd never meet anywhere else. As I talked, I watched the raindrops chasing each other down the flat windshield of my Volkswagen, and I felt noble and convincing, but I feared Leah would see I was a sham. On many days, I couldn't talk myself into this career I'd undertaken. How was I going to convince Leah, who met me the month my father died and knew me when I had more hopes than plans? Leah, in a small but firm voice, asked me again. "I understand what you're saying," she said, "but I still don't understand you and medical school. Do you really want to be a doctor?" I explained some more, and then I explained again. Finally I started the car and said, "Leah, I just need to do this, OK?" She let me go at that, and we drove back to my apartment.

But I couldn't let myself go as graciously as Leah had. A day or two later, I wrote in my journal that "much has been happening" and listed Leah's visit first. I had also talked with one of Carl's roommates, a vibrant young Jewish woman studying social work. The warmth with which she spoke about her clients and profession contrasted starkly with the distanced way we talked about our "patients" and my own strained emotions about what I was doing. Then I accompanied a visiting nurse on her rounds and met a mentally disabled woman with severe epilepsy who had just come home with her new baby. She'd had serious problems with her pregnancy and delivery, and the doctors had not easily let her leave the hospital with her baby. After her interview with the nurse, who clearly had a good rapport with the new mother, the woman turned to me and asked me if I was a doctor. I pointed to my short white coat and told her I was only a student doctor. She responded with a screed about the medical profession, ending with a phrase I recorded in my journal: "And that's why, if I had a gun in the house, and you were a real doctor, I'd shoot you." I understood her fury, but I also understood that it would do no good to try to distance myself from the profession: if I intended to be a doctor, then I needed to live up to the best construction of that role. Could I do that? I didn't know.

I attended readings in Cleveland by poets Cynthia Macdonald and David Ignatow around that time as well. Macdonald's witty and disturbing poems stood in such contrast to the standard gendered language of medicine and made me question again the wisdom of following my father's path rather than my own. Ignatow discussed the difference between verse and prose poems, and I wrote in my journal a disquisition about a theory I favored over his rather pedantic distinction. Each encounter made me ache for a life of the mind and emotion I could embrace wholeheartedly. But if daytime encounters struck me hard, then dreams struck me harder. A week after Leah's visit, I wrote down a dream in which my brother was dying from asphyxia and my mother from a degenerative disease. In the dream, my sister had called to report their conditions in a forceful but detached tone, asking me to call her back, but she hung up before she could give me a number to call her. I finally reached her in my lab at school, where we were in the process of moving our lab desks. In my desk was hidden a small, ornate safe containing a terra cotta statue of a man and boy. When I went to move the fragile statue, the father's head broke off and dissolved in my hand. Carl tried to console me, but I brushed him aside by saying, "It's all right. It doesn't really matter," and found I could move my desk. I woke up again feeling my situation was nearly intolerable but convinced myself to go on to class anyway.

After my run-in with Dr. Smith, I had been telling everyone that I was leaning toward pediatrics. Celia's parents approved, my aunt approved, and my lab partners Tommy and Saul thought it sounded right for me. My grandfather cared only that I got an MD, and my mother remained silent on the issue. Carl was probably going to pursue pediatric neurology, so he thought my decision perfectly reasonable. Even Carl's roommate Erica, a nursing student I admired and an outspoken critic of the male culture in medicine, agreed that pediatricians were the "exception to the rule." I contemplated that life in a journal entry: "It was so powerful, so shining that I could even stop reading & writing & feel I was still alright. Fixing up kids is such a moving profession." But once again I was "buffaloing" myself, as my father might have said. A specialization wasn't the point if my heart wasn't in medicine to begin with, and a good pediatrician has to be twice the scientist of an internist because the patients can't say what hurts; only a veterinarian has a greater challenge in diagnosis. In a mid-November journal entry, I lectured myself in my best Woody Guthrie voice: "I don't think I'm hitting the right road in the big house. . . . I'm lying a good portion of the time, or telling no truths. This has a lacquering effect on the soul & I'd prefer to keep fresh."

What was holding me back most was simply fear—fear that I couldn't write well enough to make my living as a writer, that no one would ever appreciate my poems, that I would lose interest in art and want to go back to medicine, that I would collapse into solipsism as an overly introspective old man. The internal stress drove me to speak honestly in the journal while the external demands of medicine made me recognize that I did no one any good practicing without passion. Just before Thanksgiving I wrote:

> Mrs. G set me straight yesterday. The woman is sick, not playing, not a research project. She doesn't need a friend—at least not me for a friend, or not me as a white doctor also trying to be her friend. I must do what I

want to do so I can do it seriously and with the whole of me. . . . If I want
my humor & what good health I have to keep life and unbitter [sic], I've
got to get at the work, learn what I want & live as I love to. Fear is not
joyful & joy is what I choose.

In the last entry for November, I note that "I've begun to say aloud to
people I'm not intimate with that I'm probably leaving school, that I
want to write." Leah's questions had forced the issue, but I needed to
admit the obvious first to myself and then to others. As Paul would say
on the vineyard, I was finally paying attention.

The decision to leave freed me up to write more honestly in my
journal and recognize just what I was learning in Cleveland and why
I'd come. The entries as 1975 ended became more direct about leaving
and more honest about the struggles I was having as a man, a son, a
writer. Medical school was slowly teaching me to listen to others and
myself. I wrote about learning to use what I learned from Rose and others I'd met and to listen to myself better and recognize my own needs,
too. I began to recognize, perhaps for the first time, the effect that my
childhood had on my "restlessness, my aversion to close friends." I'd
been holding a dual image of my father, in control as a doctor while
being controlled as a soldier. Really, he was merely a man who made
choices and died too young, not a long-lost hero. And I scolded myself
for my attitude toward books as sacred objects. Poetry required interpretation, not reverence; lines resisted a single meaning in favor of the
meaning the reader constructed. I had grown so much from even this
one semester in medical school, and I had more to learn before I left,
but I wanted to apply this growth to make me more responsive, more
attuned to my surroundings and to my own inner rhythms.

Still, I couldn't rest as the semester came to a close. We had another
final exam in the second week of December, and on the following day
we were to meet our cadavers. This was a huge event for all of us, but in
the exhaustion of exam preparation, I dreaded meeting the dead body
that would mean so much. No group dinners after the exam, but Carl
and I smoked pot together for the first time and managed to work ourselves into an extremely depressed state. He had gotten some bad news
from his former girlfriend and realized his relationship was completely
over. I had no idea what I was doing with my life. I returned home and

wrote a long entry in my journal. I didn't miss Sandra, but who would love me if I left medical school? Medicine represented social privilege. Even if I resisted it, being a doctor justified me to family, friends, and strangers. Could one sustain a life in poetry? I could see my mother's mother shaking her head: "From this you make a living?" Poetry by its nature must be evanescent, and I had written so blithely to my brother about "the nothing behind / a glass of bourbon." Nothingness overwhelmed me, the fear that I would never take hold of my life. The prospect of meeting the cadaver seemed "too much sensation, too much pain." I admitted to pretending I was hard and strong, the way a soldier must be. What bothered others didn't bother me. But, in fact, I was hurting. The night before the exam, I had dreamed I was drinking a can of Coke and blood burst all over my hands. As I wrote about that dream the night after the exam, my mother's grief came up to me through my handwriting, and for a paragraph, my usually upright printing gave way to her characteristic slanted and nearly unreadable scrawl.

This haunted night proved the turning point. I questioned myself afterward and tracked my dreams but moved toward my new life. I would pass through the tunnel of the next semester, gathering everything I could for the next leg of the journey, paying attention to what was before me and not behind me. I found even the following morning that I felt calmer, more ready to work with my fellow students and join in on challenges the school year presented. We had all worked so hard for the December exam that most of us were too weary to meet the cadaver with anything more than nervous acceptance. For most of us, the body represented learning more than death. One exception to the calm attitude among our classmates was my lab partner Tommy. He had very definite ideas of what sort of cadaver he wanted. Saul and I let him make the choice for our group, and he took nearly an hour to survey the available bodies before he decided on a man in his fifties, spare and medium-sized, who had died of intestinal edema. As my journal notes the next day: "The cadaver's face was pained and his mouth partially open & stuffed with cotton, unshaven, hair sparse and partially gray. The rest of his body is stiff and any life-like features you can notice—moles, slight hair around his nipples, enormous purple scrotum—look as though they were added on for our discomfort to an otherwise lackadaisical piece of wax." I found I had no discomfort once we settled in and started making our initial abdominal incision: "I had no trouble cutting, & actually had to contain my enthusiasm for the dissection since it is one of the most enjoyable activities the school's given us. I felt very clean and unencumbered working with the knife." And yet dissection didn't capture my thoughts very long. In that entry, I moved from the cadaver to Carl's relationship troubles and then to the local character of human dramas, the way the poem could act as "a chapel within the landscape." I ended with a warning to myself that I had to "keep making my imagination engage with the real world." In large part, that was what I had come to medical school to learn.

Over the break, I visited my brother in rural North Carolina. He was quite happily making pots at a community college with an excellent ceramics program, and he was starting to think about going to art school. In the meantime, he was getting a serious dose of southern country life. He and another guy lived with a fellow student who owned a house far from town, and they regularly had barbecues called "picks" that could last all day. Soon after I arrived, the three housemates decided to have a Christmas "calf pick." We went out early in the morning and dug a hole, started a fire, threw metal mesh over the coals, and then put on a side of a calf to roast all day. We sat and talked through the afternoon, slowly drinking beer and whiskey while we dutifully basted the meat. I loved my brother for his ability to be comfortable in a place, to make friends easily and work alongside anybody. He owned a dog, drove an old truck, and threw pots. He had begun to read when he lived in the woods of western Massachusetts and could talk about books, but he didn't pile them up like sandbags against a rising river, as I did. I was tired of fighting my environment, of holding myself away from experiences right in front of me. As afternoon turned into evening, people they knew started arriving and the party got lively. Late that night, Aaron and I were talking to the wife of another student. She had grown up in central North Carolina, and after a while she admitted that she'd never met a Jew before.

"You all are Jewish, right?"

We looked at each other, but the party was too friendly to stop now. "Yes. Yes, we are," my brother answered.

"I've always wanted to ask this question to a Jew. You don't celebrate Christmas, right?"

"No, we don't."

"Well, I hope you don't mind my asking. How do you all celebrate the birth of our Lord?"

My brother had to go on living there, so I let him answer the question. But the whole visit woke me up from my self-absorbed funk. I was just another person like anybody at that party, a little bewildered, a little unsure about where to go next. Medical school didn't change my membership in the human race, and leaving medicine wouldn't make me more or less than what I was when I started. The Christian lady cared more about our church affiliation than my medical career or Aaron's decision to go to art school. Life turns into people living if you let it.

Another significant visit that winter break was to my Beloit friend Sylvie's house outside New York. She and I had been exchanging letters since California, and now suddenly we seemed to be more than friends. I wasn't prepared to start anything serious, but Sylvie challenged me to stop hiding. She had no trouble with the idea I might leave medical school and supported my plan to go somewhere, get some training in a trade, and focus on my writing. I had known her family since I had visited early in college. On that first visit, her father had asked me to leave soon after I arrived because he wanted more time alone with his daughter. Then he promptly pulled his car out of the garage and dented my car and had to invite me to stay till it was repaired. They were a big Jewish family, kind and complex, and in their large, rambling house I felt unconditionally accepted and at home. Sylvie was leaving San Diego and her job as a manuscript assistant to a scholar studying Martin Buber. She was beginning at the Reconstructionist Rabbinical College in Philadelphia the following fall. One night after we had been to the theater in New York with her parents, Sylvie asked me to come with her to Philadelphia. I told her I needed to think about it but admitted I wanted to keep seeing her as more than a friend. We agreed to keep talking about next year through the spring.

Once I knew I was leaving Cleveland and maybe even where I was going next, daily routines became so much more bearable that at times I wanted to stay. After some initial trepidation, I made a deal with an older classmate I hardly knew to move into the third floor of his old Victorian house not too far from campus. Renting from Stan would be cheaper than living alone, but it would also be more comfortable, and I was willing to concede that I needed a bit of comfort. Stan had piloted air force cargo planes in the Vietnam War and had a houseful of furniture. He lent me a rich Oriental carpet that covered nearly the entire living area of my attic room, and for the first time I felt I could truly relax at home. He didn't accept that I needed to leave medical school when I told him and remarked clinically that perhaps it was a case of "unresolved emotions," but we came to be friends and easy roommates. When we could spare time for conversation away from our books, we talked about the way he tended to look outside for engagement while I wanted to turn inward, though extrovert or introvert didn't quite describe either of us. We could discuss the heart/lung lab or the dinner menu with equal intensity. Stan had learned yoga and meditation in Asia, and we developed a regular practice of doing sun salutes and breathing exercises together silently before breakfast.

After the move to Stan's house, I was able to look around me and appreciate the return to my hometown. I felt less need to hide who I was or what I liked to do, and I actually began to enjoy living in Cleveland for the first time. The new neighborhood was a leftover from the counterculture late 1960s, with a bookstore and little shops and the movie house where Leah and I had seen *The King of Hearts*. I explored the nearby residential streets and figured out how to walk to Bubbi and Zede's old brown brick apartment building, where my father and his brother grew up. I allowed myself the time to go to a farmers' market on the West Side and marvel at the fresh greens and peppers, breads and meats. I listened to people speaking Russian and Chinese and admired the high windows of the market hall. I found I could actually use my senses again. The few people I told about my plans to leave urged me to reconsider because, they said, I was "warm and sensitive" and medicine needed me. I had often dismissed my tendency to be nice to people as a weakness, a vestige of my nomad childhood when I wanted friends desperately and didn't have the good looks or physical prowess to attract attention. Calls for me to stay flattered me and tempted me with the need to change a system I thought inhumane. Suddenly, sensitivity had a value even for a doctor. I could see that medicine was a viable version of home, especially here where my father had grown up and my cousins had lived. But when I went back to my books and my poems, my letters to friends, words formed a home where I found joy and solace, substance and forgiveness. The journal took on greater value not only as a physical location to jot down first drafts, dreams, or crackbrained ideas but also as a refuge for reflection and an archive for news of the day. I now dated every entry and dedicated myself to keeping as full a picture of internal and external developments as I could—even questioning whether I'd been writing honestly enough for the journal to be useful if I ever went back later to reconstruct the year. If I learned anything from experience, the journal would help me manage the process.

Meanwhile, Rose was moving closer to her due date, and I was nearly as excited as the prospective parents. I had watched films of childbirth, heard lectures on delivery and newborn care, watched a cesarean section performed, and debriefed with classmates who had already gone through the experience with the women to whom they were assigned. I felt prepared intellectually, but emotionally I needed to put aside my own vacillating to be present on the day. Our class had collectively amassed a bit of wisdom by February; out of the 170 of us, many had already attended a delivery and were now in the pediatric phase. Some had run into very difficult situations tangential to but crucial to the birth. Peter, for instance, got involved with the care of his patient's mother, who was diagnosed with cancer even before the grandchild arrived. In keeping with his fiery personality, Peter fought hard against a particularly dismissive head resident who accused him of paying too much attention to the family. The resident asked Peter why he hadn't gone into social work if he cared so much about the extended family. Peter—groomed from childhood to be a physician—fired back that if the resident treated people like that, why hadn't he become a veterinarian? The resident warned Peter never to show his face on his ward again. We all thought Peter was a hero in that battle.

But we medical students weren't the heroes of our stories. The mothers, along with fathers and other relatives, carried the day. I spent hours in the hospital when Rose went into labor. Her husband was too queasy to be involved until the last phases of the delivery, but he was there when the little girl was born and took her from the obstetrician's hands. I felt tremendous joy and pride in the whole experience and affection for Rose and her husband and their little girl, but I knew I was not a central character in the drama. I also realized that all the little tasks I did during the labor—noting vital signs, helping Rose with her breathing, getting the nurse when she needed medication—I wouldn't have had the time to do as a medical student on rotation or as an attending physician. I was training to be a technician, one who could diagnose a condition or perform a procedure safely and effectively, but I was most interested in the human interaction. The high-handed resident's criticism applied more to me than to Peter. I had neither Peter's drive to practice medicine nor his ability to balance care and technical knowledge, as a good physician must. I happened to be standing in the prep room when a third-year med student, also on duty at the time, was making small talk with the attending physician after Rose's delivery. They were looking at a fetus that had been aborted earlier in the day. The med student said: "Doctor, I know you have a moral objection to abortion, but you must admit that this fetus is fascinating to look at." The doctor looked at the young man with tired eyes that pitied more than seared, and then he walked away to care for another woman in labor.

Carl's roommate Erica lectured Carl and me about the difference between nursing and medical orientations: nurses focused on health while doctors focused on illness. She described the elaborate training that nurses receive about how to approach patients, make them comfortable, anticipate their needs. She was outraged that we merely practiced on an orange once or twice before we gave the babies their first shots. In her training they saw videos, read manuals, and practiced for hours before giving their first inoculation. I began to see that medicine was not simply about facts of the body but involved a complex indoctrination that was both planned and steeped in unexamined tradition. We learned implicitly to carry our privileges into the clinic with us. The stirrups used in the delivery room came to symbolize our privileged position to me. The birthing stool, which let gravity help in the pushing, had been replaced by stirrups so that the doctor didn't have to get on his knees to catch the baby. I began to ask where patient care stopped and systemic convenience began. Everything we read in books or learned in lecture seemed couched in the privilege conferred by amassed knowledge backed by huge social investments in hospitals and clinics, libraries and drug companies. Doctors did good for people, yes, but what material conditions shaped the way we thought of ourselves and responded to other humans, our "patients"? Society needed to believe in us and we needed to believe in ourselves; medical students had to undergo a magical transformation to take on the mantle of physician, an individual representative of a complex and costly system. I began to look for edges where medicine was stretched by extremity beyond traditional understandings or hierarchies.

In an elective at the Cuyahoga County Jail, I interviewed inmates about health conditions and in the process learned a great deal about what lands people in jail. One young arsonist was a glue sniffer who had drifted away from his family and gotten into a violent fight with his girlfriend's father. Another prisoner told me he'd been minding his business, walking down the street, when somebody opened a window, handed him a cash register, and told him to run. A few inmates spoke in whispers about the notorious child molester locked up in solitary because he would have been killed in the general prison population. Their stories shocked me into recognizing that, despite my adventures hitchhiking and working at various jobs, I was still twenty-three years old and knew little about how people lived in the United States and beyond. Once again I began to think about psychiatry, though I did not know if I could handle the training or face the suffering I would encounter. Blood and wounds could be gruesome, but already I could see how one might grow comfortable treating gunshot wounds or broken bones. Diseases of profound psychological trauma or behaviors learned in violent neighborhoods, these seemed both intractable and tragic, reflecting the suffering of hundreds and thousands rather than a single individual. Meanwhile, in the prison they needed doctors, any kind of doctors, and I felt like a slouch wanting to walk away. One day we got a call in the prison infirmary that someone had collapsed in the parking lot. The three of us students followed the nurse toward the elevator when suddenly she turned to me and thrust a stethoscope into my hands. I had no idea how to use the thing in an emergency, but I stuffed it into the pocket of my white coat and felt the rush of pride that we could actually save someone in crisis.

I joined a committee discussing quality of care issues with faculty and students. The committee included some of the older students in our class, men and women like Stan my housemate, who had already served in the military or started other careers. Some had families, as my father did in medical school. More mature people faced the same pressures as the rest of us, but they carried additional burdens of debt and expectation because they'd given up much to study medicine. In one case, a classmate left a promising career as a concert musician to study endocrinology. Another had been an officer in the US Army Special Forces, the Green Berets, who were heroes to some and villains to others during the Vietnam War. These classmates understood the health-care system and the stakes for average people far better than I. Our committee organized a trip to the Frontier Nursing Service in Leslie County, Kentucky, a rural district where the needs of family medicine and obstetrics/gynecology were met mainly by nurse-midwives and nurse practitioners trained in their own school. A system that centered on women as providers struck us as revolutionary in the best sense. We met a few male doctors involved in rural medicine, and in one meeting I realized that, both for political and economic reasons, doctors of either gender should not be primary providers as much as managers and architects of programs. Systems of care based on a range of health workers could support widespread wellness better than even the most heroic single docs, working their hearts out sixty or seventy hours a week. Administration didn't seem like a job for me, but for the first time I understood what a good administrator could do. The perspective on medicine in rural Kentucky challenged me to think about health crises in a new way. Excellent care needed to go to individuals—like the epileptic mother who wanted to shoot a doctor or the glue sniffer who set fire to schools—but also to whole communities such as the Hough section of Cleveland, where Rose lived in need of services, not charity.

The single most memorable political lesson I learned that year came in a lecture after classes one afternoon in the spring. The speaker was a doctor who had been asked by Salvador Allende to advise him on the overhaul of the medical system that Chile undertook during his presidency. Allende had been trained as a physician, a public health doctor, and his vision of health care radically challenged the traditional medical hierarchy. This doctor started with an account of the shift from private to public funding for medicine in Chile. He described a clinic in the mountains, where few people had ever seen a doctor. The team of doctor, nurses, and various other helpers not only brought professional care to the area but also acted in concert in such a way that each one's expertise could be valued. They all wore the same uniforms, so that doctors were not distinguished by their long white coats nor orderlies singled out for their lowly costume. The doctor was in charge of establishing diagnoses and dispensing medications or performing surgery, but the nurse was fully in charge of patient care, and housekeeping staff maintained the safety of the clinic environment. Discussions about treatment included a range of workers, and the pay differential was not as great as in city hospitals.

Then the speaker described the anger that built up in the medical establishment over these innovations and the larger economic changes Allende introduced. When the coup came in 1973 and Allende was killed along with so many others, some doctors who served in the new health-care system were thrown into prison. The speaker had himself documented a number of cases where established doctors not only conducted torture on prisoners of the coup but conducted torture directly on detained doctors. There were perhaps fifty people in the audience, and the room fell silent as he spoke. The only interruption came when an academic doctor from Chile asked a few hostile questions, defending the Pinochet regime for bringing necessary order after the Communist chaos of Allende's reign. I left that lecture hall feeling just how fragile our systems were, how easily ideological struggles can turn violent, and yet how much is at stake in getting a system to function both effectively and equitably.

Every day at school I found reasons I might stay, but every evening when I came home to my attic room I grew more certain that I had to leave. Sylvie came to see me for a week that spring, and when she left I still wasn't sure I would go with her to Philadelphia or find a job elsewhere for a year, but the relationship gave me hope that I could have a life without medicine. While she was in town, I went with her and Stan to Bobby McGee's, a bar in town where an open-mike night was held once a week. A small scene of poets gathered there and read in between the musical acts and stand-up comics. I had decided to read a few of my new poems there, even though I wasn't a bar entertainer and didn't have a smooth patter like some of the regular acts. The crowd was rowdy that night, and a bluegrass band had folks up on their feet dancing. I started running through pithy comments I'd make to get the audience on my side, and I grew more and more nervous as the music ended. The act ahead of me was a classical guitarist, a slim young man in a white shirt. Through all the noise and smoke, he pulled up a chair to the microphone, sat down with his guitar, and without a word to the audience began to play. He played beautifully. The rowdies at the bar paid him no attention, and the players around the pool table went on with their game. But he played his Bach and Villa-Lobos without a flaw, stood up for a quick bow, and left the stage. His performance wiped out all my jitters. I thought: This is about making art. If they like the work, fine, but I'm not going to twist myself up trying to make them like me. I'll present what I do and move on. When they called my name and announced I was a poet, some guy at the bar yelled out, "Get that faggot off the stage!" I walked to the mike, read my poems with an emphasis on the rhythm and sound, sometimes looking up to find the eyes of my friends and a few others who seemed to be listening, thanked the audience, and walked off the stage. I didn't need to explain myself for what I wanted to do.

When Sylvie left town, I was lonely but hopeful. I was buoyed by our closeness, the hope we had in the next year. But I had to face my worries about leaving a profession with secure earning power and prestige for the sake of unknown work and years of writing with little expectation of recognition or support. After all, who earned a living as a poet? Some could get academic positions, and others could command fees for public readings like the poets I'd seen in Cleveland that year: Cynthia Mac-donald, Philip Levine, Michael Harper, David Ignatow, Russell Edson, Adrienne Rich. But they were all well known, at least among writers, and I figured that none of them depended on honoraria for their money. Sylvie was going to be a rabbi. Did I need a profession, too? Would I end up doing the household chores while she guided a congregation? In an April journal entry, I considered going for a master of fine arts degree in writing, but I feared being "a frog in academic muck." I wrote that I wanted to come at my poems strongly, "crack open the little heads and suck at the juice & meat." Teaching seemed possible, but I didn't want to "gut myself for the pay of it." For all my tough talk, without medicine I had no automatic claim to male privilege.

As I neared the final days of my year in Cleveland, I found myself drawing closer to friends I had made in that short year. Probably because

I was leaving, they confided in me their own misgivings about medical school, about their relationships, their families. I realized how much of a community I had among the students and instructors, this network of driven people struggling to maintain their own humanity. Stan and I talked over dinner about all the women who paraded through his life; I sympathized but couldn't quite hide my amusement and jealousy. Three or four classmates told me privately about intellectual interests in history, anthropology, and music they feared would fade out of their lives. At the same time, I became involved with the diagnosis and treatment of Rose's husband, who was suffering with a skin condition caused by toxic chemicals at his job. This brought me even closer to the family I had come to know intimately over the year. I gave their daughter, Lena, her shots in June and realized sadly that I was sacrificing the chance to follow Lena and her family for another year.

Samuel and Martha, the parents of the infant Celia who had spent all that time in the hospital with a hemangioma, were far more religious than the rest of the Lev family. They belonged to a Chasidic shul, and this community had given them added strength during the ordeal with Celia. In June, Samuel invited me to the bris of their first boy and gave me the honor of holding him while the *moyel* performed the circumcision. I wrote in a poem later:

> Pale men in dark coats,
> among them the boy's father, davened
> in a circle around us. The child
> should've been holding me, the least
> observant Jew. I hadn't shaved for months
> but still my beard lacked conviction.

Bob Lev found the orthodoxy too much and spent most of the party after the ceremony drinking orange juice with his niece and other women in the kitchen, but I sat with the *frumishe* men at a narrow table, eating herring and challah and drinking whiskey. A tall young man with a pointed reddish beard bent toward me, tapped a matchbook with his slim fingers, and said confidentially, "You can learn something from anything," indicating the man and woman facing each other on the cover advertising a correspondence school. I nodded gravely, though I had no idea what he meant, and soon we were all leaning on one another, chanting and pounding the table to the rhythm of wordless songs in the traditional minor key of Jewish music, half laughing and half weeping.

The mad scene might have been far from the mystic tales Buber tells of Chasidim in Eastern Europe, the ones Sylvie was studying in California, but it made me love Sylvie and Celia and Bob and Lena and her parents and the whole Cleveland *mishpucha*. The year had forced me to embrace a passion for connection in myself that I feared and needed. As relieved as I felt at the prospect of following my art, leaving the logical confines of science and the relentless expectations of service, I was terrified I would not find community through writing as I'd found it at Case, my father's alma mater in his hometown. I would never find my father again as I'd found his gregarious enthusiasms in the clinics and wards here. Medical school left me little time for myself, but I always knew that people needed me. Writing offered the pleasure and perils of the imagination but also the isolation of my writing room. Would writing cut me off from lives I valued or from those who valued me?

Before I could leave Case, I had to make my peace with psychiatry. My horrific experience with psychoanalysis in high school didn't leave me much respect for the profession, but I had to admit that if I stayed— or if I returned after a leave of absence, which was how I left things with the college—I would probably go into that specialty. I signed up for a brief elective with a child psychiatrist I'll call Dr. Selig, whom I had met when the ancient Eric Ericson lectured at the school earlier in the year. Dr. Selig assigned me a few articles by Anna Freud on children's literature, and we met at his house in his study. I found the articles maddening for the way they approached literature as a rational, interpretable phenomenon to be assigned its territory on a rather abstruse mental map. Where was the imagination? Didn't a child's mind have immense healthy possibilities rather than dark, circular purposes? Dr. Selig grew suspicious as we talked and finally asked me if something were bothering me besides the reading. I admitted to him that I was leaving medical school in order to write. He looked at me empathetically and asked what I was really searching for. I tried to explain, but nothing made sense in that comfortable suburban home. He asked why I didn't just take the straight route and go into analysis. When I commented on the frustrating limits of science, he smiled. "You see that stethoscope hanging on the hook over there?" he pointed to the door.

"My kids make me keep it there to remind me I'm still a medical doctor. My days are spent sitting in a darkened room, and my patients come in one at a time to consult. At the end of the day, I turn off the light and go home. I've helped people, and I never use the science I learned in medical school." I thanked Dr. Selig for the tutorial and the advice and told him I'd think about what he'd said. I didn't tell him that his account of medical practice was the most frightening I'd heard all year. My last possible perch in medicine had proven to be no place at all for me.

Sylvie came back to help me pack up my apartment after the last comprehensive exam was over. After many journal entries and a visit to Ithaca to search for work on an academic journal, I had decided that I might as well jump off into a big city and join her in Philadelphia. Coincidentally, my brother had been accepted into art school there and was starting in the fall as well. I had no reason to go anywhere else and so following the signs to Philadelphia in the bicentennial year seemed the right next step. Perhaps I could work at a medical textbook company, or maybe even finally find a job as a printer's apprentice. The thought of being part of a couple again appealed to me after a cold year alone. Our relationship depended upon shared outlook more than physical sparks, and that seemed a major improvement over the spectacular failure of my last romance. We cared about art, spirituality, and connection with others. We believed in an equal partnership between a man and a woman. I imagined forming some kind of an ideal school with Sylvie and Joel and other friends we'd met along the way. I wrote in that last week about the paradoxical state of "alone together," where partners or communities could respect the needs of individuals to form independent lives but still find joy being bound together. Just as we were packing up the last of my furniture in the U-Haul truck, the mail arrived. Among the circulars and Stan's bills was a postcard addressed to me from some fellow in Canada. He said he'd read a poem I'd published in a little magazine months ago. He liked the poem so much that he wanted me to notify him when my first book came out. Sylvie and I laughed about the obviousness of the sign, but I figured I might as well go east to fill his order.

## 7

## Entering Philadelphia

AT THE END OF June 1976, right after my last exam, Sylvie and I packed up my things in Cleveland and drove back to her family's grand house in Westchester County, outside New York City. We stayed nearly two weeks. In short visits I loved being around her two brothers and two sisters, her mother and father, in a house that seemed to go on forever and displayed art by people whose work one usually sees only in museums. Although they carried their wealth lightly and welcomed me without reservation, after a few days of wonderful meals and drinks at the pool and long talks about politics and religion at parties with people who actually knew how these things were done, I began to doubt myself more and feel a directionless hostility. To Sylvie I railed at her family's class privilege, while to myself I wrote of the chaos in my life and declared, "Art is within me and will live, but it will not overrule me any more than wealth." Above all, I would be "tending toward the good man—not moderate but tender & true seeing w/o disbelief" (7/7/76, soon after I began dating my journal's entries). I spent much time reading books from her father's art library, and I lectured Sylvie about Willem de Kooning and the contradictions of his women figures in the midst of the abstract expressionist move toward pure painting. None of my fulminating could drive away the uncertainty ahead. We were moving together to a new city where our individual projects held no guarantee of success, and we had never spent more than a week together at a time.

My journal flips back and forth between ambivalent dissections of James Wright's poetry or quotes from commentaries on de Kooning and then long passages about whether or not my love for Sylvie could survive. What would I do if yet another relationship collapsed because I couldn't find my way? Then I would rededicate myself to her, my loving companion who needed me to help her face the impossible challenge of rabbinical school. Sylvie had a deeply compassionate personality; large, knowing eyes; olive skin; and a wild head of black hair. She gathered the world to her in a comforting and ancient embrace. Her extended family on her mother's side had produced thirteen generations of rabbis. She would be the only one to study for the rabbinate in her generation, and the line would stop with her if she didn't reach ordination. Perhaps a dozen women rabbis had been ordained at that moment in the world, but Sylvie was no surer about this path than I had been about medicine. She loved making pottery and weaving in undergraduate school even as she majored in religion, and she wondered if art wasn't her calling rather than professional spirituality. Her ambitions and doubts had drawn me to her, partly because they were familiar and partly because they gave me relief from my own.

I admired her father immensely and began to imagine that I could one day accept him as a second father, but I was also wary of his wealth, his self-assurance, and his calm demeanor. He asked me one day to kiss him on the cheek as Sylvie did when we came down to breakfast, saying, "That's the price you have to pay" (7/6/76). I complied with some pleasure but also trepidation. Could he become my new father at so small a price? He had made his money in public relations—Sylvie called him a "psychiatrist for corporations"—but he had also worked in government under Kennedy. Everybody loved him and trusted his rumbling voice. Why shouldn't I? Sylvie and I would talk to him in the kitchen, his Pall Mall cigarette held between his lips till it burned down nearly to his flesh. The world he represented was complex and luscious with possibilities, stable and populated by just enough reasonable men to survive. Our world seemed jagged and precarious by comparison, lit by pools of mysterious light, pocked with more pain and poverty than we could see from their marvelous kitchen. Sylvie's family had certainly known pain and dispossession (their stories are not mine to tell), and this gave all they stood for a somber solidity I had not known in other houses. They opened themselves to be my new family, and I felt eager to be accepted in their home despite my principles.

Perhaps I wanted so much to join Sylvie's family because I was still some years away from making peace with my own. While visiting Sylvie, I traveled into the city one day to see my mother's father, Max. He had helped finance my year in medical school, and he was not happy about my plan to leave. My journal entry after that day describes our interview: "Grandpa talked to me for 2½ hours today how I'm being vain & foolish, wasting a perfectly good career as a doctor for the pursuit of some nonsense I would appreciate much better once I'm well put up & can always fall back on something" (7/8/76). He wanted desperately for me to "replace" my father, though he seldom spoke my father's name aloud; the stability and respect a medical degree represented for the family mattered a great deal more to him than the proclivities of individuals. I could feel for my grandfather. He had loved my father, at least to the extent that he could recognize others at all, and he worried about my mother and her fatherless kids. He thought both my brother and I were irresponsible hippies, spoiled by the rebellious times and possibly fated to "search for ourselves" aimlessly as we aged. He admired degrees and wanted all his grandchildren to be educated, although he himself had started working well before he finished high school and never took a college course. He believed that hard work and secure prospects far outweighed books—written or read—for survival. He hoped that, if I got serious about Sylvie and her well-to-do family, I would see my error, or at least Sylvie and her family would convince me to return to the safety and respectability of medicine.

In fact, although I would never have admitted it to my grandfather, I had tried desperately to replace my father, even to the exclusion of my own life, and I would have welcomed a viable way to earn my living that did not directly involve my poetry. But I couldn't be my father. Running from his stern Orthodox family in Cleveland, he had no money, but he did have a knack for making things with his hands and a mind for solving problems rooted in human biology. I couldn't explain to my grandfather what poetry gave me that maybe surgery gave my dad. I had truly enjoyed moments in medical school, especially once I decided to leave, but what annoyed me most was exactly what my grandfather wanted for me: the automatic social status, the expectation that I would command others, the guaranteed financial security. I did not think our family needed saving. I would have gone back to Cleveland had I believed my medical career would make my mother and sister less lonely, would patch the hole Colonel Harry Goldblatt left in us all. But medicine wasn't going to solve our problems.

Finally, in July, Sylvie and I left her home to stay with friends in Hillsdale, New York, just across the state line from Massachusetts, until we made the move to Philadelphia. Nina was the oldest daughter of Shirley and Bob Lev, my family's friends in Cleveland who had been so warm to me during my year there. Nina was married to Dick, a carpenter who had been building low-income housing in the area under a contract with the federal government. When my brother had wanted to become a carpenter and work in the DC area was scarce for a young, unskilled kid out of high school, Nina and Dick invited Aaron up to learn the trade from Dick. I didn't expect to repeat what Aaron had done because Dick no longer had much work, and after all, I'd agreed to go with Sylvie to Philadelphia, but Dick offered to pay me for some jobs around the house they were rebuilding. Nina was beginning to counsel in a women's health clinic in town, and their little girl, Beth, occasionally needed looking after. Sylvie and I could do our own work much of the time and put in some days helping Nina and Dick, and in exchange they would let us stay in their barn and share food with us when we wanted to join them. It was the countercultural retreat both of us needed before Philadelphia.

It didn't take us long to set up our few belongings in the loft of their barn. I made a space for a writing table and books. Sylvie set up her small handloom by the wide hay-loading door. Bees flew in from the meadow to store their pollen in a hive above our bed, and some afternoons I would lie on my back and watch them building and carrying, moving in single-minded flight paths from meadow to home and back out to new flowers. I was letting go and living without a map. Doctoring was behind me, secrecy and silence were behind me, my father's life was behind me. I had no solid prospects, no special qualifications to help me land a job, no confidence in love, and no place to call home. I was free to write poetry and read in whatever direction I wanted, but I had very little to hold back the waves of anxiety and self-doubt that washed over me every day.

On the days when we weren't working for Nina and Dick, we would sit by the open door and look out across the meadow, Sylvie weaving while I read. I wrote that first week: "There is a low forested hill forming the arc of our view from the front door, a pond half dug & in dispute to one side of the barn & Nina & Dick's half built house on the other side. Whenever Beth is home she is either crying & whining loudly, or laughing" (7/13/76). This was the way we wanted to be. We didn't need more degrees or bigger jobs; we had plenty to do of our own choosing. Sylvie still had some editing for a book she was working on with her Buber scholar in San Diego. I started reading Joyce's *Ulysses* as the first of the books in my rapidly expanding self-education program, now that I was free of science. I had always been strict with myself that I should read only poetry or criticism, perhaps a little history or philosophy, but seldom fiction. Still, liberation meant opening to everything that could challenge my art, and fiction counted too. I lectured myself on fiction in my journal: "It was convenient for a time to rule it out, but can't do that now & be anywhere" (8/8/76). After all, Pound had helped Joyce survive in those modernist days. I could at least read what Joyce starved for. Sylvie and I talked incessantly about our fears that art would isolate us from others even while we could not imagine our lives without seeking and making. We were only beginning to know each other, though we thought we knew each other well. Early in our stay, I noted after one conversation, "We can both be such nutshells it's hard to believe anything will get done. But I believe it will" (7/13/76). We had the drive to "do" something with all our ambitions and yet to hide from the world of accomplishments, programs, and positions, which we regarded as distractions at best and traps at worst.

I was also reading Wassily Kandinsky's *Concerning the Spiritual in Art*, trying to reconcile the desire for meaning apart from material well-being with artistic effort, while not being drawn into any specific religious practice. I quoted Kandinsky in my journal: "The nightmare of materialism, which turned life into an evil senseless game, is not yet passed; it still darkens the awakening soul" (2). I worried about sectarianism or parochialism, but I responded to him in my journal that "Art is not religion—but it is a path following the same river as any religion might seek" (8/6/76). One day I would be digging ditches and helping Dick hang drywall, the next reading Kandinsky and trying to learn how to write verse lines of varying metrical and vowel lengths, slowly trying to bring attention and focus to every activity. At the same time, I worried about whether or not Sylvie and I were suited for each other, whether or not we wanted the same mix of politics and spirituality, art and lovemaking. I felt I needed to seek intensity and worth from every moment; I couldn't let our lives simply be. I enjoyed the times we just sat with coffee or wine and gazed out our barn door—in those days, too, we smoked cigarettes whenever we sat back to talk—but I saw the stillness as a respite from the momentous work we were undertaking rather than the ground itself for our work.

Before we left for Philadelphia, we took a brief trip to see our friend Joel at the Marlboro Music Festival. He had gotten the job of stage manager for the festival that summer, which meant that he worked all day and night making sure pianos were tuned and in place at the right time for concerts and rehearsals, that anything technical worked, that the artists, young and old, need do nothing but play music and enjoy the summer camp atmosphere. This venerable program was directed by the august and kindly piano master Rudolf Serkin, who liked to throw balled-up napkins at people after dinner so that the whole room would erupt in a napkin-throwing battle. Famous orchestral and chamber musicians of all ages walked around in their jeans and T-shirts, or casual button-down shirts, or neat summer dresses. Many came from the Curtis Institute in Philadelphia, where Mr. Serkin was director, but highly accomplished musicians came from all over the world to play with their peers and mentors. Rehearsals in halls or small classrooms across this idyllic Vermont campus went on all day, and concerts were scheduled a few times a week. Sylvie had been a serious cellist as a girl, and my mother had won a classical piano competition in New York City as a teen, so both of us were fascinated to learn more about this esoteric but vibrant world. Classical music was a prized and funded art, but it was still an art and thus had to have resonance with the arts we were studying. And this was an art world where being Jewish was quite normal rather than anomalous. Our dear yeshiva-trained friend Joel still harbored some ambition to play piano at a concert level, but his job was fast convincing him that the true classical performers functioned in such an abstracted world and possessed such highly tutored gifts that he could never join their ranks. He had crushes and romances that summer with a series of ethereal women, each reminding him one way or another that he was not of their class.

We stayed for a few days, astonished by the music played in mere practice sessions. At night we hung out at the fringes of a group of musicians our age or younger. Their scene made us think again about the dangers of art practiced in seclusion. Most of them cared about very little else but classical music, and I found only one or two among

Joel's acquaintances who had any familiarity with jazz or blues or rock and roll. Few seemed touched by the politics of the 1960s, although the circle around Mr. Serkin's son Peter had the reputation for being more tuned to the times. I gave an informal reading of my poems there, and the small audience seemed open to poetry, though they knew little about modern literature of any type. In honor of the Marlboro visit, I was reading Louis Zukofsky's book *Little*, a funny but sad account of his son's experience as a child violin prodigy, but no one had heard of Paul Zukofsky (as an adult, a performer of avant-garde art music) or his poet father, and few recognized the names of William Carlos Williams or Wallace Stevens or Marianne Moore or the old impresario Ezra Pound himself. Nor did anyone know of Georgia O'Keeffe, Milton Avery, or Anni Albers, artists whom Sylvie admired. The separation of the arts, and especially the insular environment for classical music, struck both Sylvie and me as a pernicious condition of high culture that would eventually wither the very art the system was designed to preserve. The exquisite music warned us to stay connected to the world as we pursued our work. "From the sublime to the ridiculous," Joel would intone when he was drunk enough to pronounce on his experience.

I had a dream that summer that I was the captain of a spaceship. We arrived at a planet, and I alone traveled down to its surface to explore. My journal entry recounts the dream like this:

> The planet is peopled with invisible beings composed entirely of energy. Through great effort I am able to see these beings in what I perceive as sketchy orange forms, but not with much clarity or constancy. When I return aboard ship, the beings have unaccountably traveled w/me & they swarm around the ship. But because of my effort to see these invisible beings, I'm left unable to see my originally visible shipmates. Now I only see the invisible ones occasionally, & my crew & friends not at all. The visible folks are being hurt, or are at least badly threatened & fearful by these invisible creatures & it becomes my job to destroy the invisible gang. But since I can't see the visible people, each time I shoot at an invisible form I accidentally kill a visible (formerly) person. I'm caught with the problem but the dream ended w/o solution. (7/6/76)

Here was my dilemma. I was straining to see forms in my own poetry and in the writing of others that most people around me could not see.

I believed in what I was doing fervently, but I feared my reading and writing were changing me too. Sylvie, who was becoming dearer to me as we lived together, might not be able to follow me into the poem-life I was seeking. In the same way, I might not be able to follow her into the classes on Hebrew liturgy and Talmud she would start in the fall. We would have to trust each other and call to each other across the valley created by our separating literacies. But what about others? Our families, our friends becoming lawyers and doctors and carpenters? My mother had already told me she understood nothing I'd been saying in college, and she was a highly educated woman. Was isolation and invisibility the price I would have to pay for a poet's life? Many entries during this time ended with some version of stern urgings to concentrate on my writing, such as, "To be good & easy at it I must really begin to work at it, *hard*, & with all my mind" (7/4/76), or, in a kinder tone, "I'm not going to talk myself up a wall again, just take it easy & see what comes out" (7/26/76).

We arrived in Philadelphia in mid-August 1976, just a few weeks after the elaborate bicentennial celebrations in the city. Philly is quiet, hot, and impossibly humid in August; anybody who can get out is long gone to the Jersey shore. But to us, West Philadelphia was the bustling city, studded with the sounds of fire and police sirens and trolleys rolling down Baltimore Avenue. We found a small apartment on the third floor of an old row house, with curved turret windows framing the front room, where we put an old dining table Sylvie's family had given us. I felt the space truly luxurious because, beside the bedroom, we had a beautiful little extra room in the back that became my study. Sylvie arranged her books and desk in the large front living room, where she could spread out at the table and stare out the windows as a full-time student again. She set up a wall for her wool, to remind herself that she was not just a Hebrew scholar but a weaver as well. My brother, who had moved into his own tiny apartment a few blocks away, helped us paint; the last tenants had done the bedroom in green and white checkerboard and the front room in multiple shades of purple. We left the narrow galley kitchen a fire engine red and black, in honor of the apartment's previous exuberance. In my study, we kept the tolerable blue. We felt very adult indeed, settling into our new home with more belongings than either of us had ever schlepped into an apartment before, and we prepared to live.

Our lives sped up immediately. Sylvie started classes and fell deep into assignments and anxiety by early September. She was studying biblical Hebrew and Aramaic, Talmud and history. Her education and family culture were not nearly as strictly Judaic as some of her classmates and all of her professors had experienced. The dining room table soon accumulated piles of books and papers, and one of her classmates—I'll call her Lisa—worked with Sylvie many afternoons and sometimes into the evening. Like Sylvie, Lisa had an excellent liberal education but felt disadvantaged next to classmates who had grown up reading Hebrew in much more observant homes. They struggled with the classes together, and they shared their doubts about their peers and the more conservative male professors. Even though Reconstructionists had a long history of gender equality—after all, the first bat mitzvah was the daughter of Mordecai Kaplan, the founder of the movement—still women in the rabbinical class felt the weight of a male-dominated religion constantly. Every study session, while I cooked dinner, Lisa and Sylvie talked about some snarky remark a male professor or student had made. Sylvie was consumed by the work or, when she paused for a moment, by her fears and doubts about the career choice she'd made. I wanted to support her as much as I could and believed somehow I could carry more of the domestic burden because my struggles with medical school were over. Though at times I felt the rabbinical school reduced me to invisible status at home, I thought I was strong enough to care for her and see this through. I didn't need help with my own struggles. At least I had no one telling me what to read or how to be a professional.

But in fact, I too was very much at sea. I was searching for work every day, following the want ads for printer's or carpenter's helper, talking to unsympathetic secretaries and hassled foremen who were not terribly interested in a young guy with no skills to offer. The only office job I tried for was an editorial position at a medical textbook firm, but I was surprised that they showed no interest in my application, and I soon gave up the idea that I could be an editor. My grandfather took every opportunity to remind me I could go back to medical school, and Sylvie's father hung above me as an example of a humane and yet successful businessman. Though she said little directly, I could tell my mother worried about what I would do next. But I wanted to work with my hands, and this desire permeated my writing, too. At the time, I wrote in my journal that in writing, reading, and my daily job, I wanted to build something solid in the world, inside and out:

> I must find a way that poems may truly be constructed, as sculpture or painting or music may—that is a true & substantial abstract form. This doesn't mean a movement away from sense but it does mean a turn from discursive & explanatory program music. Also into the *sheerly comprehensible* form, a form which moves into the mind directly, as a cedar cabinet or the cedar tree itself might. (9/10/76)

Later in that entry, I turn to job prospects:

> I realize I want to align myself with the workers, with those who make rather than those who think "to keep things going." The paper & shop-keep world is constantly generating raw deceptive energies . . . destructions in the street are minute instances building insistently into monuments, which later are supplanted by new monuments grown from descendant destructions. Perhaps work with the hands is not the opposing side but it seems to me happier & more sustaining. I'll want to teach, but not until I have something worth teaching.

If this sounds like Wordsworth and Thoreau recalibrated through Students for a Democratic Society, Gil Scott-Heron, and Bob Dylan, I would not have denied it even then. I was trying to anchor my own artistic practice and identity in the metaphor of construction, fabricating something palpable and unassailably worthwhile. At a time when Sylvie and Lisa were rehearsing for me every night the pernicious effect of maleness in Jewish tradition, I still could not recognize the unmistakably male cast of my own ambitions.

I finally got a job at a cabinetmaker's shop in the far northeast of the city, as far across town as possible from our house in West Philly. At least my commute was against traffic, and I took pride in getting to know a city for the first time. Every morning I drove my red Volkswagen up the Schuylkill Expressway to Roosevelt Boulevard, then up the boulevard to Cottman Avenue and into the corner of the city near the old Holmesburg Prison, built in 1896. I got up early to write, worked all day carrying plywood and shop tools, drove home, cooked dinner or cleaned up afterward, read till bed, slept a short night, and then started again. Sylvie and I talked when we could, but she studied every evening, and so I did too. I hadn't gotten into the printing trade, but perhaps on this job I would learn enough to make my living as a carpenter. I bought a metal toolbox, a hammer and holster, some screwdrivers, a pair of Vise-Grip pliers, and a small crowbar. Each night I set my tools down by the door when I came home. I was reading the Jewish Objectivist Louis Zukofsky, a friend of George Oppen's but, unlike Oppen, neither a man who worked with his hands nor a Communist. Zukofsky led me to John Skelton's strange, rhythmic English Renaissance lyrics. Reading about modern art brought me to the painter Paul Klee's notebooks. My friend from college had been studying with Anne Sexton when Sexton killed herself in 1974, and this led me to read Sexton and then the madman Antonin Artaud. I worked on a sestina for the distorted women in de Kooning's paintings, and I filled journal pages with studies of line length and scansion. I wanted my hands to harden as the history and craft of poetry assembled in my mind. Most of all, I wanted to feel I could build something in words solid enough to withstand my own uncertainties.

The owner of the cabinetmaking shop was a little German man named Jan who lost his temper easily and, on two separate occasions, lost fingers in the joiner machine. The foreman was a tall, thin young black man with dreadlocks named Ivan, a master craftsman from the Caribbean. Ivan thought it was funny to have an apprentice who dropped out of medical school, and he took to calling me "Doc." They seldom let me drive a nail, but they had plenty for me to do finishing wood panels and moving equipment in and out of the truck. One day, Ivan took me on a job to a fancy apartment in the suburbs and asked me to tack up some custom molding in the dining room. I very carefully tapped in one nail while Ivan watched. He stopped me after the second nail and said to me with amusement and passion, "Doc, look. Drive it so you mean it. You have to do the best job you can and then you say f——k it." Around that time, I was driving home on a Friday evening, feeling proud that I was managing, with so little sleep, to be a carpenter and writer too. Traffic suddenly slowed down to a crawl on the expressway. I looked over at the young woman in the car beside me, closed my eyes, and drifted into the bumper of the truck in front of me. The truck didn't even notice and never stopped, but I had crushed the trunk of my beloved little car. I drove it that way for weeks as a memorial to my stupidity, till finally my brother surprised me with a belated birthday present of a new hood from the junkyard.

One evening, Ivan and I returned to the shop late from a job, and we heard screaming in the shop. Jan was holding his arm in the air, crying, "I cut my hand! I cut my hand!" The tip of his finger hung from its stump by a thread. We piled into my Volkswagen and rushed to the hospital, Ivan yelling at me if I tapped the brake for a stop sign. They managed to save Jan's finger, but the shop itself did not thrive. On a Friday soon after the accident, I went to the neighborhood bank where I cashed my paycheck. The cashier looked at the check, looked up the account in her book, and shook her head: "You better take that back to Jan. It's no good this week." I dragged back and told Jan the news. He reached into his pocket, handed me a fifty, and told me he'd pay me the rest next week. The next Friday, Jan handed me a check and said he didn't have the money to keep me on any longer. I'd been with the shop less than six weeks, and it felt like he'd knocked me down and splattered his blood across my face. I wished him luck, shook hands with Ivan, and drove home.

I went out looking for work again. I briefly held a job with an all-black carpentry company, but the boss didn't like me because I couldn't work fast enough. I couldn't blame him for letting me go. A young man in the shop, who started the same week as I did, had never enrolled in a single training course or apprenticeship program, but he could figure out how to do any job with wood, brick, or siding. My brother could look at a wall and understand its internal structure or design a three-dimensional composition from the most unpromising materials. All I could see were solid surfaces, colors, and texture, and my mind slid off the fine points of construction just as my brain drowned in the immense material sea of medicine. Cold comfort that I could read James Joyce and Alfred North Whitehead; neither of them were hiring at the moment. I did some nude modeling at local art schools for a little money. I enjoyed comparing the attitudes toward drawing that different instructors took: some very technical, others more intuitive. I wasn't embarrassed to stand naked in front of people because, without my glasses, I couldn't see anyone anyway and fell into a meditative state quite easily. But I realized after my legs gave out from holding one pose too long—and no one tried to catch me because no one wanted to touch a naked man—that this wasn't a sustainable career option. At the same time, Sylvie developed terrible back pain from hunching over her books, the physical pain exacerbating her continued doubts and frustrations about being a rabbi. I wasn't yet ready to panic about our prospects, but I did sometimes answer our phone, only half in jest, with "WFIL's gonna make me rich!" A radio station in town was offering a big cash prize to the random person who answered the DJ's call with this catchphrase.

One afternoon, I came home from a modeling job, poured a glass of bourbon, and put on Bob Dylan's new album, *Blood on the Tracks*. As I listened to "Tangled Up in Blue," I began to think about Sylvie, her bear-hug kindness, her intelligence undaunted by sneering beards. If this love didn't work out, I wanted to say I had committed myself completely. Each verse in Dylan's song told of a fully lived moment, no matter what came at the next turn.

> Her folks they said our life together
> Sure was gonna be rough
> They never did like Mama's homemade dress
> Papa's bankbook wasn't big enough.
> And I was standin' on the side of the road
> Rain fallin' on my shoes
> Heading out for the East Coast
> Lord knows I've paid some dues gettin' through,
> Tangled up in blue.

You had to laugh at Dylan's posing, but he had a point. No need for regrets if you lived truthfully, even if you made mistakes that hurt. I thought: Why not get married, no matter what happens later? When the last chord died out, I picked up the tonearm and played the song again. By the time I'd heard the song three times and finished my glass, I had decided to propose.

Sylvie didn't take to the idea at first. She had rabbinical school to worry about, let alone marriage, but she agreed we were more committed to each other than to almost anything else beside our artwork. By the end of the week, she said yes. A wedding would be a lot of work, but her folks would help, and we'd keep it small. It was mid-November, and we'd been living together four and a half months. We were twenty-four years old.

When we first arrived in Philadelphia, Sylvie had taken me out to a Quaker retreat center called Pendle Hill to meet the former wife of the Buber scholar in San Diego. Lydia was a Greek who had married a Jew, and though their long marriage was over, she was still attached to him and the parts of Martin Buber's work they both loved. Lydia taught Buber's *Chasidic Tales* to people at Pendle Hill who were taking a break from professions or marriages or education to read, meditate, and find the spiritual thread in their lives. She was a fiercely intellectual teacher but not an academic; she cared more about her students' engagement with individual texts than about all the commentary or history she could profess to them. She spoke with loving authority about the mystical side of Buber, the emphasis on passionate community and unmediated encounter. Sylvie had already read much of Buber's work, and I peeked into the first volume of the *Tales* soon after we met Lydia, but I feared the all-embracing world his Chasidic stories conjured. I offered to give a reading at Pendle Hill from the poems of Anne Sexton and A. R. Ammons, two poets I thought the adult students would appreciate. Soon after Sylvie and I decided to get married, I gave the reading. I'd worked hard on the selection, and about twenty-five people came to listen. I mostly let the poems speak for themselves, but, standing before this open-faced group in a small wooden classroom, I felt just a hint that I could teach as well as write. The audience responded enthusiastically to the poetry, and in the discussion that followed, I saw that people honestly wanted to reimagine their neat conceptions of the normal through heightened or challenging language. I still didn't think I could teach poetry for a living—too precious to me, too close to the bone—but in my journal, I noted that the experience "reminded me of the importance of voice, the spine of 'free' verse" (11/14/76). If I avoided being overly dramatic, I could reach readers without manipulating them. Teaching glimmered at the edge of my vision for myself, but I didn't want to see it.

I finally got a job at a company called Quality Libraries that handled children's books. They ripped the regular covers off of new children's books, printed new library-grade covers, and then rebound the books, filling orders from libraries in Philadelphia and around the country. To my great pleasure, I was hired with the tentative promise of moving into a position as a printer's helper, but I soon realized I would never learn to print there. The printer was in his thirties, wore his black hair slicked back, and smelled of an old-fashioned spice that I guessed covered up his habit of drinking at lunch. He had a steady hand and a terse manner, and he didn't want a helper. That left me stacking books in the warehouse and assisting the shipping clerk, Benny, when he had too many orders to fill by himself. In the evenings, I drove the owner's elderly father home in the company car, and he would complain to me that his son was running the business into the ground and the "schwartzes" were ruining the city. The job at Quality was low-paying but secure, and I joined a union for the first time because the shop was organized. Soon after I started, I ran afoul of union rules when I did some filing for the boss that wasn't in my pay grade. I got friendly with Benny, who had a bad leg but stood all day, lived alone with his father, and knew everybody's business in the company. I listened to him talk endlessly about the lottery, catering for his storefront church in West Philly, and the foibles of the boss's family. My grumpy foreman, Madge, was heavy and stolid, with an unnamed tragedy in her past, but she tolerated me as long as I didn't ask too many questions or take her job. A few times she even smiled when I made a mistake she thought really funny. The girls in the bindery paid me no attention at all, except for the shop steward who worked down there. She watched me closely for signs that the boss was grooming me for the front office. When Sylvie's family took us to London for the Christmas break, all my coworkers on the warehouse floor enjoyed making fun of me but were disappointed I had no pictures to show. The warehouse wasn't so taxing as carpentry had been for my writing, and it taught me what it meant to work every day at a job with little expectation for advancement or novelty in the daily routine. Re-engineered versions of rock songs, a ballad version of "Brown Sugar" or a string rendition of "Mr. Tambourine Man," played all day on the Quality loudspeaker. A different label color or a new shelving system stirred excitement and alarm in the shop, and everything depended on following procedure.

Late that fall, I entered into a brief apprenticeship with Carl Jung. I was reading his autobiography, *Memories, Dreams, Reflections*, and I became interested in what he called "encounters with the unconscious." For a couple of weeks, I recorded my dreams with even more detail than usual, and I began to try to meditate in my writing room, using the descriptions in his book as a guide. I was extremely wary at first, because I didn't want to be charged by an otherworldly voice to follow some form of God rather than poetry, but I eventually let my mind travel freely. I discovered that I could, with relative ease, return again and again over a shallow sea to a vast building I named the "palace," where it seemed many of my dreams took place. I decided that this complex edifice, part movie studio and part ashram, represented the seat of my imagination. It reminded me of the corridor of doors where Alice searched for the garden in Wonderland. Through one door I saw people dying in a stormy war, while the next led to the sunlit vineyards in Sonoma County. I visited a dim control room on an upper floor, where dinosaur-like creatures paced slowly around a cold fire and mumbled incantations meant to conjure my future dreams.

In other sessions, I tentatively explored Jung's concept of the anima, the female identity in myself that I had long feared in my life as an army kid, a kid too interested in school when the other boys didn't care or didn't want to show they cared. I recognized that I grew up identifying with mother as much as father, particularly after my father left the scene. Without the muscular chest-beating of poetry apologists like Pound and Charles Olson, poetry could easily be seen as an effeminate art, an activity that got nothing tangible done in the world. This line of thinking frightened me plenty, and I did not pursue it long. I soon moved away from Jung because I needed more poetry to feed my writing, but the idea of a complex geographical place for the imagination, so reminiscent of William Carlos Williams's locations for imagining, stayed with me as the internal center for the poem-life I led alongside my job, my relationships with friends and dear ones, even the more scholarly side of mental life. Poem and dream existed in a place that could be illusory or prophetic, sealed away from politics but saturated with social pain, simultaneously private and collective.

Outside of Sylvie, my brother, Aaron, was my only friend that year. He was either completing some design assignment or working at a pizza shop most of the time. But some Friday evenings, one of us would buy a bottle of bourbon, standing in line at the run-down state-owned liquor store on Baltimore Avenue, where you felt kinship with the old guy in front of you ordering the cheap Jacquin's vodka. Sylvie, Aaron, and I would finish the bottle together, stomping around to the blues and discoursing on art, the wretched politics of Philadelphia's boss-mayor Frank Rizzo and his leather-jacketed police force, or the male dominance in Judaism and America. We doubted that Jimmy Carter could dismantle the right-wing state that Nixon left, and we mourned the end of the counterculture. Even the humiliating farce of Patti Hearst as a "liberation fighter" was now over. One afternoon, Aaron came into our apartment and, without a word, walked back to our bathroom at the end of the hall, took out his jackknife, and cut off his ponytail. We had all seen young men with long hair who were now working for unscrupulous landlords, selling waterbeds, or pushing pornography. Mao was dead, the Revolution was over, and our black neighbors still occupied the lowest rung in the city. We hardly registered the massive earthquakes in Guatemala and Turkey that killed thousands, but we noticed that The Band held its farewell concert, dubbed The Last Waltz, on Thanksgiving Day 1976, marking the end of something we could not name.

By the turn of the year, our choices had brought down great pressures on our lives. Sylvie was having more trouble with school, and at one point her teachers threatened to ask her to leave because she seemed so resistant. My job started wearing on me, the need to earn more money dogged me, and Sylvie's family was asking more insistently what I was planning to do with my career. Her father offered to help me contact people in the city he knew, but I resisted as genially as I could. Aaron came over one day and talked to us about where he would find the sources for his own artwork and wondered how he could open up to a spiritual energy without religious language or practice. He was getting tired of living alone, working every minute, being a student when he felt he was his own man. All three of us wanted our independence, but we were all serving our time.

I ran across an interview with the poet/translator Clayton Eschelman where he talked about a poet's apprenticeship, and this struck me as appropriate for us all: we had to find our sources in art, in the neighborhoods around us, in our families, but we had to transform it all to something recognizably our own. It wasn't enough for me to compare the poetics of Pablo Neruda and César Vallejo, or carry on a dialogue with the Baal Shem Tov in Buber's *Chasidic Tales*, or diagram the rhythms in Kenneth Patchen's bittersweet love poems. I had to convert all these lines and parables and practices into something distinctively my own in my poems. I dreamed I had found a beautiful necklace made in South America, but Benny at work thought it ugly and cheap, and Sylvie was too wrapped up in her books to notice. I was writing a long poem about the modernist photographer Man Ray, struggling with him as a figure of an artist I admired but wanted to be nothing like. The poem got longer and longer but never more satisfying, never escaping from private argument into song. Sylvie's former boyfriend Ross in San Diego took an overdose of prescription pills and left a note about his "only courageous act," and for weeks his death shadowed all our conversations. But I still believed a return to medical school would be fatal to much that I loved, and Ross's decision persuaded us to find more concerted ways to choose life.

In the midst of all this strain and confusion, two developments helped me enter Philadelphia. First, I happened to meet John Wilson, a poet a few years older than I and with far more definite opinions about poetry. He published a little magazine called *Occurrences*, named for a title George Oppen had used for two different poems. I believe we met trying to find a reading by John Ashbery at the University of Pennsylvania. The venue had been moved, and as we wandered the campus looking for a room we never found, John and I both agreed that the poetry scene in Philadelphia had nothing for those of us not connected to a university. We decided to form a reading series at a centrally located bar where we would get all the serious poets in town to read. John was a rather unpleasant-looking guy, squat head and big eyes and mouth that made him look like he was sizing you up to swallow you, but he was extremely well read in avant-garde poetry and had developed very demanding criteria for what counted as important writing. He drove me crazy with his strictures, but I had to admire his certainty and erudition. He was willing, for the sake of the local scene, to open the reading series to a wide array of poets, and he knew a group of established writers we could invite to be on the governing committee with us. One night, John and I scoped out a spot on the second floor of a bar downtown, and later we negotiated the free use of the place one Saturday afternoon a month. Thus, the Poetry at McGlinchey's series began that spring, and through the series over the next two years, I met nearly every Philadelphia poet who had published more than a dozen poems, and many who had published nothing at all.

In one of our first readings that winter, Toby Olson read with Nathaniel Tarn and Janet Rodney. Toby was one of the original McGlinchey's committee members and a fine poet in the tradition of the Black Mountain School of Charles Olson, Robert Creeley, Robert Duncan, and Denise Levertov. I admired him both for his generous poems and his accepting spirit in our meetings. Tarn was Toby's old friend, a British anthropologist who wrote long, mystical poems that I distrusted but found fascinating nonetheless. Rodney was a beautiful young woman who had apparently been a student of Tarn's and was now his wife; her work was not as developed as his but daring in her use of material she drew from fieldwork in Guatemala. After the reading, I was feeling particularly expansive that we had drawn more than fifty to hear such vibrant work, and we all retired to a party in a house near Penn. At the height of the party, the doorbell rang, and a tall, gaunt young man with thin blond hair came shakily through the door. Everybody turned and started whispering that Gil Ott was here, fresh from his hospital bed where he had been treated for kidney disease. Gil was already publishing a hand-printed magazine called *Paper Air* that was half a latter-day extension of San Francisco Beat poetry and half a journal for contemporary experimental writers. Everybody made way for him, and he sat in an overstuffed green chair while people asked about his health, and then the party resumed around him. In the next months, John Wilson and I got together with Gil now and then and read Olson and Zukofsky and Creeley aloud, arguing about what should or could go into a poem. Gil and I hardly ever agreed on poetics until the last few years of his life, nearly thirty years later, when five kidney transplants and dialysis made arguing far less important to him than surviving and loving his family and friends. He held opinions as tenaciously as John, but his mind was suppler and more encompassing, he had a superb ear for music in words, and for all his gruffness he cared passionately about people.

My second move into the life of the city began when I applied for teaching jobs. I couldn't keep a job in carpentry and couldn't find one in printing. What did I have to sell in the labor market except my knowledge of science? I had convinced myself that I could never teach poetry or writing, but I thought human biology might appeal to teenagers. Poetry required a level of engagement that nearly overwhelmed my waking life, but I didn't want to reveal myself in that commitment to adolescents. Science could be fascinating on its surface, even if it wasn't as interesting as poetry deep below. I imagined doing frog dissections with kids and showing them the lungs and what path blood followed to and from the heart. Science offered so much to teach; I could make physiology and anatomy fun if I didn't destroy it with facts and figures. I could always motivate kids with connections to health or sex or jobs. I had no teaching certificate, and I doubted I'd fit into the Catholic schools, where I didn't need one. But Philadelphia has an assortment of independent and private schools, and I figured one of them must need a biology teacher. I could teach other sciences as long as I didn't have to teach physics, and I could teach math as long as I didn't have to teach calculus. I took a day off from work and sat in on the chemistry classes of a legendary teacher named Herb Basso at Germantown Friends School, one of the best-known Quaker schools in the city. I forced myself to send out résumés, using a filing system I had developed when I applied to medical school, and I decided not to let any rejections discourage me. After all, I was used to rejections from literary magazines for my poems, but every once in a while a poem got accepted. I needed only one job offer to free me from the daily humiliation that Quality Libraries had become.

Rejections indeed came in. One school after another told me it didn't need a science and math teacher. I suspected that my lack of experience hurt my chances, but I simply had to push on. I was getting married, I needed to keep writing, and family on all sides wondered pointedly what I would do. Teaching looked like my answer. One day, I decided I would simply take the phone book listings of private schools and drive around the city visiting science departments. If they hadn't turned me down by letter, then I would knock on their doors. I started in West Philadelphia, and soon after I hit the road I noticed in the phone book a school with an address close to my house but listed under a name I hadn't seen before. I drove to the address and found a sagging three-story house with broken front steps about two blocks from the Drexel University campus. It was lunchtime in early spring, and kids of various racial descriptions were hanging out on the porch, dancing in the big lounge on the first floor to Earth, Wind & Fire blaring from a boom box. A harried looking white woman with frizzy hair sat at a small desk in the lobby. I went up to her and introduced myself. Before I could ask her if a science job were available, she looked up at me with a smile and bright eyes: "Eli Goldblatt? I was just about to call you for an interview. We'd love for you to visit our school!" I was shocked and pleased. Apparently, I had sent a résumé to a school with a different name that had preceded this little ragtag outfit, and my letter had been received just a day or two before. Anita, who had just been named the principal for the next year, arranged for me to come back later that week for an interview and teaching demonstration. I asked what she wanted me to teach, and she said I could come in and meet the kids in a class she was teaching called Physics in the Kitchen. Whatever she was teaching that day, I could join in.

The Neighborhood Journey School had been a temporary education facility for a runaway shelter in the early 1970s, but by 1977 it had become both a school for a few group homes run by social services organizations and a haven for kids—mostly black but also some white kids from post-hippie homes—who happened to have someone in their lives committed enough to find them an alternative to public school. When I came back, Anita was teaching a class on pH measurement in the broken-down kitchen space that served as her lab. I stepped in and talked about hydrogen ions and what could go wrong in your body without the proper acid-base balance. A big, lunky guy asked me a question that showed he knew very little about biology. I gave him too much information in return and then made a joke that barely got a smile. But the indicator colors turned from red to blue when I added baking soda, and kids said the experiment was "deep." In Amherst, I had led a few sessions for preschoolers drawing to music, and in third grade, my "special" reports resulted in fights after school. This was the first time I stood up in front of a class as a teacher, or at least as a prospective teacher. I walked away intoxicated by teaching in a way I hadn't expected. None of the logical reasons I'd given my mother or Sylvie's father or my grandfather for my new interest in teaching applied as I left the building. I just loved talking to the kids and thinking on my feet, drawing them in, pushing them to consider ideas they'd never encountered. I wanted the job. I thought I could actually teach these kids. Maybe this was work I could enjoy, be good at, and still get paid for.

Anita called later that week to offer me a position for $7,500 a year teaching biology, chemistry, physical science, geometry, and basic algebra. I was overjoyed. I could quit Quality Libraries, where I was making a little over $5,000 a year working nine to five, dodging the union and my boss while "Muskrat Love" and "I Like Dreamin'" played over the radio. Benny and the others on the warehouse floor increasingly wondered if I was spying on them for the front office, and Madge clearly worried the boss wanted me to replace her. Now I could spend the summer writing. True, I would have to plan courses for the fall, and I had no idea how to "plan a course" beyond making stuff up one lesson after another out of a book. I decided not to worry about the fall and hope for the best come September. I could tell everyone at the wedding that I would be teaching in the fall, and maybe the questions about my future would stop. I was going to be a science and math teacher in an alternative school for low-income kids, I told anyone who would listen, and my writing could happen away from everybody's scrutiny.

Despite her success organizing a conference on women in the rabbinate with Lisa—where the assembled women showed themselves to be far more powerful than they had felt in their individual roles as students or starting rabbis—Sylvie had decided to leave rabbinical school. We planned to spend six weeks that summer in Deer Isle, Maine, where she would take weaving courses and reconstitute herself. I could pick up a little money working for friends of friends who owned a bed and breakfast on the island. We asked those invited to the wedding to give us money to buy a loom for Sylvie and books for me—no dish patterns or towels or Crock-Pots—and we prepared for a life outside the shade of big, professional institutions.

We did receive a blue enameled casserole dish and a few other household items besides the loom and book money, but the best gift came from my difficult friend John Wilson. Gil, John, and I all agreed that George Oppen was one of the living poets we cared most about, and John happened to be corresponding with George and his wife, Mary, about two chapters from Mary's memoir that *Occurrences* was going to publish. John asked me to edit the essays because they were a bit rough, and with trepidation I tightened up her prose and sent it back to her. To my relief, Mary approved of my changes. The big surprise came as we moved nearer the May wedding, when John announced that George and Mary owned a small summer home in Maine, and we realized that they would be a very short ferry ride from Deer Isle. John and his fiancée, Peggy, planned to go up to see them while we were there, and John offered to get us an invitation, too. We would be meeting George and Mary Oppen, who had known Pound and Williams! This would give a reality to my work that no amount of reading could provide. I had read once that Allen Ginsberg claimed he'd slept with someone who'd slept with someone who'd slept with someone who'd slept with Whitman. This was how the tradition was passed down: by association with the people who made the poems you admired. I left medical school so that I could be a participant and not merely a spectator. Meeting the Oppens meant stepping into the writing and art stream. Sylvie and I would do this together as a married couple trying to make our way, just as George and Mary had done fifty years before.

Although I wrote in my journal nearly every day that spring, there is no mention of the wedding. In entries I'm always dunning myself for not working harder, not finishing poems, not thinking or feeling more, not knowing enough. Clearly I had decided the journal was not the place to record events or even identify specific issues arising from my daily emotional life; I was still separating my poem-life from every other dimension of living. I was reading the poetry of Lorine Niedecker and Paul Blackburn, slowly working through a critical book on American Modernist poetry by the scholar Hugh Kenner, looking at de Kooning's paintings again and again. I continued to revise and expand my long poem on Man Ray, feeling that it would help me sort out the visual from the linguistic, the modernist influence from the political and personal elements that distinguished the contemporary moment. Sylvie at one point asked me what a poet does with all the reading, and I could not answer her but noted in my journal that reading helped me "find my subject" (4/30/77), not in the sense of content but in the location of love and pain that could generate art. I was reading Federico García Lorca's *Blood Wedding* at that moment, and this passion play of death taught me just how profoundly I could engage my "subject." At the same time, I was having a rather tortured argument with John Wilson as he withdrew from McGlinchey's and almost all poetry but that which met his increasingly bloodless technical requirements. His ideas seemed to come from a rather ungenerous reading of Louis Zukofsky's Poundian textbook, *A Test of Poetry*. I argued for a more playful, compassionate function for poetry, but John would have none of it. I found myself in the curious position of arguing with a dour gentile Talmudist for a less legalistic view of human desire.

Earlier that fall, I had taken great care to write down a dream Jung recorded in his book about an idealized "real" city above the sooty place he identified as Liverpool (10/21/76). The streets were arranged like a giant mandala, with quadrants composed of smaller identical squares, each surrounding a magical tree at its center. I marveled at the specificity and emotional detail of his dream city that could contain and generate his thought. Slowly, the "real" Philadelphia was entering my dreams in this way, though with its peculiar chaos rather than the neat Swiss precision of Jung's dream. Not that my dreams took place in my new home—the palace on the water still seemed the gravitational center of my imaginative world—but Philadelphia with its frictions and felicities was becoming fecund ground in many of the rooms. In one dream that June, just before the wedding, I was a college student in Philadelphia. I was attempting to enter a trance state, a common practice among undergraduates in the dream. I struck a certain posture, embracing the sun, in a field one bright afternoon. I felt rain and other weather changes and then was aroused from the trance by a touch on the arm. The field had changed, and many people stood about me. I felt as if I'd been entranced for a long time, perhaps an hour or more. When I asked a spectator, he answered, "Well, that's one way to get through college." I asked what he meant, and he told me that I had been standing in that field for three and a half years! The dream then turned to the commuter trains in Philadelphia, where Sylvie and I were helping people who seemed to be falling into trances wherever we looked. I commented in my journal (5/2/77) that, if I counted from the moment I decided to go to medical school until my arrival in Philadelphia, I had in fact been under the spell for three and a half years. I felt that Sylvie was in a similar trance in rabbinical school and that others were regularly tempted into trances by professions and occupations that dulled them to the hard issues around them and their dearest internal ambitions.

About a month before the wedding, I recorded in my journal at least two talks with Sylvie where she wondered if she really loved me enough, or if she should be living alone instead. I took these talks seriously but did not think they threatened our relationship. She had pushed me first to get involved and many times had shown me great affection and a rich connection in our common hopes. I felt she was in such struggle for her soul in the seminary that I needed to stay with her, even if she said hurtful things to send me away. I was having my doubts at the same time, resisting the happy story of American marriage, one man settling down with one woman and building a material nest. I was drawn to young women walking in the spring streets. Still, I responded to her reservations and my own with further commitment and a defensive assurance that this must also be a part of marriage for two people trying so hard to be real with each other. I believed we loved each other. Maybe more to the point, I, at least, needed her companionship during a time of almost total uncertainty: "I can't help but feel it is quite human to want a wife & food & a house. I don't want more than that except time to work. Someone to share this mess with, is that not acceptable?" (4/22/77). I barely registered the depth of Sylvie's hesitancy in my eagerness to overcome my own.

The wedding came off brilliantly, thanks almost entirely to Sylvie's mother. We had made some choices and urged them to keep the celebration simple, but we had both been too occupied with our work to contribute much. I believe we ordered and addressed the invitations, and I know we found our own wedding outfits—Sylvie wove a piece for her dress and stitched it over her breast, and I wore a Russian peasant shirt with no jacket—and we met with her cousin who would perform the ceremony alongside our friend Rebecca Alpert from the rabbinical college. I hand-printed the *katubah*, the traditional Jewish wedding contract, in English and Hebrew, using Sylvie's text, and then practiced enough to sign my name in Hebrew along with the witnesses. On the day, eighty people joined us at Sylvie's ample family home and yard, my siblings and hers held the chuppah, and behind the two rabbis stood Sylvie's aged grand-uncle, a famous conservative rabbi. At the dinner, the families and friends mixed and probed each other. My brother took great pride in bumming a cigarette from a cigarette company executive who was a close friend of Sylvie's father. Sylvie's sisters were quite solicitous of my *bubbi*, who loved the idea that her grandson had married a rich girl. The catering was strictly kosher, in deference to my father's family, but Uncle Herb, my mother's brother, happened to peek out of a window just in time to spy my self-righteous, Orthodox *bubbi* throwing up in the bushes. She had her doubts about the religious standards of the caterer, but she didn't want to embarrass the wealthy *machatunim* by refusing to eat. My mother's father was happy for the moment but kept expecting any time that I would announce a return to medical school now that I was so well connected. It was a circus I strangely enjoyed and Sylvie, at least privately to me, did not.

I'm afraid I largely neglected my own family during this time. Sylvie's family loomed so large and took so much emotional space, but I was probably also using the wedding as a way to distance myself from my mother. My sister was growing up beautiful and smart, but she struggled to find her own place in the house alone with my mother and her domesticated grief. I could do little for them except listen to both separately when I visited. My mother asked me to go with her to my father's grave before the wedding, and I did record that experience in my journal. The starkness of my father's absence haunted me until the festivities drove the scene from my mind. I described my recognition in the cemetery this way: "The fact as I saw it when I was leaning against that tree was plain & w/o mitigation—he had left us, withdrawn & left us dust to work out, we never had a choice & will likely not see him again in this life" (5/15/77). I'm sure I meant "likely" as an ironic dig at false hope, but I'm not sure I didn't partly believe I could somehow conjure him again through crafted language. Perhaps I thought if I could become a good enough poet, I could contact him again. I wrote nothing in the journal about how my mother may have felt, or what Sharon said that day. I hated the cemetery as a site of our family disenfranchisement and humiliation, but the emotion goes unmentioned in my entry. I maintained an adamant focus in the journal on my work and myself, unless Sylvie or my mother or some other near one shocked me into paying attention to her or him. I wasn't necessarily selfish in other aspects of my life, but I was determined to be selfish for the sake of my writing, and I enforced that obligation as rigorously as I could.

We were married but still so wary of established conventions that we found calling each other husband and wife difficult, if not painful.

But now that Sylvie had left the seminary and I had embarked on a career that might provide a living and also give me time for my work, we talked more freely as we drove north. We stopped at Sylvie's family retreat, a compound of rustic houses that had been established by her great-grandparents' generation. Her great-aunts claimed that the swimming pool on the property was the oldest in the Catskills, and it certainly had the patches to prove it, but the forest beautifully supplanted the city in our minds after such a hard winter. We spent more than a week there, falling into a rhythm of work on projects during the day and cooking, eating, drinking, and talking into the night. I was starting to read Pound's early poems and Hugh Kenner's big book on Modernism called *The Pound Era* and was revising a poem about the California vineyards I had drafted in Philadelphia. Sylvie was threading her portable loom for a new weaving. Various family members and friends came up to celebrate with us before we withdrew to Maine, and I did get a little impatient to put all the intense visiting behind us, but we all still felt the afterglow of the wedding. Even Sylvie agreed, now the family pressures had eased, that we'd had a very good time.

Done with our stint at professional schools, we could see each other as equal partners in a grand undertaking, without the fear of becoming unrecognizable representatives of institutions we could not bear. We were like two young frogs, both using emergent limbs for the first time to leap in the mud. After the Catskills and all the well-wishers, we drove up the coast and across the causeway onto Deer Isle. The air elated us. Even though we hadn't yet found a place to stay and had little money to manage, we felt both hope and freedom as elements of the landscape more identifiable than pine or spruce. We stayed the first couple of nights at the inn owned by our friends Ellie and George, who had a toddler, Elena. They put us up for free, in honor of our new married status, and soon agreed to let me help them renovate an adjoining barn they were turning into a restaurant dining room. Within a day, we had located a houseboat for rent on the property of a master carpenter named Oliver and his wife, Kay.

The little beached plywood box on a hull stood at the edge of a cove five miles from Haystack Mountain Craft School, where Sylvie would be weaving. The cabin was perhaps seven feet wide and twelve feet long, with a mattress on a shelf and a wood-burning stove made of a thirty-gallon steel drum mounted on a table at the bow. They told us we could stay for a ridiculously small sum if I agreed to scrape, paint, and caulk the hull by the end of our stay, so the vessel sat on blocks all that summer while I slowly made her more or less seaworthy. When the tide came in, saltwater rose to within feet of the bow, but half the time the cove was nothing but a mud bed for boulders and scavenging gulls. Aspen and small maple saplings hid us from the main house, and we looked out our front window at a little mystic island covered in pines about two hundred yards from the shore. Oliver found an old typewriter on a wheeled table I could use, and the cabin had just enough room for a rocking chair between the bed and the stove. We kept milk in the family's refrigerator, cooked on a camp stove, and warmed up on cold mornings by burning wood in the steel drum stove. We lit a kerosene lantern in the evening. Our toilet was a portable commode set on the deck. All the birds in Maine got Sylvie up in time for class and sang to me in earnest polyrhythms the rest of the day.

At Haystack, Sylvie was happier than I had ever seen her. She wove at a big loom inside an open studio that faced the ocean or out on the deck with a portable backstrap loom. At lunch, she took long walks on the big granite chunks that lined the shore. She made immediate friends in the classes and came home with their stories, descriptions of the fabrics they were weaving, and thoughts about the ocean that drove away the mists of rabbinical school. We talked incessantly every evening and ate produce, fresh fish, and fowl I bought at the market in Stonington or the Deer Isle General Store on my workdays. We smoothed out the terrible knots that had developed between us during the tense school year and toasted cheap red wine in the sunset to the open sea of next years. Some nights we drove back to Haystack for slide shows of the faculty's work, and we returned along the narrow road drunk with art and each other in the close dark. Happiness was a language we had never spoken so well before; we had no inclination to celebrate our good fortune but only drive on into it. Sylvie listened to me discourse on poetics and didn't regard my talk as a threat or an alien force. I embraced her Haystack tales as reports from a nearly ideal society, and if I didn't approve of some speaker's conception of art, Sylvie had usually come to the same conclusion. We faced no frowning professors or violating examinations, and a life making and remarking on art seemed not merely possible but manifest. I turned to my books and typewriter each morning with pleasure and welcomed Sylvie home with equal pleasure.

Once we moved into the houseboat, I set up my library. Along with Kenner's big book, I'd brought Pound's *Personae*, the collection of his early short poems, and a volume of his translations of Chinese poets, Japanese Noh drama, the Renaissance Italian Guido Cavalcanti, and others. I had my copy of Oppen's *Collected Poems*, which I was studying and rereading line by line, in preparation for meeting George and Mary. I had brought the James Wright book I'd never finished because he represented a group of poets much in ascendance in university creative writing faculty, closer to my teacher Ammons but far from the New York, San Francisco, and Black Mountain poets I had been reading with John and Gil. They both hated Wright and anyone associated with MFA programs, but I was reading him not so much out of defiance but to test myself. Did I need to choose sides? Could I see what the academic critics saw in this kind of writing or what my friends held against it? I wanted to embed personal emotion in verse without sentimentality or melodrama, and Wright represented a very different path from Creeley or Duncan or the other poets I had come to know as my people. And then there was our old friend Martin Buber, from whom I'd been nibbling for years, and to whom Sylvie owed so much of her love for Jewish thought. I wanted to discover what Buber saw in the mystical tales of Chasidism—the joyous side of an orthodox tradition I had known as mechanistic and arcane—and I wanted to confront my own predilection for spiritual thought as a basso voice in the fugue of a poem. I also carried a volume of Emerson's poems and essays, partly because I decided I needed to read something older and American, and partly because I suspected that his transcendental vision could help connect Ammons with Oppen for me. Of course, I brought along a big dictionary, not just for Kenner's hypertrophied vocabulary but for accidental discoveries, words such as "catenary" and "brume." I could retreat to my little library to settle me down whenever my poems fell apart into flimsy, self-indulgent, or inarticulate fragments.

I worked particularly on one poem rooted in the experience of the cove. I wanted to be as present in this place as possible, but I also wanted to write a poem that created a present for readers wherever or whenever they read it—not a representation, but a meditation that was itself an experience. One morning in June, while finishing my cereal, I watched a great blue heron fishing in the cove and noted his presence in my journal:

> At moments the heron & his movements were distorted by the window glass, some panes are old and flawed. One point the heron bent low stretched his neck straight forward then down into the water for a small fish. The window analyzed the motion into consecutive pieces, fast or slow depending partly on the speed at each section's instant & partly on the curve of glass the piece flowed over as I saw it. I thought at first a naturalist might abhor this way [of] seeing. Tho I enjoyed it I felt perhaps I was enjoying the scene at the heron's expense, & at the expense of *really* seeing the heron. What I've learned of art says no, that you may subject what you see, or what is there, to whatever process you choose, trusting to the multilayer integrity of the world to yield some new thing not seen before but with its own attendant qualities. By transmuting you liberate. (6/22/77)

As I was writing, I was also living with the cove: its tidal rhythms accompanied by song sparrows and gulls in sight and song; the wind setting the aspen leaves shaking; the pine trees out of reach on the island in front of me; Sylvie five miles away developing her own life in parallel to mine; my dreams, enthusiasms, and fears, sounding my nerves throughout my physical being, cupping it all in momentary consciousness. The poem was neither a record nor a treatise. It was a thing made at maximum attention, like a John Marin watercolor or a Tibetan monk's song. My part was small but not inconsiderable. Later, the blue heron fishing entered the poem in these lines:

> the heron
> hunkered down distorted
> by my windowpane.
> He caught the fish, I thought
> tho he flowed quickly
> & slow across old glass
>
> Would you imagine
> what you love

heard in your head
threatening peace?
an I isn't much
not enough to be only a good man

My hope for a life overrun neither by the exigencies of wage earning nor the infinite demands of art making lay in equilibrium with this creature that shared the cove with me. I was a small part of the scene, but I could not honestly write myself out of the picture. I worked on the poem most days, inventing new lines, shifting the pieces, fretting that my language was too private, too emotional, too flat. I read more Kenner, broke down the prosody of Oppen poems to the very particles of vowel length and consonant pattern. What would George Oppen say about such a poem if I were brave enough to send it to him? Would he send the typescript back, torn in little pieces, or merely nod his head in silent acceptance? Would he acknowledge me as a poet at all?

After about ten days in Maine, the time came to visit George and Mary. John and Peggy had already gone directly to Eagle Island, where the Oppens lived in the summer, and we were to take a short mail boat ride out to the island for an overnight stay. Sylvie was nearly as excited as I. She had read Mary's memoirs and was curious about her. What had the organizing years been like for Mary, or the war years while George was away, or the exile in Mexico? Both of us were ready for a change of scene after our intense first days on Deer Isle. We caught the boat early in the morning and got off on a barely domesticated island with no roads or stores and only a handful of year-round residents. We didn't quite know where to go from the landing, but soon after we'd made our way into a clearing above the dock, two old people came striding around one corner of the wood. Mary said loudly, "Are we looking for you?" and Sylvie and I were both stunned by their appearance, as I later recorded:

They were such clearly etched figures they seemed unearthly to me. Mary looks like one of those beautiful older Quaker women so precise, but with all the non-violent principles stacked in bonfire fashion burning vigorously inside her. George seems tall, though he is really not much taller than I, was wearing a large blue coat but even so thin, almost gaunt with his deep cut wrinkles & gray hair wild at the top of his head. (6/30/77)

They swept us away immediately to their small cottage in the woods. I believe it had electricity and running water but few other amenities. All they had in great abundance were stories, one vignette or carefully observed instance after another in a torrent that lasted all evening. But they also listened and wanted to know about us in a way I had never experienced from an older adult, let alone ones who had witnessed personally the great upheavals of the twentieth century in art, politics, economics, and war. Sylvie and I were transfixed but not struck dumb. We asked questions, ventured opinions, talked about our work, told our own stories. George and Mary took us seriously as artists, with no hint of condescension or expectation that we would eventually capitulate to the commodity world. Sylvie and I went out with Mary and collected mussels for dinner. Peggy and John had been there a day or two already, but Peggy was bored, and John couldn't respond to their kindness with any intimacy of his own—I could see already this was the end of our friendship. In the morning, George woke us up with the question: "Is there a weaver here who'd like to be sailed to Sunset?" Their boat was too small for four people, so they chose Sylvie, who had sailed in camp as a kid, to sail back to the Deer Isle dock at the little village of Sunset. I rode back on the mail boat with John and Peggy and said good-bye to them as they got in their car for the long drive back to Philadelphia. Meanwhile, George and Mary had made coffee on their boat and were sitting prettily on the tiny prow waiting for me. I could have been jealous of Sylvie's trip alone with our new friends, but I was too pleased that Sylvie enjoyed them as much as I did.

Back on the houseboat, I pushed harder on the long poem I'd started at the cove and also began drafting a short poem that came out of conversations with George about levers and language, about the communal and the private experience of speaking to another person fully. He had liked the image of the lever, which came from a unit in the physical science textbook I was going to use in the fall, and told me I should use it in a poem. George listened gravely and actively, and his attention made me feel I could write and act in the world as he had. At the same time, I felt I had so far to go, so much to learn. The Oppens had jumped into organizing and working alongside people disenfranchised by the Depression. They had rejected the artist lives they set out to pursue in their early twenties because it meant ignoring the suffering around them, but they did not reject the drive to create art that clarified, consoled, investigated. They were irreverent—at one point, they allowed that, had they been Joyce's editors, they would have cut long passages from *Ulysses*—and uninterested in the marketplace of literary reputations. George warned me to resist the temptation of the avant-garde. I nodded, but I did not really understand what he meant. George had run away from a wealthy German Jewish family and only late in his life had begun thinking about how Judaism might have affected his poetry. Mary was more outspoken about the problems with American religion and electoral politics, but both of them harbored no nostalgia for the old Communist Party that had so dominated and distorted their lives at one time. They had lived, and George had shaped his spare, unsparing philosophical poems in the forge of their experience. Their example gave both Sylvie and me hope, but at times I felt how impossible it was to put the world into poems and still be in the world myself in some productive way.

I also spent some time with Martin Buber after visiting the Oppens. I had brought with me *Hasidism and Modern Man*, a book that collected essays on his vision of the mystical religious tradition based on holy rabbis called zaddikim and their followers, the Hasidim. The eighteenth-century founder of Hasidism was the Baal Shem Tov, a humble teacher who had an ecstatic way with prayer. I was fascinated by Buber's insistence on dialogue with both God and man, but his reflections about Hasidism seemed to have direct bearing on the way I was coming to think about my poetry. Buber emphasized the need to reach the divine only by becoming more human, and in the stories the zaddik is always so tied to his followers that no matter how lonely his mystical endeavor, the community of Jews around the rabbi mattered at least as much as his devotion to God. Ecstasy in prayer stood in the middle of the Hasidic system Buber described, but service, intention, and humility completed an equilibrium that balanced yearning for the divine with earthly engagement. I surely wanted my poetry to touch spiritual and emotional locations not bound by the material realm. However, the Objectivism I learned from Williams and Oppen, as well as the meandering discourse of my old teacher Ammons, insisted that a solid world surrounds the poet, a world that cannot and should not be ignored. At the same time, I read "service" the way my mother or father would: paying attention to others in need. I could not have said it then, but I was looking for a poetics consonant with my Jewishness, which meant social commitment even more than ritual to me. Teaching could fulfill a part of that commitment, even if I didn't yet know what teaching would mean, but my poems themselves could not be centered on me or my ideas or emotions alone.

I finally got the nerve to send the two poems to George, and he wrote back promptly with a few kind words for the poems and an invitation to visit them again on Eagle Island. Alone with George and Mary on that second visit, we grew closer to them and to each other. Mary and George told fewer stock stories and spoke more openly about the trials in their lives together: the Communist Party, the war years, exile in Mexico. They felt the longevity of their friendship represented their greatest achievement—far more important than George's Pulitzer Prize—along with the shared work in raising their daughter, Linda. Like me, Linda had turned away from medicine, although she'd finished all four years before deciding to train horses instead. For all their difficulties over the years, the Oppens seemed to have few regrets and took much joy in each other, Linda and her family, and the homes they had made in Maine and San Francisco. Sylvie and I felt immensely strengthened knowing them. Without ceremony or pretension, George and Mary accepted us among the company of artists and organizers and stalwarts they had joined over the years, those in "the world, weatherswept, with which / one shares the century" (5), as George had written in the first poem of his first book. Above all, they gave us a greater sense of the preciousness of marriage, not as a social pact but as a unique partnership that could be a work of art in itself.

8

## Beyond the Fathers

AT THE START OF my second year of teaching, all the kids arrived for a half-day orientation to meet their teachers and hear about their courses. Four of the school's six faculty had been new in the previous year, but this year we all felt we knew what we were doing. I was again teaching eleventh grade biology, the tenth grade introduction to physical science we called Energy, a much attenuated chemistry course for seniors, as well as geometry and basic algebra. I was also reprising a course I'd developed called Sexuality and Reproduction, teaching half the year for a class of kids who then switched with another group taking law with my friend and colleague Dave for half the year. The previous year, Dave and I bonded as the only ones on the staff with not a lick of previous experience; the other two new teachers had taught elsewhere for a couple of years. Only Anita, the principal, and James, the art teacher and her boyfriend, had taught at the school a few years and knew the kids well. All of us were making up the curriculum and daily lessons as we went along because we were constantly in search of hooks and ladders to draw our students into the game of education and away from the far more attractive social scene they lived for. It was the hardest job I'd ever done, but unlike carpentry or printing or grape farming, I knew a little about the subjects and fancied myself a natural.

The Neighborhood Journey School occupied a smudged gray brick colonial, grand in its day, with a wide porch badly in need of rehab and paint and an inviting interior stairway leading off the foyer, with large rooms on either side. It was a makeshift affair from top to bottom. Classrooms and an office were in bedrooms on the second floor, and an open third floor room served for Maryann's English classes. My science room was to the left of the stairs on the second floor, next to the office. We had no bell system or even a reliable clock. Because my room was centrally located, I volunteered to be the one to signal class changes. I kept time with my watch, and as long as I didn't get carried away with a lesson, I would walk around the halls ringing a funny little brass bell with a dowel.

A magic closet in my room held such treasures as a couple of nearly complete molecular models, an array of very old chemicals and glassware, springs and other physics toys, and a roll of rumpled anatomy charts among the half-filled workbooks and old math texts. I hadn't known until the second year that the state would pay a little for lab equipment and specimens, and so I was proud that year of the new dissecting kits and pans, a classroom set of earthworms, a pot of preserved frogs, and a fetal pig I'd ordered and received. That orientation morning, I had ushered kids in and out of my room, telling them about what I would teach that year, exhibiting my fresh dissection specimens, brandishing brand-new copies of *Our Bodies, Ourselves* for sexuality class, and demonstrating a cool science principle with one of the gadgets from the closet. At the end of the morning, I was standing on the stair a few steps up from the foyer, waving good-bye as the last kids went out the front door, thinking how monstrously Tommy and Kelvin had grown over the summer, when I heard a sickening crash upstairs. I ran up to the second floor and into my room, where plaster smoke was still thick in the air. The entire ceiling had come down in response to the troops of kids pounding down the steps all at once. Ten minutes before, the ceiling would have landed on the twelve kids and me in my last period class. At least I'd put the fetal pig away safely in the closet.

I loved inventing my classes as I went along. In every course, I plotted out an ambitious curriculum week by week at the beginning of the year, based on the books we had for the class, but often the weeks unfolded very differently from my plan. Since I knew nothing about lesson planning, let alone curriculum, I often had too much for class on a given day—like the one class session I reserved for Darwinian theory in biology or the three sessions I budgeted in energy class for properties of light, the electromagnetic spectrum, polarization, lasers, X-rays, and wave/particle theory—so some periods I would have to wake my students up with an activity on the spot, pull something from my closet, or have a "discussion" on a topic I thought might occupy them. In math, we dutifully worked through chapters, and there was always another problem set I could assign, but I knew instinctively that I needed to go slow in math because most kids had high anxiety around numbers. In science I really did have to present a demonstration or hands-on project at least once in a while or kids would rebel. Occasionally I could stun them with the intensity of my lectures, but I got exhausted talking so much, and even on my best days, half the class wasn't really listening. Of course, I gave quizzes and tests and homework and study questions, just like a teacher is supposed to do. In fact, I had at least one stack of papers, and usually more, in my backpack to grade every night. Before bed, I would check that I had a topic and a thing to do in every class the next day; sometimes my activities worked and sometimes they didn't. I especially liked when I made up a clever analogy that the kids responded to enthusiastically, and those days I rode my bike home thinking I was a pretty damn good teacher.

But many days I felt like a complete failure. My geometry class was one of my favorites, and in a moment of casual camaraderie my first year, I mentioned to the students one morning that I'd never taught the subject before. They immediately fell silent, and it took me a week to get them reengaged without snide remarks about how I wouldn't know if their answers were right or wrong. One high-maintenance student I'll call Carole would lose her temper regularly in the middle of Sexuality and Reproduction, and I wouldn't know how to stop her from lashing out at her classmates and stalking out of the room. Jasper would spend the entire Energy period annoying a girl half his size, or Tommy would stroke his wispy mustache through my most impassioned speeches in biology, until I asked him a question that revealed he had no idea what we were talking about. My quizzes came back almost blank, my tests showed little progress, even if I gave out all the answers beforehand, and I was lucky if homework came back at all. The more I strained to teach the kids, and the more I learned about their stories from talks after school or briefings from the social workers or the rare teacher/parent conference, the more I wanted to teach them, but the less sure I was how to do it. I couldn't just dump knowledge from my brain to theirs. The reproduction cycle in molds or electron orbit filling of nonmetals in the periodic chart existed only as lovely but isolated patterns in my own mind. Such arcane topics made no impression at all on them. I couldn't give inspiring speeches every day because urgency soured readily into nagging, like sweet milk turning nasty in the heat. Girls in my sexuality and reproduction course got pregnant; boys in Dave's law class got arrested. They were good kids, but many had spent years in foster care, or came from families with too little for too many, or simply never attracted attention in the large, faceless public schools they had attended before. Often it seemed our best moments of school time had no reality for students once they left the premises. My effectiveness quotient fell in inverse proportion to my fondness for the students, but I comforted myself that at least I was working hard and showing up every day. Kids seemed to want to be in our school, as opposed to the high schools they'd left behind. They did sit in our classrooms, but they weren't exactly lapping up what we fed them. Neighborhood Journey School was no *To Sir, with Love*, not only because I didn't look like Sidney Poitier but also because nobody had let the kids in on the happy ending.

James didn't look much like Sidney Poitier either, because he was too short and talked too fast, but he was a good-looking African American man who connected with the kids much better than the rest of us. He'd come from the projects in Pittsburgh and got out because he had a talent for drawing and painting, but he'd only really come into possession of himself when a well-known African American painter taught him in a summer workshop in Maine. After the painter watched James tossing off work in his spare time between parties, the older man dragged James out into the woods surrounding the studios, pushed him down, and sat on his chest. "This isn't playtime," the painter said. "If you want to be an artist, you'd better work your butt off. Nobody's going to pay a black man to be a fool, at least not for very long." James had become driven and disciplined in the eight or ten years following, and he brought to his classes a wonderful mix of kindness, understanding, humor, and strict discipline. I loved to sneak down and watch him with his students in his basement art room, and sometimes I'd stay late after school to hang out with him in his personal studio in a small space off the English room on the third floor. He worked late every night after the kids left, preparing for shows he was getting at galleries. He used to joke with me about my poetry. "Eli, sometimes I get discouraged about painting," he'd say, "and then I stop myself and think: 'Well, it could be worse. I could be a poet.'"

We had the most trouble with students after lunch. We had no lunch program, so kids would go across the street to the Greek's, a pizza parlor with decent greasy cheesesteaks and hoagies. They would come back late and, frequently, high. James would throw kids out of his class if he thought they were stoned, but I didn't quite have the clout he had. Even if I tried to swagger in my torn jeans and the black leather jacket I bought in a thrift store for five bucks, or if I talked about issues in their lives as directly as I could in class or after school, I was still a white man with a fancy college education. At least I was proud kids hardly ever skipped my class after lunch, the way they sometimes did in Dave's sociology class. He and Mr. B, our history teacher from Tanzania, would have to go out on the street and herd their classes back into the building. My students always trooped in, almost on time, and sat quietly when I lectured or demonstrated. After work, Dave and I would go to a bar nearby and commiserate over pony bottles of Rolling Rock. I would listen to his tales of mouthy pupils and snoozing students and secretly pride myself on being the better, more natural teacher. They failed my tests, but at least they showed up.

Finally, one day I was in the middle of a bodacious lecture on theories of atomic structure. I drew Rutherford and Bohr models on the board and acted out their experiments, explaining along the way why the Heisenberg uncertainty principle was important for our lives today. I was undoubtedly brilliant, funny, and eloquent, but suddenly I realized I wasn't teaching. I was performing. They weren't learning anything because they were too stoned and too passive to engage in anything I had to say. They were spectators enjoying the show, and I was the dancing bear. I wasn't doing any better than Dave or Mr. B or anybody else. I was a soft liberal teacher, and my students would never be learners if I didn't find a way to make THEM do the work. I myself comprehended the basic science much better as a teacher than I ever had as a student because I had to make the material make sense to a tough audience. My students had no other obligations in my class except to write down on tests imperfect versions of what I had told them in class. Most of them received the same meaningless grades from me that they had received in school all their lives. I told myself I loved these kids, but I wasn't doing them any good.

Meanwhile, Sylvie and I were starting our second fall as a married couple in 1978. We'd weathered a hard previous year while I was beginning to teach and Sylvie was trying to find a graduate program or a job that would allow her to bring together her interests in art, therapy, and religion. Nothing seemed right for her, and often she was terribly unhappy. Then her parents—who had seemed the model of marital commitment and mature love—suddenly announced their divorce because of the infidelity of her father. This threw us both into confusion. The man we both admired and loved, the one man I was beginning to accept as my new father, no longer seemed the same. Sylvie had considerable trouble recovering from this emotional rupture: where the problem had been to find a way to earn a living and still follow her interests, now she had to recover the solid ground of family she had always known. I felt I needed to be a better husband, but my father hadn't lived long enough to demonstrate what a husband should do. In fact, given what feminism said about the destructive roles men played in women's lives, I could see no good model of husband behavior around me. The closest I had was the care and sacrifice model my mother offered as a single parent. I grew more bound to Sylvie as I focused more on her needs, but I condensed all my needs into my "work." Everything that wasn't reading and writing could be for her. Sylvie was taking a class with the famous Jewish mystical leader Zalman Schecter, but she felt restless around people she knew who were still deeply rooted in Judaism. Philadelphia seemed tiny and dry. We talked about traveling to South America where Sylvie would study weaving. I would learn Spanish to read Neruda without the bewildering screen of translation.

The McGlinchey's poetry series, which had started with such explosive force in its first months, continued to attract good crowds but grew old for me. The well-known names, from mainstream poets associated with the *American Poetry Review* to the avant-garde editors of L=A=N=G=U=A=G=E magazine in New York, didn't seem very interested in anyone they didn't already know in Philadelphia. The hungrier poets appeared at our readings in the hopes of getting a reading for themselves, and at times I looked around the room and felt that most of those in the audience were listening to poems in order to compare them to their own. I laughed to myself about Kenneth Koch's great lines in "Fresh Air":

> "Oh to be seventeen years old
> Once again," sang the red-haired man, "and not know that poetry
> Is ruled with the scepter of the deaf, the dumb, and the creepy!"
> And the shouting persons battered his immortal body with stones
> And threw his primitive comedy into the sea
> From which it sang forth poems irrevocably blue. (55)

I loved the scene and especially enjoyed running the open readings with the young poets hoping to stake out their territory and try on new voices, but I began to get discouraged about why people were writing and whom they were addressing. Why write only to yourself or to a close circle of friends? My friend Gil and I argued about what sort of writing was called for in that moment. He was working for the Painted Bride, a small-budget community-based art center that specialized in dance and performance, and he still published his magazine with whatever funds he could scrape up when his transplanted kidneys would let him. He was reading the work of Mayakovsky and contemporary experimental poets in San Francisco and New York while I was trying to understand where the various American poetic streams came from. I told him I was more interested in poetry that investigated rather than experimented, but he thought I was too emotional and not current enough on formal innovation and literary theory. Neither of us wanted to be academics or have anything to do with universities. We both knew graduate students and professors we thought staid and opinionated, unresponsive to politics or history, and we wore our tiny salaries and outsider status with honor tinted by envy.

After months of looking, Sylvie finally got a job in an economically stressed part of the city known as Fishtown. She became a counselor for women who were in abusive relationships, and the new responsibility immediately seemed to give her a purpose and tapped into strengths she was waiting to use. From the very first client, this job brought her face to face with incredible brutalities, but the center where she worked gave her enough of a structure to act in response. Working with women, on a staff of women, lifted her spirits. It woke us both up to the horrors of domestic violence, and this became a major topic for conversation between us. Not long after Sylvie started her job, we heard a commotion on the street below our dining room window, where Sylvie and Lisa had spent hours studying when we first came to the city. We opened the window and looked downstairs. A man and a woman were screaming at each other in a car. The car began to shake; the woman opened her door, but the man dragged her back inside and seemed to be punching her. We called the police immediately, and they came within a few minutes. But as we watched from above, the cops pulled the woman out of the car, handcuffed her, and put her in the back of a van. Sylvie was furious and ran down the stairs to find out what was happening. When she learned that they wanted to charge the woman with disturbing the peace, she started yelling at the cops. I joined them downstairs and tried to mediate, but the cops thought we were simply interfering with their duties. They let the man in the car drive away and took down our names as witnesses.

This was Frank Rizzo's Philadelphia, and his cops still controlled the streets. The next morning, I was driving my Volkswagen on my way to work when I heard a siren and slowed down, but after a block or two, I realized that the police car didn't want to pass. He motioned me to pull over. The stocky white patrolman who got out had been the lead officer in the incident the day before, and he quickly identified enough violations—a taillight out, an inspection sticker just expired, my failure to pull over immediately, and a few other petty sins—and told me he could write me a ticket for over two hundred dollars. Then he smiled at me and said he would let me off with a warning but that he'd be watching to be sure I got my car inspected right away. We didn't mention the incident, but he was clearly warning me about something more than my taillights. I hadn't controlled my wife's tongue, and she had questioned Philadelphia police officers. I needed to recognize where I was and who kept the peace in our neighborhood.

Rizzo tried to change the city charter in the fall of 1978 so that he could run for a third term as mayor. This caused great consternation in the black and liberal communities, and lefties in our neighborhood joined the campaign to stop the charter change. I volunteered to be a poll watcher, but on the day of the vote I woke up with the flu. I was running a fever and sweating, but I didn't want to miss this historic battle against forces that looked truly evil. I was assigned to a polling place in a barbershop in an Italian neighborhood of South Philadelphia, Rizzo's stronghold. Most of the day I sat in a corner, making sure that people voted in an orderly way and nobody dead voted twice. The clerk of election for that ward was an imperious woman in her fifties, with big hair and no time for me, but everyone treated me civilly and even offered me doughnuts and coffee. I just held onto my chair and shivered, trying to smile when I could. About three in the afternoon, the barbershop door slammed open and a broad man in the leather jacket of the Philadelphia police, but with all its badges removed, stormed in. "Who's the faggot working against Rizzo?" the man thundered. I looked around and raised my hand, too sick to protest or run. He strode over to me and snarled down, but before he could say another word, the clerk behind him spoke up sharply: "Joey, you take that attitude outta here. This is my place, and I will not have you intimidating a poll watcher. Get out NOW." He glared at her and then glanced back at me. "All right, Ma. But Rizzo is gonna win!" he muttered and closed the door quietly as he left. I stayed that night till the very end in order to record the final counts on the machines. Rizzo had won in the ward, but more "no" votes registered than anybody expected. Charter change was rejected across the city, and a liberal named Bill Green replaced Rizzo in the following election. Green's managing director was Wilson Goode, later to be the first black mayor of Philadelphia.

When I thought about the troubles Sylvie was having with her life's direction, I consoled myself that I had made my choices: I would teach science and write poetry. I often wrote in my journal in the initial months at the school about my frustration with the amount of attention my students needed, the time it took to prepare science and math lessons, and my disappointment in the little progress my poems were making compared to my brother's leaps in drawing and sculpture in art school. However, I'm missing a crucial record of that first year teaching. I had just completed a spiral notebook in April 1978 with four months of entries when I brought it in to show my homeroom what personal reading and writing looked like. After a midafternoon break, the journal disappeared. We all knew who took it—a very troubled skinny white boy I'll call Kelvin, who had stolen other personal items from kids and adults in the school and had been the only one in the area of my room at the break when it went missing—but I could never prove he stole the notebook, and he never admitted to the theft. I had developed a good relationship with Kelvin, done much for him along the way, but I finally realized that the journal would never come back no matter how I wheedled, cajoled, pleaded, or threatened. His bulky mother, who still took baths with her teenage son sometimes, was no help in the process, and I decided that Kelvin needed whatever help we could give him more than I needed my journal back. I had kept notes on my reading of Chaucer, then Dante's *Commedia* and *Vita Nuova* along with other readings, in preparation for starting Pound's *Cantos*. I missed my journal like a father must miss his lost child and wrote soon after, "Just remembered some notes in that lost book—where could that book be goddamn I feel like I should be able to see it & go to it wherever it is lying" (5/6/78). All those drafts and dreams gone, but at least I'd done the work. The verses and commentaries were now inside me, in marrow or synapses or fatty tissue, wherever one stores cognitive transformations. Now I could not depend on notes to prove I'd read this or thought that; my growth had to travel to prove real. Any drafts of poems I thought worth keeping had been extracted long before, so my loss was all in the record of beginnings and origins. I mourned that loss but accepted the lesson like a rebuke from a *zaddik* to his disciple or a Zen *roshi* to his follower. I needed to let go of words even as I struggled to master their power.

We made a brief return to Deer Isle and the houseboat that summer, limited because Sylvie had started her counseling job and could no longer take a full course at Haystack. Much to our disappointment, we missed the Oppens, who had been unable to make the trip that year. We did spend some time with my brother's old high school friend John Landreau. John was related to George and Ellie, who had given me work the summer before, and was earning a living on Deer Isle as a carpenter and, like me, trying to write. I admired his carpentry skills and his independence, his deep focus on reading and his apparent ability to live happily without engaging much with people. I got so involved with my students' lives that they occupied my dreams and waking hours, and I consciously had to block them out of my writing room. I felt ashamed that I couldn't keep quiet like John; I always drifted into conversation with people on the job or in stores or even waiting for a bus. In the city, I felt I was "talking to social purpose only" and "losing hours, evenings, weekends to bunk" (4/22/78) because I couldn't say no to people who wanted me to be their friend or help them in some way, even if I didn't particularly enjoy their company. John seemed to take his work so seriously and know how to live on his own, but he was terribly hard on himself and would not show me anything he wrote. Sylvie and I had a wonderful, long conversation with him one night about art making and politics, "all of us in common isolation as artists and uncaptured people" (7/3/78), trying to do more with our lives than simply earn a good salary and drive a nice car. As much as we all enjoyed the exchange and the wine that night, I felt the tension of wanting to maintain the closeness Sylvie and I had built on our Maine trip, develop this new friendship with a younger writer, and yet encourage a bond between John and Sylvie based on their own commonalities. The writing life, no matter how removed, was still a life with people, and people complicated everything.

Before we left for Maine, I had finished assembling a collection of poems, despite great doubt and misgivings, noting at one point that "I was imagining meeting Pound and Williams in heaven, their shaking my hand, exchanging half bored half pitying glances & walking away from me" (7/14/78). I'd gone on a little fiction venture and read two Virginia Woolf novels and Proust's *Swann's Way* while writing a rather labored short story about a woman fighting Philadelphia police brutality from inside the police force. On our return to Philadelphia, however, I returned to poetry. I noted in my journal that on July 23 I started *The Cantos*, an eight-hundred-page march in addition to all the commentary, history, politics, and doubt this undertaking would entail. I wondered if my imagination and intelligence were sufficient for the test, if my mind could "climb steeply enough" or be trained in "rigor and constant attention" (8/14/78). Even if Pound himself did not possess the superior vision of his senior William Butler Yeats, the philosophical turn of Wallace Stevens, the discipline of H. D., or the amused wisdom of Marianne Moore, Ezra would be my examiner and my guide. I was beginning a new stage of my apprenticeship, one where I could cut no corners nor skip any lessons. I was fully prepared to argue with the impresario of Modernism, but I wanted to stand in Pound's full rainstorm of culture and history and still make my own small poems. When I finished a month later, I wrote: "I have lived thru the Cantos, am myself now on the other side. . . . Now its sorrow & history are stitched into my back. I can hardly see it, but I know I won't be able to let it go" (8/22/78). One permanent change I noted was that Pound had rendered light a palpable quality, "not so much a wash applied to tint the leaves but a bodiless live substance occupying the space around & the surface of trees" (8/22/78). Pound also left me with the conviction that the vast canvas of history as well as the minute refractions of language figure in the composing of verse and that to write means to breathe in one's own time among the centuries. Teaching loomed again, and with it both science and the stressed lives of my kids. I wasn't a bit ready for classes, but I felt sure the new school year would go more smoothly than in my first year.

Sylvie and I started the school year with much tension between us at home. I was unhappy starting work again, realizing that I "seem to need to form up 2 separate lives & live them equally" (9/14/78), both to write and to teach. When I closed my eyes, I saw school situations—kids in classes, homework to grade, planning to do—but I wanted my mind clear at home for writing. I dunned myself that I wasn't selfish enough to be a writer. Sylvie didn't know what to do with my unhappiness. She seemed to be over the sorrow caused by her parents' divorce, and she was becoming more and more invested in her job. She had trouble focusing on our relationship and me. One night in September, she went out with a work colleague and didn't come home till after two in the morning. I paced up and down in our little apartment, fearing that something had happened to her, but when she returned, she was annoyed by my concern. She had simply been out late talking with a close friend, and she recounted their conversation in detail. Soon after that, I went out to McGlinchey's bar to see the second Ali/Spinks fight with my teaching pal Dave. The next morning I lay in bed late, looking at the light on the big loom we had bought with our wedding money, and I began to compose in my head the first lines of a long poem about the Greek figure Herakles, the strong man/god Romans called Hercules. I almost never watched boxing, but I was struck with the beauty of Ali's style, the power of his punches. These big men gracefully pummeling each other comforted a growing unease in me.

My journal became largely the record of my drafting this new poem, soon transformed into a Greek-style drama, about Herakles after death. I took notes on all the Greek plays I could find while my own play grew from monologue to scene and then to act. Still, the daily tension appeared in my writing. A sentence or two occasionally recorded that Sylvie and I weren't able to talk to each other, or that we'd broken through our impasse and would weather this hard time. Once she came home and told me she couldn't go on without religion; she missed Judaism but it just never gave her enough. The conversation recalled close talks we'd had the year before, but now it was mostly a replay of a conversation she'd had with a friend at work. She brought her intense work dramas home at the same time I was trying to leave my day-to-day life in the school building, allowing struggles with kids and teachers to burst into my journal only now and then at the mention of a student conflict or a classroom setting for a dream. The school was being threatened with closing by the social service organization that funded us, but I mention that threat in the journal only once, in passing.

Sylvie and I were reading Mary Daly's *Beyond God the Father,* and in January I quoted in my journal a passage that stays with me still: "It is not necessary to anthropomorphize or reify transcendence in order to relate to this personally. . . . Why indeed must 'God' be a noun? Why not a verb—the most active and dynamic of all? Hasn't the naming of 'God' as a noun been an act of murdering that dynamic Verb?" (33). I accepted Daly's anger at patriarchy as a matter of course and tried to incorporate her thought without struggling to understand my place in her decidedly woman-centered worldview. I was making more place in my journal for women scholars of ancient Greece such as Sarah Pomeroy and Jane Ellen Harrison as well as the Modernist writers H. D., Gertrude Stein, and Marianne Moore, but my writing was still fixed on men such as the Greek dramatists and American poets like Pound, Rexroth, and Oppen. Mostly the journal is filled with lines and notes on *Herakles.* Each time Sylvie and I had another convoluted talk, I discovered more to write about this figure in between matriarchy and patriarchy, god and man, man and woman, strength and weakness, madness and wisdom, black and white. I developed a sense of spirits haunting my actions and my words; I dreamed of kissing my grand-mothers, one alive and one dead. In the final entry of the fall semester, I recorded a dream in which I was handling scientific glassware in a basement, then windowpanes spattered with paint from my brother's carpentry jobs. My brother and sister told me how to handle the panes, but I couldn't follow their sensible advice: "I woke up frustrated with the memory of brittleness . . . the tiny snaps of broken glass felt in my hands, ears & jaw" (12/16/78). I didn't even recognize the dream's pun on handling "the pane."

A day after that dream, Sylvie told me she had kissed another woman, her friend at work. I felt hurt, but I could not believe this would end our marriage. She still loved me, and I loved her enough to see her through the exploration she needed to do. We talked earnestly that Saturday and worked together all the next week to help her mother, who had drifted into a debilitating depression after her divorce. The closeness I felt with Sylvie contradicted the simultaneous feeling that she was slipping away. Later during the winter break, I went on a trip with my brother and sister, just the three of us driving alone to a shore hotel in South Carolina, and I admitted to them and to myself for the first time that Sylvie and I were having trouble. By mid-January, Sylvie had made love with her friend. At the news, I punched out a panel of a wooden cabinet in the hall of our apartment and cried, but I still could not accept that our marriage would dissolve.

In my journal, I was devising a theory of emotion derived from Einstein's theory of gravitational frames and relativity. It promised a way to understand individual emotional states in terms of social frameworks like sexism and racism, terms within which Sylvie and I felt increasingly encased. I accused myself of writing merely in the hopes of proving myself a genius, to justify an image of myself as better than everybody else. I had so much to prove—to the army, my Orthodox grandparents, the suburban high school, psychoanalysis, the Ivies, medical school, Sylvie, and even the kids I taught—that I could be brave, smart, nonsexist, understanding, real. I wanted to show my father that "a landless monkish Jew" (12/27/78) could write poems even Christian literary scholars would accept in American libraries. I read Goethe's *Faust I* and *II* for his handling of men's desire for intellectual and spiritual power, while in my *Herakles* the hero refuses the commands of his father, Zeus, to return to Olympus from Hades and instead returns to Earth to discover that his one true lover had been the queen in a lesbian court. I made a three-page list of my ignorances: authors I needed to read or reread, music still to know, languages to learn. Sylvie couldn't be ending our marriage. We had met George and Mary Oppen together and admired their long love partnership as a great human accomplishment. We planned to leave this commodified country and live in Latin America, absorb its arts and revolutions. We wanted to grow old and wise together so that young artists would seek us out for advice. I had worked so hard to be a steady and supportive partner, neither a Rizzo cop nor a sneering rabbi. Why couldn't she see me and preserve our common home?

The feminist singer-songwriter Holly Near gave a concert at the University of Pennsylvania that January. Sylvie wanted me to come along, and, though I was wary of being hurt, I went to show that I could be happy in our new consciousness. The auditorium was packed, but I was one of perhaps only a dozen men in the audience. I sat through the familiar songs—Sylvie played Near, Meg Christian, and other feminist singers all the time now at home—and the music rattled me awake. As I listened, I had a vision of what was happening to us. This wasn't just a matter of two people who couldn't stay together; our particular story was a part of a great human movement changing the shape of gender relations. Still, I thought, I have just my little life to live. Afterward, Sylvie and I had coffee together, and I told her I pictured us on a long journey through forests and beside rivers, the two of us encountering adventures along the way and always moving on together. Then we came to a meadow where women were dancing. In my vision, Sylvie asked me to wait on the road while she joined the dance, promising to return soon. She came back now and then to tell me excitedly what they were doing, but she always returned to the dance alone. I waited and waited. Finally I called to her, hoping to get her back on the path with me, but she no longer heard me. I stepped ahead slowly, expecting her to catch up or call to me, but after a while I realized she would not. I would have to leave her and move on.

The next months were a jumble of waiting and action, sorrow and fear and occasional exalting hope. The poetry manuscript I'd sent out with great hope came back from yet another small literary press, with a sympathetic rejection note that "the weaker poems detract from the finer ones" (3/9/79), but all I could do was laugh and rail at them and figure out a new place to send the poems. Sylvie wanted me to stay in the house even though she really wanted nothing to do with me. I could not face my anger and instead kept telling myself we could get back together if I could be patient, that I was learning so much about myself, that Sylvie needed my support for her difficult decisions. *Herakles* literally seemed to write itself in my journal and typescript as our private drama progressed, and the growing stack of pages gave provisional relief from the pain of sleeping beside her alone. At rare moments, I realized how hard this arrangement was: "the difficulty of the work right now is that it is so centered in my life. I literally sit in my wound as I work" (2/20/79).

I took up reading Kierkegaard and found his analysis of Abraham's willingness to sacrifice Isaac modeled the sacrifice I needed to make for a new way of being male. When we talked, we talked about feminism all the time now, and I was beginning to feel that my dear friends, the Modernist poets, had betrayed me. Reading a collection of essays about Marianne Moore one day, I realized how much the women poets at the time had been vilified and diminished by critics and even lovers, while the men had talked themselves into godlike status. I doubted those I had admired, and qualities I had excused began to look like deadly male sins: "Eliot & Pound are both snots, one nastier than the other . . . Williams himself comes out in his essay as an intense little boy" (2/8/79). These were no longer fathers I could believe in.

John Landreau, who introduced me to Kierkegaard's work, had moved to Philadelphia that winter and was living in a small apartment above Aaron. The two of them listened to me tolerantly when I couldn't stand being alone, put up with my tears, and avoided saying anything against Sylvie. They supported me with sympathy and alcohol. They were the only tenants in that building, and one night we stayed up most of the night, drunk and high, drumming rhythms for hours on empty cans, table tops, anything that would sound. They put up with my long justifications of Sylvie's needs and my rants about the horrors of patriarchy. In March I finally left the apartment I shared with Sylvie, after I suddenly recognized one afternoon that the couples therapist we were seeing had no intention of helping me. She saw me only as an impediment to my wife's process of coming out. I had to stop taking care of Sylvie and start taking care of myself. I moved briefly to my brother's place down the block and then to a rooming house around the corner, where everybody, including the Dutch Indonesian landlady, was so lonely I frequently had to leave the house in the middle of the night just for enough air to get back to sleep. The day Aaron and John helped me move out of the apartment, the man in the downstairs apartment was beating his girlfriend. She was screaming for help. Aaron ran for the cops, who always hung out at the steak and pizza shop nearby, and warned them the guy was dangerous because we knew he held a black belt in karate. One cop buckled up his leather jacket and remarked, "He can't punch a bullet." They did stop the beating, let the girlfriend go, arrested the guy, and carted him away. I finished packing my few things and left.

Around that time, the school, too, had to move from the old house near Drexel. The school's sponsoring agency was continuing to make noises that it couldn't afford to support the school, despite the fact that we educated all the kids in their group homes on the most minimal salaries possible. The building was in such bad repair that it needed major renovations to be safe enough for kids to walk up the front steps; we actually feared that the whole front porch would collapse if kids danced too hard on their way out the door. But we had to find a way to keep the school going. The principal, Anita, found a hospital in West Philadelphia that had moved its operations out of town and was willing to rent us the upper floor of the otherwise abandoned building. This new place was spooky, but it did have regular heat, and we could use whatever tables and chairs we scrounged from the lower floors. I even found a twenty-foot-long blackboard for my classroom, and with my meager carpentry skills it took me most of an afternoon to hang it on the thick ward wall. The day we moved all the desks and books, James, the art teacher, returned to the old building for one last load of materials he'd left behind. He happened to look in the furnace room and caught the boiler just as it was about to blow up. I noted in my journal, in one of the very few comments about my day job during that intense time, "The school is in such disarray, I can barely teach there" (3/9/79).

Teaching became a blessed distraction. I needed those kids as much as I needed my writing and my friends. I would teach a class, release them when it was time for me to ring the bell, go into an empty class next door, and cry till I had to ring the bell for the next period. The kids kept me in the present, even though I was still doing silly things to get their attention and put myself in the spotlight. When I was teaching electricity, I came across Maxwell's four equations for electromagnetism in a physics text. Though I couldn't understand them myself, I wrote them out on my long blackboard to show my students that they could pick up elements that they could understand in the most complex mathematics. I performed a sex change operation on a paper bag to show them that the penis could be converted into a vagina with the proper cutting and tucking. But I was beginning to balance performances with more openness to the kids themselves and their stories. I brought my chess set to school one day because I had no place to keep it in my new little room. A white kid named Chase in my algebra class took an interest in the set and wanted to play me. Chase would throw fits in class when he couldn't calculate in his head. I found out talking to him over chess that his absent father was an Oxford mathematics professor who had briefly married Chase's mother while on a visiting lectureship at the University of Pennsylvania. Chase beat me within ten moves three times in row. One of the angriest kids in the school, a wiry African American guy I'll call Rodney, from a rough neighborhood in North Philly, saw us playing and wanted a game. I stepped back and watched Rodney beat Chase three times in a row. After that, I just took the board out whenever kids wanted to play but did not play much myself. Rodney later decided he wanted to do better in school and voluntarily signed up for an Upward Bound program in the suburbs, which he left abruptly only after doing very well most of the summer. Later, Rodney made a successful career in the Air Force. Chase moved in with his pregnant girlfriend and left school. I never heard from him again.

I watched the kids I'd taught geometry and biology graduate, some of them headed to college. I'd taken one young man to an interview at a small nearby college that specialized in science and pharmacy and another student to the police academy, much to my consternation. One or two of our kids got college scholarships; others went into the military. They all had those impossible smiles as they walked in their caps and gowns and their families cheered. Perhaps I had done something for them, but I didn't feel like much of a teacher. What had I taught them? They taught me that I'd better pay more attention to them. I needed to recognize that teaching wasn't about proving my brilliance or turning them into little versions of me. I had to listen more actively, shine the light on them, and judge myself by what they learned rather than by what I said. Teaching took so daggone much time and energy, but I had to admit that conducting frog dissections or leading discussions on domestic violence with teens suited me better than constructing walls from two by fours or hanging drywall in old houses. I felt more at home in a classroom than anywhere else I'd ever worked. At the same time, I decided not to return to the school in the next year. I'd spend the summer in California with Joel, do carpentry again in the fall with John, and then go to Latin America for as long as my little savings would last. But clearly I'd be back in a classroom, if I ever came back at all.

I finished *Herakles* as the school year ended. Although I wasn't writing for my students or my colleagues, somehow teaching suggested a solution to the problem I had with audience for my poems. I couldn't run from all those kids I knew in the army and on the wrestling team, from my coworkers on the vineyard and in the book warehouse, but I still wanted to write poetry out of a tradition that didn't include any of them as readers. If I filled my consciousness with as many types of people as I could, then when I wrote I would be writing with them as a part of the total environment. Perhaps that would at least keep me from falling into the tacit assumption that readers were all white and college-educated and mostly male. Everyone yearned and hurt, thought and felt, and my poems needed to grow out of more than my personal pain or intellectual preoccupations. *Herakles* was not a populist tract or a best-selling novel—perhaps no one would ever see it at all—but the play taught me both that I could not keep my private life out of my "work" and that even the most arcane language traces to a common base. Words move in and out of people's mouths and cannot be regarded as pure or sacred; words are particles in a shared human stream. My little drama with Sylvie dominated my waking and sleeping life that year, but it didn't make me special. Thousands of people were suffering worse in my city alone. My writing had to earn its consciously wrought language and address an audience and a self with humility and openness, not with judgment and condescension. Pound had taught me much, but his bluster and pretension and hatred held no more luster for me.

Summer in Oakland with Joel meant I could leave my room in the boardinghouse behind. Joel was working in a group home for autistic kids again and wasn't very happy in Oakland. Once I got there, we glowered at each other some days for what we couldn't say to each other. Our saving grace was his big old sheepdog, Pax, who would dig a pit in the little front yard every morning under a eucalyptus tree and remain there all day till we took him for a walk in the Berkeley hills. I was reading almost exclusively women writers, especially Virginia Woolf's *A Room of One's Own* and the poetry of H. D. and Emily Dickinson, except for when I was reading minor writing by William Carlos Williams and despising him for how he portrayed women. I was a dupe for believing his generation of men could teach me how to write! Joel was less guarded than Aaron or John with his criticism of Sylvie and more particularly of me. He didn't approve of the way I waited for letters from Sylvie and wrote to her immediately when one came. He let me know I was a damned fool, as I'd been with other women before. I should just stop complaining about gender and do my work. When we were getting along, we talked about music and travel and politics. He supported my plan to pack up and go to Latin America. Nicaraguan revolutionaries called the Sandinistas had just defeated the dictator Anastasio Somoza that July, and I decided I'd go and help out in the reconstruction of the country. After all, most of the members of the ruling junta were poets or novelists. It would be a new experience to see a country ruled by socialist writers. I would gather my shreds of self in a bedroll and set off for a world that valued poetry. I'd just have to learn the language somehow, and not in a classroom.

While I was in Oakland, I visited George and Mary Oppen in their beautiful little row house in San Francisco. I feared they wouldn't remember me, but they welcomed me like a grandson and showed no sign that they were disappointed with me that Sylvie and I had split up. They wanted to know how I was, and they shared their own concerns. Mary's autobiography, *Meaning a Life* had come out, and there seemed to be a resurgence of interest in George's work, but they didn't really want to be bothered by earnest dissertators and condescending critics. Mary took me aside at one point and told me that George was repeating himself more and more and regularly forgetting where he'd put things. She was clearly worried about Alzheimer's, but she maintained her warmth and the intimate tone of their conversation. At one point, we went out to look at the ocean, where they had seen people diving off cliffs with giant kites. Mary needed to pee, and she got up and walked down the open trail to some bushes. I was amazed that someone in her seventies could be so free and unconcerned about propriety. They convinced me that I should go off to Nicaragua and see the revolution for myself, no matter how lonely it might be. As we sat in their apartment that evening, Mary asked me how old I was. I told her I was nearly twenty-seven. George took a puff on his pipe and said, "That's a respectable age."

I returned to Philadelphia in the fall to earn some money and make a start at Spanish. I had to sell my beloved red Volkswagen but in the

process discovered a crack in its frame that made the car both dangerous and unrepairable. An inventor acquaintance generously gave me a
hundred dollars for it, and I could not help but laugh at the self-parody
of my silly life. John and I started a company called Ten Penny Carpentry and picked up steady work pretty quickly. I wasn't much help
to John, but I could carry things from his old Chrysler and drive a nail
wherever he told me to put it. Together we managed to make a little
money despite our profound lack of business acumen. We underbid
jobs and underestimated construction time, but we talked constantly
and kept away loneliness while we worked. I lived in a half-finished
apartment the size of a large bathroom, renting from a crooked landlord
whom John and Aaron referred to fondly as the Fat Man. I wrote a few
desultory poems I didn't bother to revise. I read the poet Octavio Paz
on Mexico and various texts on Maya archaeology, made lists of writers
in Spanish I would have to read, and decided my trip should focus on
old mythologies and new political struggles. I ate cheesesteaks, drank
most nights, and put on an extra twenty pounds. But I did study at
a Spanish school where beautiful Colombian women laughed gracefully at my pronunciations, and I learned how to order pork chops in
Spanish even though I didn't eat pork. I saw Sylvie once or twice and
disciplined myself not to hope for anything from her. I was leaving on
the trip we had once planned to do together. I wouldn't hear her voice
for a long time, though some nights I wanted to crawl back to her on
my greasy knees. One evening, while John and I were completing a job
in the home of academic friends who had hired us to insulate a wall of
their tall and narrow Center City home, I was cleaning up in a rush to
get to my Spanish class. I came hurtling down the steps with a bundle
of insulation on my head, turned a corner on my way to the basement,
and ran full force into a chandelier in the sitting room. Two globes
from the fixture came loose, and I watched them fall in slow motion.
I offered to pay for the damage, but our friends knew I had no money.
The globes were hand-made. We finished the job but never mended
the friendship. It was time for me to get out of town.

## 9

## *Viajeros, Extranjeros*

I WOKE UP IN a bright green room in the cheap section of an otherwise splendid white adobe hotel in Merida after a warm December night in 1979, my first in Mexico. Tourist prices would consume my trip if I let them, so I sought out *barato* accommodations where Mexican migrant families and young international travelers, or *viajeros*, paid only a few pesos to stay. Vigorous bedbugs left little bites on my arms and head. I forgot to carry toilet paper with me into the bathroom and had to use the newspaper torn in strips beside the toilet. But I figured out where to throw used paper when I was done and managed a shower, even though my part of the hotel offered only cold water. Those first joyful days away from America reassured me I could manage a traveler's life. I met *viajeros* from Quebec almost immediately, and then French travelers, Danes, Australians, and Brits. I felt alone but also a member of a restless class of wanderers, some looking for drugs and romance, others for knowledge and politics, or art and architecture and song. We strained to use the common language of Spanish with each other, but few could muster more than a sentence at a time. One new Quebecois friend suddenly burst out with a long disquisition to me in French until his companion explained to him in halting English that I understood even less in their home language than any of us did in Spanish. We laughed at our clumsiness on the balance beam of language and shared what we knew about eating and sleeping on a traveler's budget.

I had stopped on the way to Merida to see my sister in Chapel Hill, North Carolina, where she had transferred after an unhappy start at the University of Pittsburgh. Sharon was making an adult life for herself, waiting tables and studying psychology and children's literature. Restaurant work, she declared, was like theater; the staff prepared a different show for guests each night. Sharon was always one for the grand gesture, and she hid her pity for her big brother with characteristic grace. I must have been transparent, frightened and hurt while I masqueraded as an adventurer who no longer cared about life in the States. I also had a physical ailment to attend to: I'd dropped a board on my big toe on a job, and the wound under the nail had grown infected and sore. Sharon helped me find a doctor who tore off my toenail while we looked on in silent horror. The doctor sterilized the wound, and I left her office feeling I could walk across Mexico. When I said good-bye to Sharon, I was saying good-bye to the last person for a long time who would be good to me just because she loved me.

I had read *Paradise Lost* in Chapel Hill and, without a hint of irony at my choice of reading material, I railed in my journal at Milton for being "an insidious prophet of Power, Hell, & the Manly God" (11/27/79). Once I hit Mexico, I turned to Lawrence's fascist classic *The Plumed Serpent*— a weird modernist fantasy about primitive blood and sexual striving and the individual (white) soul—a book I could rant against for its masculine venom and racist portrayal of Mexican Indians. Would Sylvie hear my righteous indignation so far away? Lawrence invoked gender in a way feminists had taught me to despise. Marriage was an ideological trap and heterosexuality a vast mythology based on rape, but I was tiring of rage. I would put aside the wars in my brain and shift my focus to Maya anthropology and Spanish for a while. I had brought along one new literary magazine I admired, *Montemora*, which was publishing the mystical fragments of Edmond Jabès, a French Egyptian Jew whose poetry lingers over questions about Jewishness and the silence left by an absent God. Sylvie was building a life with her new partner, the poetry circles at McGlinchey's would carry on fine without me, and even my kids at the school would find their way. I could remake myself here alone among travelers, ruins, and political turmoil. But first I had to break the habit of mentioning Sylvie to everyone I met along the trail.

I struck up a friendship in Merida with a young Dane named Eric, not far out of high school but mature and curious about this southern world. We traveled together for two weeks, sharing our stories and common interests in politics and science. But most of all we speculated on the character of the *viajeros* we met: the bold and loopy Quebecoise Nicole, the forthright Australian woman named Jelly who had trained horses in the outback for seven years, a couple from England's Cambridge who were taking a break from their doctoral studies before plunging back into their dissertations. Eric, who was tall and blond and far more attractive to women than I, met two black-haired Basque nurses in Merida on their way to Nicaragua. We shared an intense evening of political talk but no romance with them the night before we left for Tulum. Eric and I stumbled through the language barrier—they spoke little English and no one but Eric spoke Danish—but they held to their sharp focus on revolution and their own homeland struggles. Their nationalism made me feel righteous for heading toward Managua but damned for my country's policies and muddled by my personal drama. As in black neighborhoods of Philadelphia, I couldn't resign from my white skin or my privileged education; all I could do was listen and learn. Perhaps someday I would do something to help people my people had hurt. My Jewishness didn't excuse me from being American, male, and white. Other nationalities could love their country, or their particular clan, with a pride that wasn't available to a white middle-class *viajero* from the United States with a conscience or a consciousness in 1979.

I had little time to write in my journal during that first week traveling from Merida to the ruins at Chichen Itza, Uxmal, and odd little Tulum. The first two sites were grand, open spaces with pyramids, palaces, and ball courts, overrun with tourists and dominated by a classical sense of military power. I forced myself to sit and draw the buildings called "nunneries" and temples. Sketching kept me from running away from their scale and hawkish decorations. Tulum, on the other hand, was diminutive and nearly funky in its odd angles and skeletal paintings. According to Michael Coe, the expert on the Maya I carried in my backpack, the small structures in Tulum were in a "degenerate" late style, but I found the site intimate and congenial to my modernist tastes. I used drawing to admire them in silence. The process gave me scaffolding on the page to observe details closely over time, to stay with the lines and shadows before me long enough to absorb them. I'd drawn people and landscapes in the past, but from those first days, drawing became an alternate language for me to meet the landscape and shut down my penchant for too much talk. Sketched lines on a page brought me closer to the present, while lines in a poem created their own reality quite apart from the room and even the city where I composed. People tended to avoid me when I drew. Unlike painting on canvas, drawing in a notebook is a private act done in public, and so people didn't stare over my shoulder.

In Tulum, Eric and I stayed in a *pensión* composed of huts near the beach not far from the ruins, and there we met travelers who had no interest in the Maya or their remains. A very young Israeli couple just out of their army showed little enthusiasm for this land that was, to them, not as spectacular as their fiercely remembered country. They seldom visited restaurants so as not to "eat their vacation" and instead prepared meals like those at home on the kibbutz to which they would soon return. Eric remarked to me that the Israelis' particular chauvinism seemed to provoke me into amplifying my Jewishness when we ate with them, and I took his point. My parents had traveled in Israel before they were married, and some part of me felt I should be there learning Hebrew rather than in a Catholic and pagan country learning Spanish. But I'd made my choice. The *viajero* must stretch the self without breaking character, and it was so early in my journey that I didn't yet inhabit my traveling persona. A lithe Australian woman with a wild head of sun-bleached hair also stayed nearby. Four years out from her country, cocaine and her boyfriend in Brazil captivated her more than the Atlantic waves breaking a hundred yards from our campfire. An older American joined our group too, though he said very little until we prompted him. He'd hung out with Ginsberg in San Francisco's North Beach years before, but he wasn't so much a literary man as a sad character seeking a little sanity on the road.

Buses served as a liminal space between locations. We met travelers from other countries on buses, talked or gestured the best we could to local poor farming folk called *campesinos*, sat next to wizened old women with live poultry in cages or sleeping men with machetes on their laps. As Eric and I passed from Tulum inland to Palenque, for example, we met a Quebecois traveler who got into a shouting match with an immigration officer. The officer may have wanted a bribe, but in any case he clearly disliked the French-speaking *viajero* even though the Quebecois also spoke fluent Spanish. The argument almost came to blows till an older officer diffused the situation. I happened to be standing nearby the whole time, unable to follow the conversation but unwilling to look away. The Quebecois then confided to me that he produced a news program for a radio station in Montreal and that he was working on a master's thesis about the Nicaraguan revolution. We talked about history and politics, and he gave me the name of a history professor to look up in Mexico City if I wanted to find out more about Nicaragua. The interaction made me realize what a vast undertaking it would be to write about Nicaragua and its recent civil war, that I knew nothing but a few random facts and some rousing clichés about the country. In fact, often on buses I learned how little I knew about people or places or language. I looked forward to these long, bumpy rides as a way of clearing out unrecognized arrogance. Whatever I knew from one town would need to be recalibrated when I traveled overland to the next.

Eric had been away from home six months, and he was on his way back when I met him. We traveled east to Palenque together because he was headed toward Mexico City and a plane to Denmark, and I was winding south into Guatemala. We spent a couple of days exploring the temples of Palenque, broken but commanding architecture that seemed far more soulful than anything I'd seen before. Eric was not particularly moved by Maya archaeology, and so while I spent time drawing in the ruins, he walked around talking to people he met. We had grown close in those two weeks together and were frankly tearful when we said good-bye the morning he took the bus to Mexico City. Forming a new friendship helped get me started on my path. Sylvie's confusions had turned all friendships in my mind to muddles of sexuality and prejudice. I found comfort that I could travel with another man, reveal to him intimate details of my last year, and feel a bond with him that was not forged either of repressed homoerotic desire or shared misogyny. Straight men could be decent human beings. I was glad to be alone now, preparing to move on toward Chiapas, the southernmost department of Mexico, and from there to Guatemala. Not far from the border, in the town of Huehuetenango, I had reserved a place at a Spanish language school where I planned to learn finally what people around me were talking about.

From Palenque I took a rocking, pounding ride over the mountains to San Cristobal de las Casas alongside Nicole from Quebec, whom we'd met in Merida. She was an exuberant character with strong features and new age opinions. She seemed to be somewhere between her early twenties and mid-thirties, but she reminded me of old ladies you meet in the subway who wear boxy hats and talk a little too loud. Still, she was a sharp observer and spoke both English and Spanish with complete disregard for grammar or decorum. I quite enjoyed our jagged conversation when we weren't worrying that the packed luggage racks would come down on our heads. I remember looking out of the bus window at a stop in a tiny village and realizing that no one on the street was speaking Spanish. Until that time, I'd thought my poor Spanish prevented conversations with local passengers, but suddenly what I had read about Maya Mexico and Guatemala became clear to me: my bus partners themselves knew only basic Spanish. Their birth languages had survived the Spaniards' conquest and still defined their lives at home. Languages differed from village to village from here to Belize, and many women spoke little or no Spanish. I was walking a mottled ground of speech—among *viajeros* and tourists, *campesinos* and immigration officials, professors and tortilla vendors—for as long as I stayed away from that homogeneous American language landscape where I had lived and taught and written. I had always treated other tongues as foreign, at best seeing them as intellectual challenges and sources for spiritual or literary meaning. Now "language" meant a particular channel for immediate human interaction. I thought about the Mexicans I'd worked beside in the vineyard and wondered for the first time what other languages they had spoken at home.

San Cristobal de las Casas in Chiapas tempted me to stay forever. People in modern and traditional dress moved through winding streets lined by white rows of low houses accented in blues and reds and orange, or azure houses trimmed in white, all roofed in terra cotta tile. Even more than in Merida, the streets of the colonial city lay lightly over the deep Maya substratum. The churches and colonnades on the *zocalo* presented the colonial face of religion and state, but Lacandon Indian faces outshone the blonde-girl beer signs, and Coca-Cola jingles could not mask the far older rhythms of the market where I bought mangoes. The cathedrals were ornate and imposing, but just outside the town, in the village of Chamula, the blocky church contained religious fervor for gods barely touched by their Christian saint names. In San Cristobal, I found a decent room in a *pensión* connected to a Turkish bathhouse, and I set up my writing desk to stay through the Christmas week. The guests were a mix of Mexicans visiting for the holidays and *viajeros* on their way to and from Guatemala. I also discovered a café called Olla Podrida nearby, a place where travelers and locals mixed and there seemed always to be someone interesting to meet. A Belgian painter named Marcos greeted most everyone who came in. I managed to hold conversations with artists, poets, and musicians in Spanish where at least I thought I grasped what we were talking about. This was a scene I had been hoping to find.

The guidebooks said San Cristobal had a library called Na Bolom, the House of the Jaguar, which had been established by a Danish archaeologist and his Swiss journalist wife in the early 1950s to collect scholarship on the Maya and Lacandon peoples of the area. The rose-painted house trimmed in ochre sat on a leafy street on the other side of town from my *pensión*, and it was a revelation to enter. Immaculately kept, with a central garden surrounded by an arched portico, Na Bolom offered sanctuary along its brick paths and tile floors. Before the library/museum closed for the holiday, I managed to work a few days in the small but fine collection, reading about Maya history and mythology, taking notes on the calendar system and the debate over what wiped out the civilization in the so-called Mayan Collapse. My notes roam across subjects, images, and themes; I simply wanted to record everything I could find about the people who had lived in these parts before the conquest. A student from Brandeis I met at breakfast as I prepared to go to Na Bolom asked me why I cared so much about the Maya civilization, and I found I had no answer for him. At the time, I answered mechanically, "I'm a writer," but the more I thought about it through the day, the less sense that made. I could be writing about food, or love, or traffic patterns. After much speculation and a day of study, I wrote in my journal, "Mostly it seems to be my present condition & I leave it there" (12/22/79). Perhaps I was retracing the obsessive study Charles Olson undertook in his "Mayan Letters," a work that had influenced me years before. Or perhaps I associated the sudden collapse of the culture with the inexplicable collapse of my marriage. In any case, I needed to connect with the people around me, and learning their history seemed the most compelling way. History and art could anchor me in this foreign place. I wrote most of the next day in my hotel room, drafting a poem for the first time on the trip, hearing myself think and trying to release the voices in multiple languages I'd encountered in the mere twenty days I'd been away from the States. Writing settled me, lowered the volume in my head, but left me alone in my crumpled core. I missed Sylvie with the same intensity I'd felt the day I left our apartment not quite a year before: "Much has been purified out, but a center I can't understand remains" (12/22/79).

While I was working in the library, I heard guitars and firecrackers outside. I looked out the door and saw trucks parading by with young actors dressed up in elaborate robes and makeshift sets on the flatbeds. They were holding dramatic poses in tableaux to celebrate the birth of Jesus, and children in gangs shouted for Christmas. I had hardly noticed the holiday except as an annoyance, but now it was everywhere. When I got back to my hotel, lights were strung and people were drinking. I met two French documentary filmmakers at the Olla Podrida and felt very proud that my Spanish got me through the rich conversation. When I returned home, the owner's son barged into my room and wanted to know if I knew any rock and roll songs to sing. He was drunk on bad Mexican brandy, and we sang songs like "House of the Rising Sun" and "Angie" while he strummed his guitar. He thought it strange that an American knew no songs from Kiss or Black Sabbath and dragged me out to a house party of teenagers drinking. A sleazy Mexican lawyer also staying in the hotel followed along and soon started selling drugs to the kids. I left the party feeling as alien as I had during my childhood in Germany during Christmas, the unmoved Jew in a culture of celebrants.

But Christmas Eve was different. Marcos, the painter from the Olla Podrida, had invited me to his house for a party that night, and I felt honored. The invitation directed me to walk up into the mountains outside of town, and I expected to have to ask someone in the deserted darkness, but I easily discovered a small, well-lit house with gardens around it and Bach coming from the open windows. Inside I recognized a few people I'd met in town earlier. Paintings and prints by Marcos covered every wall, and every surface held pots, figurines, and weavings he'd collected on his travels. He had six shelves of anthropology, poetry, and art books. We ate exquisitely prepared meats and savory pastries and drank red wine and Belgian vodka. One couple I particularly liked were Ricardo and Ruth. Ricardo was a compact, dark-skinned Mexican with a narrow beard and quick eyes who promoted documentaries for UNAM, the national university in Mexico City. Ruth was an American poet with shoulder-length dark blonde hair and an inclination toward tranquil curiosity. She had lived in Mexico for nine years and seemed utterly comfortable in the country. They were a bit older and world-lier than I, but they accepted me, and occasionally Ruth would speak English to be sure I knew what the conversation was about. The talk ran quickly and pleasantly, even though I was lost much of the time, especially when language would shift into French to please Marcos's friend Gilles, who spoke no Spanish. Marcos showed slides of his recent trips to Afghanistan and Central Africa. Then he put Nigerian music on the record player, and we all danced together and separately, each in our own way.

Well after midnight, three Spaniards and a Frenchman arrived. Traveling with them was the Frenchman's girlfriend, a stunning, light-skinned black woman who turned out to be from Trinidad. The group cast a somber spell on the party, and talk turned to politics in a way I felt more than followed. When the late visitors made ready to leave, they offered Ricardo, Ruth, and me a ride into town, where they were dropping off the Trinidadian woman. Along the way, we stopped at the Spaniards' rented house, which looked to have been converted from stables. We sat in a large white room hung with masks, and in an open-hearth fireplace at the center of the room, a smoldering fire gave off heat but little light. They produced glasses and bottles of Spanish wine. A mellifluous conversation unfolded in friendly tones charged with genteel hostility. I could see Ricardo grow tense and sit up straighter as he answered the Spaniards' slouching remarks. Their Castilian accents turned into pure music in my ears, and I imagined the strangers on Arabian stallions, trampling the local corn on their way to the sea. I could barely make out single words, let alone understand sentences, as if I witnessed the scene from under water. Ricardo sulked, and Ruth seemed locked in a metaphysical battle with these disdainful Europe-ans who wore cloth ponchos and tied back their long hair. One took out a guitar and played a melancholy ballad. No one paid the slightest attention to me, but finally the lead Spaniard looked straight at me and then over at Ruth and hissed in Castilian, "He doesn't understand a word we're saying, does he?" It was practically the only full sentence I had understood all evening. I answered quickly, "I understand a little." We left soon after, and I did not see Ruth and Ricardo again till I looked them up months later in Mexico City.

The next morning, a profound sense of filth and ignorance shadowed my hangover. I took a shower in the bathhouse and walked to Na Bolom for comfort, even though I knew it would be closed. I couldn't enjoy the quiet of Christmas Day. I went to the Olla Podrida and felt a kinship with the *viajeros* there but no connection with anyone in particular. What was I doing in this place where I understood nothing and felt like a lost child most of the time? At the hotel again, I wrote that I was hiding from myself: "Almost I'd like to pack up now & run home—as tho I had somewhere to return to. Could I return to Cleveland & draw the white sheets over my head. Good bit better to be a little lonely in Mexico" (12/26/79). I was feeling abundantly sorry for myself, not an unpleasant or unfamiliar sensation. The only thing to do was pack up and head to Huehuetenango, over the border in Guatemala, where I planned to settle down and study Spanish. At least then I might know something, though miles and mountains of my ignorance lay ahead of me still.

I hitchhiked as far as Comitan, the sweet colonial town in Chiapas on the border with Guatemala. Not a gringo in sight, or at least no one who did not speak Spanish fluently, and I felt like a "cow in the sea" (12/27/79) of this beautiful language. I drew myself, staring in the mirror of my hotel room, wondering how I could exist—traveling, smiling, invisible—and yet in love with Aimé Césaire's words I read in the *Montemora* magazine I carried about his return to the island of his birth: "And above all, my body as well as my soul, beware of assuming the sterile attitude of a spectator, for life is not a spectacle, a sea of miseries is not a proscenium, a man screaming is not a dancing bear" (15). Enough time pretending I was a doctor, a teacher, a poet, a brave traveler. Labels merely hid my inclination to look on, hang back, play the innocent army brat who just arrived with his family from their last posting. Yes, I had to learn, but I could not use ignorance as an excuse for disengagement. I was not training for my life anymore; this was my only moment on the planet. Had Sylvie convinced me that love couldn't exist without loss? Had she freed herself from me to move into her own life? I never wanted a muse, but perhaps I had asked too much of her and not enough of myself. My poetry would be made of these shards but also of the live world around me, cultures torn down and built again. I knew so little about Guatemala that I couldn't even imagine its landscape or the look of its people, but I would find out as soon as I got off the bus the next day. "This is an exile, but I want to embrace it" (12/30/79), I wrote soon after I arrived in Huehuetenango.

The military presence struck me first in Guatemala. Soldiers and police stood on every corner of little Huehue. Young men in fresh haircuts carried automatic weapons—sometimes two at a time—and wore combat fatigues and heavy boots. No mistaking the conditions on the streets. People passed by as though they had somewhere else to go, not scurrying or furtive but purposeful and internal. Only when I looked up from the guns could I see the astounding mountains, the beautiful Maya faces of the townspeople, the children shining shoes in the park for coins. As I grew used to the town in my first days, I began to feel its gentle patience, but the sustained poverty enforced by a ubiquitous army made Guatemala unlike anything I had seen before. I grew up seeing uniformed MPs with guns in Jeeps patrol my home, but in those days, soldiers were a source of comfort against the Cold War outside. These soldiers bared their teeth, displaying their undisguised aggression. I'd seen political graffiti on San Cristobal walls, but those slogans seemed abstract compared to the telegraphic messages here, equating the governing party with death or calling for unity with the Nicaraguan revolutionary Sandinistas. One message read: "*Solidaridad con el Pueblo Nicaraguense. Lucas y Somosa son la misma mierda.*" Even I could translate the sentiment: Solidarity with the Nicaraguan People. Lucas (the Guatemalan president at the time) and Somoza (the recently deposed Nicaraguan dictator) are the same shit. I walked out of town on a small mountain path, and a mile from the town, among corn planted in tiny plots on steep ground and shacks roofed in corrugated metal and fiberglass or tarpaper stapled over slats, helicopters passed regularly overhead. One didn't need a graduate degree to read the tension scrawled across this terrain. The government and the people were at war.

I started at the Proyecto Spanish Language School two days after I arrived. The school moved me in immediately with the Diaz family: a father and mother, five children, a very young woman as maid, and a two-month-old puppy. The family gave me my own room, while everyone else crowded into the rest of the three-room house. I was paying rent, and that mattered to this family, but they also welcomed me warmly, which was not the case for families of some other students in the school. I played with the kids when I was around, and clearly I was going to learn much of my language from them. During my first week, Francisco Diaz took me on his motorbike up to the small Maya "ruins" outside the town, a truly ruined site where United Fruit had years ago trapped original stones in modern concrete, creating an American-style family park you might encounter in rural New Jersey. They had, however, inadvertently neglected to destroy a secret ancient tunnel that started there and led to Quetzaltenango some fifty miles south. Francisco told me people hiding from the army occasionally escaped that way. The park did provide us a secluded place to talk candidly about the situation of his family and the town. From what I could understand of his careful Spanish, Francisco was a teacher up in the mountains some four hours away. He earned a small salary and was gone most of the week when school was in session, especially during rainy season when it was nearly impossible to drive the dirt roads home. One of his sons, Jorge, had developmental delays and physical limits from a difficult birth, but they had little money for medical expenses. Francisco tried to explain the politics of the country to me, but I followed him only well enough to know he was angry that the army had kidnapped many boys in his village. People in Huehue had disappeared in recent years too, and some had been shot on the street. He also tried to explain his evangelical faith but assured me that he would not pressure me about his Lord. Back in town, the family fed me on rice and beans and, occasionally, chicken. It was sometimes difficult to eat when I saw that the kids received less meat and more salsa. One day they proudly served me an egg over *arroz y frijoles*, but when I looked up, only the father also had an egg on his plate next to the rice and beans. I tried to give my egg to Jorge, but the parents discouraged me. My small housing fee contributed to the family's budget, and I decided to raise no more questions about how they divided the food.

My schoolmates at Proyecto were a fascinating collection of eager scholars. Some were simply *viajeros* bent on drifting farther south. Others were professionals who worked regularly with Spanish speakers and wanted to be more communicative in their jobs. Most came from the States—midwesterners or Southern Californians, especially—and had heard that Huehue was an inexpensive, low-pressured place to study. Some were college-age adventurers, like Bobby and Ted, two surfers from Los Angeles who wanted to follow the coastline as far as they could go. Others were five, ten, fifteen years my senior. A middle-aged Catholic priest named Charles had moved to the region a few years before, long enough to raise a three-hundred-pound pig named Sunshine and new piglets Sweetpea and Sugarbaby. A doctor named Susan, in her early thirties, worked with farm migrants raising apples in Washington State. I admired her quiet ardor for the job. She wanted to make her patients' lives better, and that meant fights with growers as well as with microbes. She made very little money in her clinic, but the passion for her patients' health clearly drove her. Her stories didn't call me back to medicine, but I could understand her choices in a way others could not. I was drawn to Susan but made no attempt to get closer. I couldn't possibly contemplate an intimate relationship, even if she might have looked at me as more than a directionless kid.

The staff of the school vigorously welcomed new students. Young and clever, methodical and funny, they showed an active curiosity about us but were undistracted in their role as cultural ambassadors. Unfortunately, they also felt aggrieved with their work situation. School policy discouraged students from using English during the day, but soon after classes began for me, I pieced together from brief English asides that our teachers hadn't been paid for at least a month. They were contemplating a strike, a serious decision in Guatemala. The government discouraged work stoppages of any kind, and such an action could bring down gun butts on their heads. The kindly American representative who spoke to me when I called from the States left the school within days of my arrival, and the American manager who acted as the representative of the school's ownership looked exceedingly nervous as the week went on. I was too untutored to catch the whispered Spanish at break, and the one-on-one sessions with my assigned teacher stuck strictly to fundamentals. I waited for what would happen next, and near the end of the week, the pay finally came through. For the moment, tension released and we all went out to play volleyball, where I learned my first Guatemalan slang.

Guatemala was a perfect place to learn Spanish. Native speakers enunciated so slowly and distinctly, far more lingering and courteous than the singsong and idiomatic Spanish of their northern neighbor or the rushed and consonant-starved accent of El Salvador and Nicaragua. Perhaps to a Spaniard's ear, Guatemalan speech sounds drawled and unsophisticated, but the Guatemalan manners provided just the learning speed I needed to discover all those little mysteries of tense and vocabulary I had longed for since I arrived in Merida. Every hour revealed some phrase I needed for a thought, some idiom for a common observation. All the drudgery of language drill in American classrooms vanished here in a country where I wanted to know everything and I understood nothing. My instructors and I went over grammar and usage exercises, but we also held real conversations that filled in blanks for me about soldiers on the corner and cultural habits in restaurants and bars. My new Huehue friends seldom cursed, and they looked at the world with a discretion that came from years of suppressed freedom. Because they didn't know me, my teachers didn't speak openly about politics, but they indicated with all their jokes and gestures that deeper secrets lay ahead if I proved myself trustworthy.

One student stood out for me as a congenial colleague. Bill Lamme refused adamantly to speak a word of English on school property or after classes ended, but even in Spanish I could tell he had a dry sense of humor and a deeper purpose. He hung out with Mindy, whom he had befriended in earlier weeks, and the three of us shared dumb beginner jokes in Spanish and hiked up to the ghastly United Fruit ruins. Mindy was going back to the States soon, but Bill was planning to head south, like me, to try to get work in the massive reconstruction effort in Nicaragua after the revolution. Unlike me, Bill had a skill they could use. Even through the screen of Spanish, I gathered that he had recently trained as an electrician and had at least some experience in factories repairing large machinery. I hoped to do some carpentry, but realistically I was probably better suited to teach English or science or math. Bill and I decided that we would drop the ban on English for one evening and go out and get to know each other well enough to decide whether or not to travel together.

We met on the *zocalo*, the town square where locals and tourists promenaded in the evening, and we walked over to a brightly lit bar, quite empty early in the evening. We were a bit of an odd pair: a short Jewish guy with uncombed curly hair and a tall blond WASP from Dayton, Ohio. We ordered the clear liquor of the place, "Indite Especial," distilled toilet bowl cleaner pretending to be vodka, and we started to tell each other our stories. First we discovered that we'd both gone to Cornell, Bill graduating in history two years before I transferred there. We took a drink and discovered next that I'd lived in the same apartment house he had three years earlier. Another drink and we realized we'd rented the same apartment and camped in the same tiny triangular bedroom. After these bonding revelations, our stories came tumbling out. He had been a conscientious objector during the Vietnam War and had worked with youth at a church in Iowa for his service. He'd lived in a communal house and helped raise a child collectively. Once he left Latin America, he thought he'd move to Chicago, where he would find factory work and join a leftist group whose organizing he admired. His politics were far better articulated than mine, but we agreed on the wretched history of American foreign policy and the rightness of the Nicaraguan revolution. He knew little about poetry or archaeology but seemed inclined to listen to me rant. By the time the *indite* tasted almost sweet, we had become friends. We decided we might as well travel on together when we'd finished our studies.

I developed the flu, and in the midst of my fever I had my first dream in Spanish. A circle of Spanish speakers surrounded me, quizzing me about a game I'd played in the States that involved cardboard boxes. I could describe the action, but I couldn't remember past tense and so felt awkward and stupid. I woke up still sick but with a sheepish pride that I'd at least tried to explain myself without resorting to English. Proyecto forced me soon afterward to leave the Diaz family because of some administrative change, and I moved to the somewhat more affluent home of one of my teachers, Julia. As a favor, I went to an evangelical meeting with Francisco Diaz and his family one night, and the shiny-suited pastor tried with his best lilting command—"*Pase adelante, joven!*" ("Come on down, young man!")—to invite me down to accept Jesus as my personal savior, but I wasn't moved. Francisco took solace in his religion and felt the Catholic church had abandoned him, his family, and his people. He also knew evangelicals heavily supported the dictatorship and the military. All public institutions seemed arrayed against the poor, but the poor stubbornly used available resources to survive with dignity.

In Julia's family home, I had a quieter room and more ample meals, but the atmosphere was more formal. Her husband, who supervised construction projects, treated me warmly but did not share much about his life with me. Their two little girls played in the enclosed courtyard of their house, as the Diaz kids had played in the dirt behind their kitchen door, but Julia's girls were shy with a stranger in the house. When one of the girls developed a mysterious fever, for the first time since I left medical school I chastised myself for not completing my training so I could treat a child. How self-indulgent I was for giving up a chance to help in Latin America! But the spell passed with her fever. I could barely remember how hard I'd tried to make myself a doctor, but enough traces remained to warn me I still couldn't go back.

I wrote more poetry in this new house, but I also began to understand enough Spanish to read newspapers. On January 31, soon after I moved, *campesinos* occupied the Spanish embassy in Guatemala City to protest army violence against them and their brethren in the highly contested northern area called El Quiche. The Spanish ambassador received the peaceful group sympathetically, but President Lucas called out the police and army, who stormed the building and set off a fire (debate still rages over its origins) that killed thirty-six people, including protesters, Guatemalan politicians, and embassy staff. The military blocked anyone from leaving the burning building. It seemed an outrage that would bring down the government, but instead Lucas and the generals tightened their hold on power. I went out to the school to see some familiar faces. I asked Julia and her wisecracking colleague Blanca about organizing a silent protest or poetry reading at the *zocalo* later that week. They thought the idea appealing but dangerous; I had never seen Blanca so quiet. They both recommended I speak to Yolanda, a teacher who usually taught more advanced students. Yolanda was a slender young woman with dark, frizzy hair and an immediate smile, but as she listened to me, her face remained cool. Perhaps the informal collective of language teachers might help sponsor it, she suggested, but she could not be involved. I could hardly believe what I understood her to say in Spanish. She'd spent a year hiding underground after her boyfriend was assassinated for helping to organize a miners' strike. She had shaved her head and lived as a boy, never staying more than a few days at any one house, and she still felt traumatized. Every time a policeman walked behind her in the street, paranoia nearly overwhelmed her. No, she could not help me with the rally.

I spent much of the next two days working on a long poem in response to the massacre:

> A woman carries her roll of cloth
> to market early, with every other shot
> of weft she had moved the sticks
> to make her pattern
> > Shall the sons
> of dollars break her body as
> they tear her cloth beneath their weight?

Alongside, I wrote a furious eight-page letter to my mother. Letters from home had been precious to me, and I usually enjoyed writing back, crafting a description that also gave my correspondent some sense of my state as well as of the complex and simple beauty around me. In this letter, I tried to settle into print so much that had been thrown into the air over the last weeks. I recounted my understanding of what happened at the embassy and translated what the right-wing newspapers described, with their talk of psychotic terrorists lighting themselves on fire. I related to her my fear that the United States would send troops to prevent a popular uprising, and I told her of my growing conviction that US poets should play a more active role in the world than as professors of literature: "Why shouldn't the women & men who have trained themselves in *subjective* observation be out in the world reporting back the downright evil our government has worked here & elsewhere? Objective analysis is such a wonderful cover behind which the perfect teeth of the greedy mouths can chew firebombed flesh" (2/3/80). But I warned myself in my journal that my rage mixed easily with personal grief and that in "the sense of exile I have, I [should] not confuse these griefs w/the ones I encounter here" (2/1/80). I needed to live in beauty as well as anger, reaching for the emotional clarity George and Mary Oppen had talked about in Maine.

Later, I met three teachers from Proyecto on the street. I asked them if they would help me organize a peaceful vigil, and their responses echoed the fear and paranoia Yolanda had described. One teacher, a leader among the staff, immediately tried to silence me and explained that such American ideas wouldn't work here. Pablo, the second teacher and one of our favorites because of his fiery attitude and brave pronouncements, immediately said, "Great idea! I'll bring the dynamite!" The third teacher mounted his bike and rode away without a sound. For the first time, their fear penetrated me. What if my passport didn't protect me, if my own government wanted to see me dead? For just a moment I felt truly afraid, the terror of unreasoning state violence. I did not yet understand a tenth of what I needed to write about this country, let alone act in its history.

Bill took off to visit friends in Antigua, near the capital. Yolanda and Blanca formed a small new school, and I followed them, though I stayed at Julia's house. Blanca was the best teacher I'd had in Huehue, and while she drove me through the remaining verb forms all the way to subjunctive, we also chatted incessantly. Spanish was becoming less like a blunt pointer in my hand and more like a work glove over my fingers—rough and ill-fitting but manipulable enough to pick up small objects. Through a day of instruction, Blanca joked, cajoled, and filled me in on stories of teachers we both knew. Occasionally she would whisper a bit of history, such as the story of the 1978 "Massacre of Pansos," when over two hundred men, women, and children were killed and buried in a mass grave. She showed me a picture of Yolanda's boyfriend marching at the head of miners carrying signs. He had been gunned down in front of his office, not far from the *zocalo*. But our chats were not largely political. I talked to Blanca about my marriage in the States and my doubts about ever having a relationship again. She scolded me that "love is in your veins" and hinted that Pilar was interested in my attentions. I had noticed Pilar, a young woman who still taught at Proyecto and was a widow with two small children. I fantasized about settling down with her in Huehuetenango, writing every day and making a living by translating or teaching English. I could barely understand her or her friends once social conversation whipped up into laughter outside the classroom, but love would teach me best, and perhaps not being able to talk so much would counter the complications of relationships up north. I was so lonely I could taste solitude in my mouth. Blanca urged me to speak to Pilar alone, but I never did. I stopped taking classes and spent my days writing in my journal and trying to read in Spanish, but I soon recognized it was time to leave Huehue. I had stayed nearly two months. Bill came back to town, and I said my good-byes to the Diaz family, Blanca, Yolanda,

Pablo, Pilar, and as many of the others as I could find. I had gained a sense of the language here, rooted in friendship and drama I barely understood. Though I was far from fluent, I was ready to be more than a student in Spanish. We climbed on the bus to Guatemala City, the next step toward Nicaragua *libre*.

I had seen very little of the country except the mountains north of Huehuetenango, and Bill hadn't seen much more. Though we were anxious to get started in Nicaragua, we decided to take a circuitous route and flew up to Tikal from Guatemala City. Tikal is a grand and massive archaeological site, and I could have spent weeks there drawing and studying the temples, but I was no longer driven to know the past as I had been on the first leg of my journey. Now politics gave dimension to everything, and even the monkeys and quetzals couldn't keep us in this ancient world dominated by contemporary tourists. Bill and I took an all-night bus from Tikal to the beach town of Livingston, bouncing around on potholed roads while we tried to sleep. Early in the morning, a military detachment stopped our yellow school bus and pulled everyone off. They had no interest in two hippie gringos, but they searched the Guatemalan men carefully and barked at them, pushing them around. Finally, the soldiers let us go without stealing anyone for service. We stayed in Livingston for nearly a week, resting up from our travels and studies and looking ahead to work in Nicaragua. I still had anxious dreams of swallowing parasites or witnessing murders, but by day Livingston treated us well. We shared meals with travelers from the States and Europe, some of whom were also hoping to work in the post-revolutionary reconstruction effort. We hung out with a Belizean who called himself Junior, and he told us much about black Caribbean history, so rooted in slavery and yet parallel to the oppression we had come to know in Guatemala.

Bill and I sang Beatles and Dylan songs, told stories about family and friends, and grew to trust each other. Our sensibilities complemented one another. Bill was as open a man as I'd ever met, but he wasn't much for describing his own emotional states. He found it curious that I wanted to talk about my feelings. He thought hard about politics the way I thought about poetry. We talked economics and culture when we were drunk or sober, over breakfast or on the beach, at communal dinners with Frenchmen and Swedes or squeezed next to sacks of corn in the back of old buses straining up mountain roads. I began to conceive of the book I wanted to write on this trip as being "an honest charting of politics over against poetry," not just about the Nicaraguan literary tradition but about "how or whether the investigative yearning & individual spirit of the poem can be found in a socialist revolution" (2/21/80). Bill warned me that a first book on so big a subject would need years to develop because I had to take so much history and personal struggle into account. But he did not dissuade me from dreaming and took my hazy ideas seriously. We both agreed that Marx and Lenin should not be read in the isolation of libraries but instead in study groups, preferably ones associated with organizing and action. He spoke Spanish better than I did, or at least I thought so, and we regularly challenged each other with new words or idioms we ran across in conversations or reading. Seeking work in Nicaragua would be a real test for us, and we wanted to be as ready as possible for the day we arrived.

From Livingston we traveled by boat, bus, and rattletrap minivan into Honduras, stopping off at Copan to see the ruins there. Few tourists made it to Copan, but the large heads and ornaments were lovingly carved. Part of me just wanted to stay and wander through this "lively intricate site, obviously a place of art & intellect" (2/24/80), this stark and controlled record of the past. But the gravitational pull toward Nicaragua had grown too strong. My time for scholarship and language preparation had ended; I needed to meet history unfolding now. We soon got back on the bus to Tegucigalpa, the last big stop before the Sandinista border. Once in the dense Honduran capitol, we met a street guy named Pedro who, after a beer and a meal, talked to us freely about the politics of his country. Honduras looked to be in less turmoil than Guatemala or El Salvador, but Pedro warned us not to be fooled. Assassinations and suppression of dissent happened here too, he said, but the corrupt government controlled resistance better. We needed to understand the Nicaraguan revolution in the context of Central American history, and each conversation opened up a new aspect of peoples' lived experience. Bill hung back to buy a paper when we were boarding the bus to Nicaragua, and as I settled into my window seat, I looked down to see an old woman selling *chicharrones* from a basket. Pigskin cracklings sold on the street lay at the far end of the kosher spectrum from my mother's shabbas chicken dinner on a Friday night. I gave the vendor a coin for a newspaper cone full of the crusty things, to test if I could eat them. Up close they stained the newsprint with grease from a thick layer of fat under the skin, and swine hair poked from the pitted surface. I took a bite and nearly vomited out the window. Even Bill, who could eat almost anything, could not finish a whole piece. We gave the rest to fellow passengers as the bus pulled out.

We arrived at the border of Nicaragua on February 26, only seven months after the Sandinistas had driven Anastasio Somoza Debayle out of power and declared a new government led by Sandinista Front (FSLN) leader Daniel Ortega and four others. The border resembled others we'd crossed, but a palpable national pride informed the proceedings. Many soldiers stood around with guns, but none yawned or scowled or stared off into space. Officials examined our papers carefully and searched our packs for contraband and weapons, but they were generally friendly, and no one expected a bribe. We were quite prepared to hug everyone we saw, and the many posters of Augusto César Sandino, Carlos Fonseca Amador, and other heroes of the revolution added to our excitement, but officials had seen enough enthusiastic foreign supporters that they merely welcomed us calmly and asked our business. Both Bill and I told them we were there to help the reconstruction, and no one questioned why *norteamericanos* would want to do such a thing. Within a half hour we were on our way to Managua.

Managua was a city still recovering from years of war on top of a devastating earthquake that had occurred in 1972. Soon after our arrival, I wrote in my journal that

> walking to the post office is like walking thru the country fields except that once every block or 2 a building still stands—perhaps w/its top floor ripped out, & certainly w/o windows. People live in these torn structures, squatters who have no place else to go. There are signs up for shoe repairs or small *tiendas* [shops] on buildings w/windows boarded up, or doorways still blockaded for military action. The cockroaches here are *bastante grande*, big as my thumb, but I haven't seen rats yet. (2/28/80)

Bill and I landed in a little *pensión* a mile or more outside the center of town, where many *extranjeros*, or foreigners, came to stay while they looked for work in the reconstruction. The Nicaraguans called us *extranjeros* rather than *viajeros* because the emphasis was not on how we got there but on where we belonged. We were no longer travelers; here we were strangers hoping to prove we could contribute. The *pensión*, an elaborate rambling shack reaching to a second story in some places, had grown like a series of afterthoughts. It looked like the owner just tacked on another room every time he needed to accommodate another paying guest. We shared a room with five others on cots and the floor. Jules, the French Red Cross worker, had his own room because he'd been there months already. The young German socialist reporter and his schoolteacher wife staked out a double bed separated from the rest of us by half a wall, but the hotel owner had given the Salvadoran Pedro a free week to give that bed up to them and sleep on the floor. Pedro didn't have much money anyway, and we all took turns buying him meals. Fifteen or eighteen guests used one bathroom, but the Victoria beer was cold after a long day of dragging from office to office only to find that yet another office had the form you really needed to apply for work.

And we all wanted to work. Some, like Bill, had real construction or technical skills they hoped to use rebuilding schools or factories or bridges. Others, like me, were primarily sympathetic intellectuals or curious travelers who were willing to carry bricks or paint walls or clear debris if we could contribute to the national moment. Frida from Sweden represented the nongovernmental agency Oxfam, and Tina from Stanford School of Education had long pursued her interest in teaching dispossessed people of Latin America. I wasn't sure how Ramon fit in, but he was certainly charismatic. He had been a leader of radical students in Spain during Franco's dictatorship and fled the country after a strike in 1968 when he feared he would be jailed or killed. He landed in Sweden, learned the language, and carried a Swedish passport. He casually cultivated a Leon Trotsky look: chin beard, wire-rimmed glasses, bald head. His fiery support of the Sandinistas and trenchant critique of Latin American dictatorship articulated what many felt, but his wry analysis of day-to-day problems in post-revolutionary Nicaragua sometimes bordered on the cynical. Bill didn't trust him from the beginning, but I thought Ramon was the most colorful character among us.

Our first days in Managua were quite glorious. The country was so small that it seemed you could meet anyone doing exciting national projects in the arts as well as economic development or plumbing. Bill and I visited offices of people we'd been told about either by Nicaraguan Solidarity groups in the States or by travelers we'd met along the way who had contacts in Managua. Most contacts met us coolly at first but warmed quickly when they saw we weren't arrogant Americans. One woman, a US citizen associated with the national film institute through her Nicaraguan husband, generously drove us up to see Volcano Masaya just outside town. As we stared down into the smoking throat from the crater's edge, watching sulfuric acid and water vapor rise in the air, I felt I had really arrived in this country I'd imagined since I left the apartment with Sylvie a few thousand miles ago. Bill and I went to the national theater for a concert and dance performance based on folk cultures around Nicaragua, and the next day we met the main singing group in a parking lot of the Ministry of Culture. Everywhere, people were talking possibilities. If people could rise up and throw off the Somoza family and drive out the generals, then they could remake the country into a place where work brought dignity and basic human survival would no longer define daily life. Despite the debris and ruin of war, the air itself seemed new. Little children would jeer at us on the street as we passed, calling out *"Fuera la CIA! Fuera la CIA!"* but once we told them we loved Nicaragua and hated the CIA, they wanted to know if we knew any baseball players on the Orioles of Baltimore. All politics aside, baseball was the favorite sport in the country, and the great Orioles pitcher Denis Martínez was a national hero because he was the first Nicaraguan to play Major League Baseball in the United States. Bill and I went to the opening day of the postwar baseball season. Fans cheered wildly for bunts and homeruns and booed balls and strikeouts, no matter what team made the play.

I took Bill to hear Father Ernesto Cardenal, one of the poets I most wanted to see on my trip to Latin America. Cardenal was the Nicaraguan poet best known in the United States. The poems of William Carlos Williams and especially Ezra Pound had influenced Cardenal during his two years studying literature at Columbia University. He'd meditated with Thomas Merton, the famous Trappist monk who wrote poetry and religious texts. But Cardenal was as deeply political as he was religious and artistic. He served as a member of the Sandinista leadership, much to the consternation of the conservative element in the Catholic church, who felt that a priest should not be associated with godless Communists. As the new Minister of Culture, Cardenal set out to use poetry, visual arts, music, and film to draw into the public sphere people who had never lifted up their voices before. The ministry hoped to use creativity and imagination to heal a society nearly destroyed by dictatorship and violence. He read a few poems that night, but mostly he talked about a place where he had worked in the south and showed some slides of paintings done by *campesinos* there. I didn't follow his lecture very well because he spoke Spanish rapidly, with the Nicaraguan tendency to drop consonants. Later I read in the paper that he was talking about Solentiname, the islands in Lake Nicaragua where Cardenal had helped establish a religious community based on the arts and social justice, a place despised by the Somoza regime. His work in Solentiname would be the model for Houses of Culture, centers where people could paint and write and make music that his ministry planned to sponsor throughout the country. I decided to interview Cardenal if at all possible. I would ask him many of the questions I had been asking myself about poetry and revolution. Perhaps I could publish the interview in a literary journal or in a political news magazine like *Mother Jones* in the States. In the little restaurant where we often took meals, a young man named Roberto told me he worked with Cardenal in the Ministry of Culture. He promised to arrange a meeting for me with Father Cardenal in a few weeks' time, and I filled my notebook with questions I wanted to ask the poet.

The Sandinistas, however, were understandably wary about who they allowed to help in the reconstruction. They feared subversion or sabotage, but even well-meaning outsiders might interfere with the community bonding among Nicaraguan people finding their own strengths. The crew of *extranjeros* we met seemed to pose no threat, but many lost patience quickly when they had to wait on line out in the sun for hours, only to find that the person they sought had gone home for the day. I myself chased all over town to find a gringo poet named Mark who worked for the ministry and was supposed to be in charge of vetting *extranjero* writers trying to work in the country. I waited for him three days in an office where he never showed up. When I finally caught Mark, I talked to him for over an hour. I learned the depth of commitment it would take to stay in the country as an active writer and the level of my ignorance about Marxist aesthetics and the history of Nicaraguan literature. Wherever we went, it seemed another bureaucrat had a reason to tell us no or ask us to stand on another line till the day was over. Bill went to factories to offer his services, but people were literally too busy to talk to him about what he could do. *Extranjeros* would gather at night in a circle on the concrete slab in front of our *pensión*, drinking beer and grousing about the day or arguing about what direction the government should take tomorrow. Frequently, young Nicaraguan men would join us to hang out and talk, but we guessed that many of them were simply keeping tabs on the strangers to see if any of us meant trouble. Ramon grew loud in his dissatisfaction with the red tape and the long lines. Bill and I avoided the gripe sessions, preferring to talk to Frida and Tina, who had better connections and thus more luck talking to officials about their projects. The two women focused on the difficult work the nation had to do and maintained perspective on the day-to-day annoyances.

I began to lose hope that I could find work, but I wanted very much to stay. I began visiting the national university regularly, hoping to find a sympathetic soul who would give me a job teaching English or maybe math and science. Finally, I decided to look up private high schools for foreigners' children and located an American school in a wealthy neighborhood. I walked miles to get to the compound, low beige stucco buildings surrounded by barbed wire. I managed to talk my way inside, and the headmaster agreed to speak to me. He was a corpulent man from Iowa, and he looked skeptical when I said I'd come to help in the reconstruction.

"What did you major in at *Cornell*?" He emphasized the college to let me know he didn't believe a thing on my rumpled résumé.

"Classics," I said.

"Oh, that's a useful major!" he said, looking away like an exasperated businessman on an American sitcom. I was taken aback. In the nearly four months I'd been away, I had become accustomed to people growing animated when I said I was a poet, but this man apparently agreed with my grandfather: no study mattered if it didn't lead to a respectable job or a professional title. Art and literature counted only to add a patina of culture to the economic man or nurturing woman. We talked a little more, and he allowed that he might need someone to teach biology if I were still around in September, and I thanked him for his time.

When I returned to the *pensión*, I was absolutely beside myself with rage at this philistine, this parody of an American academic, this dog trainer of diplomats' children. I sat in the circle of *extranjeros* in front of the hotel with my cold Victoria in my fist, ranting to Bill about know-nothing American educators and their disrespect for literature or social conscience, wealthy people who want their children "finished" in an American school. Bill let me go on until I was well into my second beer. Equally frustrated about the job search, he was ahead of me about the lesson we were learning.

"So when are you going back home?" he asked calmly.

"Not for years. Maybe never. If I can't get work here, I'll keep going south to Bolivia, but I'm not going back to a place where it's shameful to be a poet!"

"But that's why we have to go back. We can take our time, but really our fight isn't here, Eli. Don't you see? These people are rebuilding their own country. They took their country back from generals and capitalists. What are we doing for poor people in Chicago or Philadelphia down here? We've got to learn in Nicaragua, but our fight is at home."

Easy for Bill to say—his family had been in the United States for generations. Was the United States really my home? Yes, Aaron and John still listened to the trolleys roll by at night on Baltimore Avenue. Gil occupied the back room of his parents' house in the Philadelphia suburbs, recovering from yet another kidney transplant, editing *Paper Air*, and writing his unassailable poems. My mother lived alone in Maryland, working for the feds under President Carter. Ronald Reagan, RONALD REAGAN, might be her next boss! What would that mean for Nicaragua *libre* or for wars heating up in El Salvador and Guatemala? Sharon was an adult in college, distancing herself from Mom's pain. The kids at Neighborhood Journey School showed up every day at the abandoned hospital that served as their building. Sylvie had no doubt settled into her life without me. Carlos and Hilario and the others tied vines in Northern California while Paul yelled across the field that he wished some damn body would pay attention. Joel remained in Oakland, working with autistic kids and playing Renaissance music concerts on recorder.

I had traveled thousands of miles away from the people who knew me best. Where was my place, and what did I have to offer any country? I wrote in my journal:

> There is so much trudging to be done before I find a home (*Callate*, Mr. Frost)—but what is trudging & what is home? Every minute is a new lesson a new infinite world. I have forgotten whatever conception I once had of a home, but strangely a new more solid one is forming—even tho I am also becoming convinced that a home may be impossible for me to have. As always, writing seems v. difficult. (3/9/80)

I thought I'd come to Nicaragua to help the people in their reconstruction, but of course I'd come for my own. They were rebuilding a home, but the only tools I had for my own rebuilding project were my words, spoken and written, in Spanish and English, among friends as well as enemies and always alone. Bill's logic began to sink in. I noted in that same entry: "Nicaragua is a real country & not a radical dream" (3/9/80). If I could find productive work, fine, but I had to be honest about what I sought for myself. The next day, after a frank talk with the Spanish Swede Ramon and the Red Cross Frenchman Jules, I wrote:

> I realized how much work I do have in *mi proprio pais* [my own country]. . . . The Nicaraguan revolution is for Nicaraguans. They must indeed close themselves off from us, who excentuate [*sic*] the differences between the people here, ask the wrong questions & misunderstand the answers. That is not to say we can't know what a country is, but surely we can't know it in weeks or months, & we always see more of ourselves than of the inhabitants. (3/10/80)

I didn't regard the trip as a mistake—far from it—but I needed to recognize my role and gather my strength to go back both to my writing and the people I had left behind.

Bill and I decided that, if we weren't going to be able to find work, we'd better make an effort to see more of the country and learn what we could to take back home. We took a trip with the Swedish Oxfam worker Frida to the Pacific resort town of Poneloya, where we squatted for the weekend in a vacation house abandoned by Somoza sympathizers. The pool was empty and cracked, the garden overgrown, but we had three rooms and a kitchen to ourselves, with the beach beyond our tiled porch. The night we arrived, we met an old lean *campesino*, who came by to meet the *extranjeros* staying in the vacant house. He showed us a workbook the Sandinistas had prepared for the national literacy campaign scheduled to begin later that week. It had pictures and sentences and places for him to write his own words. He mentioned that the government had done this sort of campaign in Cuba after their revolution. This was the first time we'd looked at materials from the campaign up close, though we'd seen signs saying *"Puño en Alto / Libro Abierto"* ("Fist in the Air / Book Open") all over Managua. He couldn't wait for his teacher to arrive from the city so he could begin reading his book.

The next morning, I went for a swim early and walked back into our bedroom to find Bill in bed with Frida. It was quite reasonable; women we met usually fell for Bill and considered me a friend. I had actually been more attracted to serious Tina back in Managua, although I knew she poured all her attention into the schools of the New Nicaragua. We laughed about it and had a pleasant bus ride back to the *pensión*, but the incident shook me. I didn't blame Bill—how could I?—but I began to question myself once again, to wonder if I could ever sustain love with a woman. Was I too weak, or my desire too strong? Did my inability to settle in a place or follow an occupation mean I could never have a relationship? I admitted to myself that I missed my people, the ones who simply knew me. I wandered down into Managua. I had no letters at the embassy. At the central square, I witnessed young men and women—the *brigadistas* of the *alfabetización* campaign, some barely in their teens—massing for transport out to the field, the *campo*, in the total national effort to improve literacy. The *brigadistas* threw their pink or green backpacks full of books and teaching manuals on to buses and trucks. They shouted and sang with excitement, bursting with energy and joy in the same way women had the week before at the first International Women's Day since the revolution. People in this country had begun to feel they could solve their own problems.

I turned away from the trucks and started drawing the cathedral across the square, with a giant flag of Sandino hung over its ruined face. I felt sorry for myself and embarrassed about my petty concerns, but at the same time I was elated by the immense optimism of the campaign. Sixty thousand youth and professionals flooded out to the *campo* to teach reading and writing where schools had been forbidden or shuttered during the four decades of rule by the Somoza family. A census had determined that over 50 percent of the country's population was illiterate, 30 percent in urban areas and 75 percent in the rural regions. Could this army of *brigadistas* really make any difference? While I sat there in a little park beside the square, three small children came up behind me and watched me draw. They wanted to know what I was doing there. One little girl had no nose because she had been caught in an explosion during the war. I handed them my notebook, and each drew pictures of people riding in trucks or flags and drums from the military parade. The girl with no nose wrote her name and a few other words, the others managed some letters. They all wanted to write in my book. Teaching required a direct, intimate connection.

I made a day trip by myself to Masaya, the little town with a reputation for its strong folkloric tradition as well as its historical role in the revolution. In 1978, an insurrection arose there in an indigenous neighborhood called Monimbó and sparked much nationalist resistance to Somoza and his Guardia Nacional. I sat in the market, drawing the women who sold mangoes and meat, and I marveled at the bullet-ridden walls and the blasted buildings cordoned off with barbed wire. In Masaya, I realized I needed a longer trip away from the bureaucrats and politics of Managua. When I returned to the *pensión*, Bill wanted to stay for one more attempt at employment in the city, so I planned to catch a bus by myself to Bluefields, Nicaragua's Atlantic coast town. At breakfast, I ran into Roberto, my contact at the Ministry of Culture, who told me he'd arranged an appointment for me with Cardenal on the following Monday morning. I left Managua with a sense of connection between my personal path and Nicaragua's direction that I had lost waiting in all those lines in the sun.

On the bus were two other people I knew from the *pensión*. One was Ramon, now openly bitter about employment with the reconstruction and ready for some time at the beach. The other was Anna, a slender American woman with very short hair, who had recently arrived at our hotel but didn't hang out with the other *extranjeros*. We rode the bus separately, but at El Rama we changed to a boat called a *panga* to travel the rest of the way down the Rio Escondido to Bluefields. On the *panga*, we three got to talking and decided to find a hotel together once we arrived. Ramon spoke Spanish fluently, of course, but with an accent that Nicaraguans didn't always understand, which noticeably frustrated him at times. Anna spoke Spanish no better than I, but she had been traveling in Latin America much longer and moved with confidence. Together we walked up from the dock to a narrow, steep street lined with modest *pensiónes*, and we found rooms at one that were both reasonable and clean. That night we went out together to a cheap but generous restaurant and talked long into the night about the revolution, travels, and home. Willie Nelson, Loretta Lynn, and Charlie Pride populated the jukebox, with a few reggae hits thrown in, so steel pedal guitar served as a soundtrack for our spiraling conversation.

Ramon told us more about how he had been hunted in Spain by the secret police after the student uprisings, how Sweden had taken him in and counterculture friends had made a place for him in a commune outside the cities. He spoke harshly about the Sandinistas, and we argued about his rejection of their plans and tactics—he seemed to want both more socialism and more license in a country not yet cooled from war—but he was so worldly and clever that he sounded more like an idealist trying to be hard-boiled than a radical shocked into reactionary politics. Anna remained circumspect about Nicaragua and had not come to seek work in the country. She had flown from California to Chile and for six months had been moving up the South American continent and through Colombia into Panama and Central America. She traveled largely alone, and she told amazing stories about adventures she'd taken by herself that I would not have ventured with a friend. Many *viajeros* have a specific enthusiasm or an idiosyncratic preoccupation, but Anna appeared to be motivated by a curiosity not limited to politics or music or drugs. She did tell some funny stories about manipulating billboards and radio for progressive messages in San Francisco, but she didn't seem particularly focused on journalism or media in Latin America. Wherever she traveled, she remained a *viajera* and not an *extranjera*, a traveling but not displaced foreigner. She simply wanted to know whatever she could about the places she visited.

The next day, Ramon disappeared early. In the morning, I worked on questions for the Cardenal interview. Anna and I took a walk into the countryside late that afternoon, and I told her more about Sylvie than I had told any woman other than my sister. Anna had been through

rough times with relationships as well. We talked particularly about differences in cultures across the Americas, and I described the individual language of the poet and the communal language of revolution that I wanted to ask Cardenal about. We found ourselves at a party back in Bluefields, a public benefit for the literacy *brigadistas* who had just arrived to take up residency in town for the next few months. Bluefields was larger than Livingston, but like the Guatemalan town it was predominantly black and mestizo, with much English spoken along with the native Miskito and various Caribbean dialects. Because you could reach the town only by plane or *panga*, it remained rather isolated from the rest of the country. Fighting had been relatively light there during the revolution. However, Somoza had done little to improve Bluefields from its original days as a pirate base and a Caribbean port, and its open sewers announced the lack of public services inhabitants took for granted. Though they seemed less enthusiastic about the Sandinistas than people in the interior, townspeople were clearly pleased about the literacy campaign. Once we paid our entrance fee, the fiesta was on: yucca and plantain, arroz con pollo, chorizo and beans, and much Victoria beer. Five dark-skinned musicians, some wearing dreds, played country-western music with a decided reggae beat. Young Nicaraguan men flocked around Anna, and I found myself eating and drinking alone most of the evening. At one point, the band struck up Kris Kristofferson's "Help Me Make It Through the Night." It was a small gathering, and I felt a swelling affection for the song.

> Yesterday is dead and gone
> And tomorrow's out of sight
> And it's sad to be alone
> Help me make it through the night.

I considered pushing my way up onstage and taking the mike, but when I went through the lyrics in my head, I realized I had never known all the words. Humming crucial lines would have made me an even uglier American.

The next night, Ramon, Anna, and I went out to the only large dance club in town. We sat down at a round table and ordered drinks, but while we were taking in the scene, a scruffy-looking pale man in a trench coat came to our table and sat down abruptly. He asked us what we were doing in Bluefields and demanded to see our passports. His aggression surprised us, and Anna asked him politely in Spanish who he was. He pulled out a gun and put it on the table. *"Somos el Pueblo!"* ("We are the people!") he declared. We didn't have passports with us, and he said he'd follow us back to the hotel. Suddenly, a chubby mestizo man in casual clothes joined us, and a tall young man of African extraction trailed the group. Back at the *pensión*, the pale officer set up in Anna's room to interview each of us in turn. They called Ramon in first. While we waited, the chubby man chatted with us on a porch outside our rooms, while the young man stood guard at the top of the stairs. The friendly official explained with a smile that he was a political agent while his partner was with the secret police. But our friend didn't exactly act the good cop. He pretended to tear up my traveler's checks, and he continually poked Anna as he stood beside her. When Anna asked what they were going to do with us, he answered in a pleasant tone: *"Ustedes van a morir esta noche"* ("You are going to die tonight"). I was near tears, and I tried to explain how we had come to help in the reconstruction and meant no harm to the new country. I was more upset by the idea that Sandinistas could see us as enemies than I was about the threat, which didn't seem credible. Still, if he had been joking, he wasn't funny.

The officer dismissed Ramon quickly, and our Swedish companion went off to his own room in a foul mood. Anna went in and stayed for a very long time. I wanted to write in my journal, but they wouldn't let me go to my room. When Anna came out, they told me to step in. I was worried my Spanish wouldn't hold up, but I found that danger focused my mind. I understood nearly everything the officer said, and I managed to form sentences well enough to make myself understood. It seemed Anna and I were in no trouble, but they had strong suspicions that Ramon was an agent for the CIA. The police had evidence that he'd run a shipment of guns to a group of anti-Sandinista resistance fighters called the *contras* on the northernmost tip of Nicaragua's Atlantic coast. I couldn't quite believe what the disheveled man was saying to me, but I felt sure I was hearing the words correctly. How long had I known Ramon? What had he been doing in Managua? I couldn't tell him much, but he seemed largely uninterested in what I said anyway, which was a relief. Finally, the officer shuffled through my passport and said they were just trying to protect the revolution from outside threats. The United States was arming a force to the south and the north, and more war was coming. They did not suspect Anna or me, but we should return to Managua immediately and avoid further contact with Ramon or they would begin to scrutinize us, too. All three policemen left with barely an adios.

Anna told me later that the pale officer had cried to her in the room. He described years in the hills, fighting the *guardia* and growing more embittered as he witnessed Somoza's brutality. He wondered if he would ever be able to have a normal life, if he could raise children with all the hate and suspicion he held inside. All he had was the revolution. The war ended for everyone else, but he would go on fighting to keep what he fought for alive. The reconstruction must occur inside the heart of each fighter, of each mother who had lost a son, of each child who had seen his or her parents murdered. He detailed the shipment of weapons that Ramon supposedly delivered and accounted for the days Ramon was in the northern jungle before he arrived in Managua pretending to be an *extranjero* in search of work. We felt sick about the accusation. If what they said were true, Ramon had lied to us and used us to cover an evil plan. If false, the secret police had made a terrible mistake that revealed incompetence masquerading as paranoia. In either case, we could do nothing but leave town. The *panga* didn't push off till afternoon, so Anna and I joined a group of innocent travelers in the morning on a jaunt across the bay to a beach known as El Bluff. I floated in the waves and let them break over me again and again. I tried not to think about anything for a change, and for a change I didn't.

When I returned to Managua, I told Bill the whole story, though I decided not to tell others at our *pensión*. Anna and I barely spoke on the *panga*, each of us staring out at the jungle as we motored by. Ramon didn't take the same boat back, and I spoke only a few words to him again when he did return. Bill didn't believe the story about Ramon and chalked it up to overanxious cops in exile from the center of action, but soon enough none of us could think about our own small dramas. That Monday morning, the day I was supposed to interview Ernesto Cardenal, we woke up to reports that the Salvadoran archbishop Óscar Romero had been assassinated in a small chapel while he was saying Mass. Everything stopped. For Nicaraguans, this atrocity recalled the

1978 murder of Pedro Joaquín Chamorro, the courageous editor of the leading opposition paper, *La Prensa*, shot to death in his car because he spoke out against the dictatorship. For *extranjeros*, the enormity and boldness of the crime shocked us once again into recognizing the desperate nature of the struggle in Central America. Already there had been rumors that the Sandinistas would register all *extranjeros* and ask most of us to leave within a few weeks. I ran into Roberto at the neighborhood restaurant, and he told me Father Cardenal had been called away to the archbishop's funeral. Perhaps we could schedule the interview for another time in the near future? Later I went to the university, hoping that a job teaching English would finally come open, but the university was utterly locked up and deserted. Everyone had gone to the *campo* to teach reading and writing to the people.

Bill and I saw no reason to stay. We could see that the *contras* were indeed arming in the north and south, and Nicaraguans had more to do than find work for Americans, no matter how much we were on their side. We got on a bus at seven in the morning and didn't stop again till five thirty the next evening in Esquipulas, Guatemala, just beyond the borders of Honduras and El Salvador. For the next two weeks, we traveled separately and together around Guatemala, ending up in Hue-huetenango to see our friends again. Our trip to Nicaragua seemed to make us more trustworthy to our Guatemalan friends, and they spoke to us with an honesty we had not known when we were students in the town. Pablo, our fiery *compañero*, had grown dangerously restless, wanting to join the guerrillas in the mountains but not able to leave his family. Instead, he had become less disciplined and wilder. A few weeks before we returned, he'd gotten drunk in a bar and denounced the government; fifteen men took him out back and beat him nearly to death. Julia, who had always been pleasant but restrained when I lived with her family, admitted to me that her cousin had been kidnapped by a death squad and found recently with multiple breaks in both arms, burnt fingers to obscure his prints, and a crushed skull. His name had been linked to a car under investigation in Guatemala City, though it was undoubtedly another person with the same name on the registration. But all the news wasn't bad. Pilar had found a new man. I was happy for her and her children and not unhappy for myself. Blanca and Yolanda continued to run their school, picking up the overflow from the original Proyecto. Yolanda managed to get money together to visit a former student in Quebec, and her friends organized a big party to send her off.

Before we left Guatemala, we took a trip up to Nebaj, a town in the mountains northeast of Huehue. There we discovered an entirely silent population. Late in the evening, when we managed to talk to a Canadian who lived there with his Guatemalan wife, we learned a massacre had taken place in Nebaj a few weeks before. A group of women had gathered in front of the army barracks to call for the return of their husbands and sons, who had been detained for no cause. The army opened fire and killed the assembled women, then trucked their bodies away. Guatemala too was no place for us if we weren't willing to stand and fight.

We traveled together over the next weeks to Palenque, Cuernavaca, and Oaxaca and ended up in Mexico City. One of Bill's parting gifts to me was a visit to a family I'll call the Seisses. Albert Seiss was a New York Jew who had married Anya, a Guatemalan working in the States, and they settled in Mexico in the 1940s. Because they had established themselves as Mexican writers and translators at the time of the McCarthy era, many writers who chose exile over persecution in the United States gravitated toward the Seisses' home. Bill knew of them through lefty connections in Chicago, and they welcomed us warmly to a meal at their large wooden dining room table one evening. From Albert and Anya we heard many stories about Dalton Trumbo and other blackballed film writers as well as lesser-known poets and novelists hounded by the anti-Communist hysteria. Finally, I couldn't contain myself any longer. I asked Albert if he knew George and Mary Oppen when they had settled in Mexico, running from the FBI and the witch hunts. Albert looked at me with surprise and said, "Know them? Why, George built this dining room table!"

Finally, Bill had to return to his new life in Chicago. We said good-bye at the airport, but it wasn't a sad parting. We knew we'd see each other again. We had become brothers through struggle, laughter, song, and language. He was wise where I felt foolish; I appreciated what he sometimes didn't notice. He helped me see politics in paving stones and economics in tortillas. I helped him see that literature and the arts are intimately inscribed in a people's destiny. We had lived and traveled together imperfectly in Spanish and English almost continually for five months. We had discussed women and love, murder and power, ancient temples and factory electrification. When we tripped on mushrooms on the hills outside Palenque, we'd barely avoided being trampled by a herd of cattle because Bill noticed the bull's hostility while I was philosophizing about the nature of roads. Bill let me cry over Sylvie and did not turn away. We have visited each other, later with our families, regularly for more than thirty years.

I stayed in Mexico City another two months, renting an incredibly cheap room at the top of the Gran Hotel Cosmos near the Bellas Artes at the center of town. I bought a portable typewriter, found an English language bookstore, and wrote and read every day. I produced poems, articles about Nicaragua and Guatemala, and letters home. This was what I loved; this was what I came to do. Despite my desire for action and worldly contact, I also needed a small, quiet space for measured words. Some days I didn't leave the hotel room after coffee in the morning until I ventured out at night for *enchiladas verdes* at my favorite joint in an adjoining neighborhood. Other days I went out at lunchtime for the businessman's special that gave you a full three-course meal for a few pesos, and then I'd work till eleven and get a plate of tacos at the corner before bed. I sent a few poems out to magazines, feeling I finally had finished work to publish. At last I possessed a stable address for correspondence, and news from the States started drawing my mind to family and friends. I also had a mirror in my room, something I hadn't been around for many months. I would read a short story by Doris Lessing or a chapter on European history or a passage from *Marxism and Literature* and then stare into that mirror. I no longer looked like a boy, and I thought I could detect my father's father's lips. The grandfather who would not let his son be buried in Arlington with the *goyim* had the thirsty lips of a scholar under his beard.

An acquaintance in Philadelphia had told me to look up a poet name Raul, whom she knew in Mexico City. Raul invited me to join a group of poets who called themselves Liberta Sumaria. Eight or ten men and women met to share poems each Friday evening in a rented room across town. I understood a little better than half of what they said, and that was enough to feel nearly part of the group. As in other places I traveled, poets in Mexico weren't particularly associated with universities. In this circle of well-educated writers, there were accountants and bureaucrats and travel agents and bankers. Their poetry sounded accomplished, at least to my partially acculturated ear. Only Raul and one other member of Liberta taught at UNAM, the national university, and the other person taught anthropology rather than literature.

Now and then, loneliness nearly paralyzed me. However, more often I could release the self-pity and enter aloneness, a place that allowed me passion and integrity, admitted the desire for human contact, but barred the desperate need for others. Then I felt tremendous joy at my freedom. I encountered art and archaeology in museums and galleries as if they were messages from planetary peers. I sought out murals by Siqueiros, Orozco, and Tamayo all over the city and visited with reverence the Blue House of Frida Kahlo and Diego Rivera in the Coyoacán borough. I would not be in Mexico much longer, and every moment felt as precious as the new air in Nicaragua on our first days there.

I went to a German movie called *Messer im Kopf* with Ricardo and Ruth, the couple I'd met months and a revolution ago in San Cristobal de las Casas. We all laughed on the walk home when I realized I'd missed a main plot twist because I mistranslated a Spanish subtitle and thought the main character was on trial for writing in his journal: "If I were an American, I would jump from this window." Instead, the movie involved the prosecution of the man as a terrorist for writing: "If I were an American, I'd shoot a gun from this window." Although my Spanish remained unreliable and my college German hadn't survived Latin America, my ease with the language had nonetheless grown without my noticing. For instance, I gave a lecture on William Carlos Williams to a literature class taught by my poet friend Raul. I must have sounded like an intelligent *burro* speaking mock Spanish, but they listened politely—without the sniggers or sneers I feared—to my disquisition on the modernist American drama of abrupt line breaks and everyday images such as plums and wheelbarrows. I shared my poems in English and Spanish in my final meeting with Liberta. They liked the one Spanish translation and what they could understand in English, with the exception of a poem I'd written featuring a jaguar as well as a stone knife plunging into a sacrificial victim's chest. "Every Mexican writes a poem like that," one friend warned me. "Aztecs are so overdone."

I considered going to the Pacific coast to write for another six months, but the money was finally running out. I had traveled eight months on less than three thousand dollars, but now I had to get a job in Mexico or go back to the States. Philadelphia called me. Aaron and John had moved into a big house in Germantown, not far from Sylvie but far enough to be safe. They said an apartment was available in the house next door to them. Gil lived nearby and might eventually move in, too. The Phillies were making a run for the pennant.

I unexpectedly started a relationship with a French woman named Rose, who stayed down the hall from me, and suddenly I could imagine having love in my life again. She did not despise me for wanting her and, despite the holes in our shared languages, we managed to talk without much misunderstanding. Rose owned a pharmacy in a small French town and offered to support me while I wrote if I wanted to return home with her. I was tempted and grateful for her kindness, but we both knew this wouldn't happen. Rose left for Acapulco, and we parted without bitterness or regret. I wrote in my journal, "But to see the world w/love in it, even if I wasn't exactly in love myself, that was a pleasure" (7/12/80). As that sweet interlude ended, an affidavit for my divorce arrived in the mail. I signed it and sent it back with more relief than sadness. My mother came to visit. We traveled by bus to Oaxaca and then visited my sister in Cuernavaca where Sharon was studying Spanish for a month with a boyfriend my mother didn't like. In my journal I noted a dream from that time. I was preparing to give a reading in an old Mexican city, "but when I looked down on the neatly typed pages, the poems were all in German translation—I had forgotten to keep the originals in English" (7/22/80). My old life had begun to mix with my new one, and though I hadn't really worked out what I would do back in Philly, I decided to go home.

## 10

## High Five at Second Base

TUG MCGRAW THREW THE final strike of the 1980 baseball season, and the Phillies won the World Series against the Kansas City Royals. I had returned from Mexico less than three months before and taken up my old job as a science and math teacher in a new incarnation of Neighborhood Journey School, now called Neighborhood Academy. The morning after the Phils won, teachers took attendance to make the day official, and then the principal let the school go. We joined the throng striding down Market, past Drexel University and 30th Street Station, to City Hall and the parade on Broad. Philadelphians of all persuasions and hues, unused to a championship team of their own, came out to yell and whistle and slap strangers' hands. It wasn't the Nicaraguan revolution, but it felt all right in the moment. Side by side with teens from a hundred schools, office workers, housewives, and retired firemen, I walked joyfully toward Center City. My brother, our friend John, and I hadn't followed sports since we were kids, but the city accepted us nonetheless.

When I took up teaching again after encountering revolution in Nicaragua and death squads in Guatemala, I slowly became committed to the occupation as a profession, if not a calling. I decided I should actually learn something about pedagogy and realized that others had in fact thought about education before me. I enrolled in a master's program for secondary education in biology at Temple University. The courses weren't challenging, but a young graduate student showed up at my school regularly and recorded everything he saw going on in my classroom. His detailed observations amazed me, and his careful debriefings demonstrated what reflective practice could mean. Anthony, the principal of Neighborhood Academy, challenged me—as my foreman Paul had done on the vineyard—to pay attention and take responsibility for my practice (Goldblatt 10–12). These and other colleagues hastened my transformation into a teacher who had a stake in his students' thriving and not just a claim on their daytime hours.

Once I was back in the classroom, I began asking myself in earnest what subject I wanted to teach. Although it took me six more years to settle on composition and rhetoric—a discipline new to English studies at Wisconsin when I went there to study American Modernist poetry in graduate school—my return from Latin America initiated the slow shift from science and math to writing. One day when I was preparing a lesson on atomic structure, I happened on a newspaper article describing quarks. I'd heard about these tiny particles that researchers identified as the building blocks of the heretofore "basic" protons and neutrons. The notion of quarks came along after I graduated college, and so I'd never studied them. I was curious, but the whole *mishigas* annoyed me: quarks possessed color charges and came in flavors like "charm" and "strange." It was all too absurd! Why mess up my neat lesson with "hadrons" and "antiparticles" when my kids had trouble enough telling an electron from a proton? Between the papers I had to grade and the poems I wanted to write, I didn't have time for such nonsense. But soon I began to listen to myself. That know-nothing impulse shocked me, and I recognized that, even if I feared teaching what I loved most, I had to learn continually or choke over dead material. After a year or two, all the hot little facts I learned in medical school would grow cold, and then what enthusiasm could I bring to science? I would die in the classroom if I didn't love the material I set before the kids. I needed to teach a subject I wanted to read about in journals, and certainly I wanted to read poetry journals more than *Scientific American*.

I met Wendy Osterweil in the late spring of 1981 on the dance floor at a house party in West Philadelphia. From our first phone conversation the next day, we talked freely about art, teaching, and Latin America. She was a dedicated artist whose studio work woke me up to the visual again. She liked a whole new set of artists I had not known before, and the bold imagery of Käthe Kollwitz, Antonio Frasconi, and Gabriele Münter challenged what I had learned of art from abstract painters like de Kooning and Franz Kline, whom I had studied alongside the New York poets I admired. She stood up to my pontifications, too. After a particularly brilliant rant I delivered in her studio that year, she looked at me calmly and said, "Eli, you can't browbeat me into liking what you like." I had to start learning new ways of seeing from her if we were going to share our enthusiasms. I needed to trust her enough to listen on a new frequency and perceive color as music I hadn't heard before.

Wendy prints on paper and dyes fabric, layering impressions in fluent reds and pod purples and dream forest textures, an enactment of composing far more dramatic than drafting in a writer's room. In graduate school, we would meet in her campus studio late in the evening, after I had spent hours in the library and she had worked all day on prints. We'd warm soup on a hot plate, eat crackers, and talk. She'd show me successive proofs of her latest prints. Proofs reveal a composition in form and color coalescing through multiple reimaginings, and her work helped me identify what mattered most to me of what I read and wrote. Her literacy with media and techniques reached toward an immediacy of affect and sensation that made my poems seem clumsy and my theoretical arguments cloudy and self-serving. Together we wanted more than virtuosity from our art. We wanted what George Oppen had called clarity.

We've grown together as teachers on a parallel path with our art. We talk over class plans and share stories of students' triumphs and misadventures. After faculty meetings in one or another of our departments, we exorcise the demons of turf battles or senseless feuds. We help each other find the nub experience in a class session that lies beneath the information load and "content" of a curriculum. Not until I read John Dewey on art, democracy, and education did I realize that we had been at his progressive project together for years. The Deweyan sense of learning by engaging in common activity with others extends to our geographic location as well. Wendy grew up in the Philadelphia area, and entering her large family helped me accept the city as my own. In fact, she accepted much about me I assumed no one would notice, let alone love, and her attention released me to trust our physical setting, to accept that no higher authority was going to order me off to a new post far away. Literacy in a city means you know its neighborhoods like a vocabulary and its history like a syntax. A city's characters shuffle in infinite permutations, but its drama is continuous and stable within the daily rhythms. Although we've left for months or years now and then, we've lived and worked together in northwest Philly since we met.

Our son, Leo, regards Philadelphia as his hometown, and that alone is worth paying city wage tax all these years.

Without the writing, I doubt I could have settled in a place as a husband and parent. The poems and journals gave me my first tenuous hold on fluid forms during my teens and twenties. Working with my hands seemed to offer me solidity, and science supplied a stable sense of the world for a time. I seized on teaching at first as an alternative way to make a living, but it has grown into a mode of being. Yet my writing continues to shape and be shaped by my inner life. Quite often, the key to writing well is hammering out a viable support network so that you have sufficient time and peace to keep the writing alive. Poets especially face this problem, assuming they do not have trust funds or unflagging patrons. Beyond the challenge of earning daily bread, the greater challenge for poets lies in finding a place to contribute and belong. Teaching emerged as the most congenial occupation to sustain me so that I didn't have to depend on writing as a way to pay the rent. My trip to Central America convinced me that I needed a profession that spoke to the needs of disenfranchised people, and I decided teaching could be that for me if I dedicated myself to the right school and the right population. What I hadn't anticipated is that teaching would meld with writing to clarify and sharpen the differences and similarities between working with students and addressing readers. I had no intention of mixing poetics with pedagogy, but along the way, my clearly drawn lines blurred and my neatly plotted boundaries no longer made meaningful distinctions.

In large part, my drive to read and write grew initially from an early ambition to be known. My father hadn't been widely recognized for his work when he died, and as a young man I looked back on that service medal the army gave him as a pale remembrance of all he'd done for the military. Like many young poets, I sent out my first batch of poems to the *New Yorker* because I grew up with the magazine so many middle-class people admired. I wanted people I knew to see my poems and admire me, even if they didn't understand what I wrote. Later, I began to put that individual ambition into a more collective context that guides my work as a writer and educator: writing and reading grow from and create relationships with people, living and dead. Writing connects me to distant authors, to my own father and others our peripatetic life left behind, and to the quickly flying present I want to encounter. I write to belong, and every piece of writing defines the threads by which we connect with others across time and space. One is clearly always alone and never alone within a written text. Human conversation fostered by media such as print or symbol, moving image or sculptural form, envelops us in relationships even as the media themselves seem to block face-to-face exchange. The challenge is to find a purpose more valuable than self-justification or solipsistic tautology in the metaphor of literacy as relationship.

Some of the stories I've told in this book may seem to have little to do with literacy. I'd have to write a second book to trace literacy fully in my narrative, but in this chapter I want to linger over three themes I recognized in the telling. The story of my love for writing hasn't ended, but I pause in 1980 because that moment marked the beginning of new loves that complicated the plot. Through the 1980–81 school year, I grew increasingly more serious about teaching as more than a job. I met Wendy the following spring, and our relationship radically widened my sense of how two people could trust and share their lives. Teaching and loving again in Philadelphia forced me to see the city as more than the latest post in my journey. Philly became my hometown, and as I settled in a place, to be a writer no longer seemed a distant honor I could never earn. I had been writing seriously for ten years. Though I had published barely a handful of poems and only my friends knew my work, by August 1980 I felt I'd finished my apprenticeship and, in matters of the craft, considered myself a journeyman. I didn't need a Pulitzer or even a book to prove I wrote; I just needed to keep writing. The three themes below––the individual and collective nature of text, the materiality of language, and the desire for human connection that words embody—combine to form a conception of literacy both bound and animated by relationships.

## Writing the Individual, Reading the Collective

When I first started writing poetry seriously in college, I took out a long-term mortgage on the isolated writer myth. Blake and Keats served as my historical geniuses; Pound and Williams updated the tale. John Berryman, the first live poet I saw, represented in his drunken persona a compelling internal struggle with words and emotion that seemed to me noble and genuine, precarious and mystic. I wanted to join the tradition, and that drove me to look backward. My art, I thought, compelled me to master the literature, to know who used certain images and told what stories. Indeed, I held myself responsible for the language itself. As a displaced kid from army schools, I felt uneducated and therefore low-class entering a suburban junior high. I didn't know about negative numbers and couldn't handle grammar or spelling the way better-dressed kids in the upper tracks did. I didn't even know what color socks to wear. No matter what recognition I gained in high school, no matter how many wrestling matches I won, the fear that I'd be found out as shallow and ill-taught shadowed any achievement and recalled the shame I felt when my lack of Hebrew disqualified me from mourning my father properly. In college, I worried about mispronouncing a name or misapplying an idea. I built a nest of books and records and pipe tobacco in my college dorm room, defending myself against any charges of ignorance, reassuring myself that I belonged among the clan of scribes. I imagined poets scattered over languages and time but united in the sacred pursuit of the poem. I wanted to join the hunt.

At the same time, however, I understood that the poet needed a unique vision and a distinct language. My language needed to be mine alone, even though I knew very well that words carried histories and could not be owned. I was constantly testing myself to see if I could compose alone. As I started college, I adopted two inflexible strictures to govern my spoken and written behavior:

- *Better to write like Catullus in American English than to sound like Frank O'Hara in his own language.* This left my poetry truncated and half-expressed, lest lines or images look too much like a poem I admired. I wanted the concision of dream but also its unresolved quality. At first my lines seemed merely cryptic, avoiding the cadences of Williams or H. D. or Hart Crane or anyone else I was reading. My prose became hopelessly muddled as I resisted formulas or common organizing patterns. At times, my few readers must have thought I was translating from another language. To some extent, I was.

- *Better to struggle articulating a complex position than to utter the obvious.* This led me into silence or incoherence in undergraduate classes and emptied my academic papers of examples or concrete instances on which my general statements could draw. I knew how to write more coherently, but I did not want to be found out for a dope.

Perhaps my only hope as a college writer was my mother's insistence in high school that I write reasonable assertions others could follow, even if they didn't agree with me. But, of course, a young man in college must try in every way to distance himself from the mother's voice in his head. The uncompromising demands of science in premed and medical courses—disembodied and male—gave me relief from the argument on discourse I was having with my mother. Science taught me that simple responses were not necessarily simplistic, and the emotional torsions of medical school left me no room to lie to myself about what mattered most to me.

Making friends with other young poets in college proved crucial because I learned I could do this work without maintaining complete isolation. My friends also showed me that words emerged from a number of sources and that writers didn't all live with the imminent death sentence my father placed on me. I could laugh, I could play, I could love without sacrificing my claim to seriousness. My grandfathers, one with his black hat and the other with his tinned fish, couldn't be appeased by either secular study or literary success. My sensible sociologist mother and my problem-solving doctor father simply had not cleared any space in our lives for the ambiguity and invention of art. I felt ashamed that my family was not artistic; I couldn't see the strength in their ethics and practicality. The Christian world of T. S. Eliot and G. M. Hopkins and Robert Lowell, and the apparently pagan worlds of Wallace Stevens and Ezra Pound and H. D., offered the comfort of anonymity for a Jewish boy in a vast country governed by metaphysical rules my relatives simply never knew. If I worked hard enough to learn art and literature among the *goyim*, perhaps I could remake myself as an individual with a past I took from other people's traditions.

Medical school, Philadelphia, and especially Latin America cracked me open. Language came in waves, not from distinct individuals but from constellations of disciplines, neighborhoods, regions, and histories.

I needed to speak like everyone else just to keep from drowning. Medical training, especially in the first two years, largely involves language immersion; clinical syntax organizes an arcane vocabulary of the body that lay people aren't privileged to acquire. Ways of talking and thinking, pacing of question and answer, gesture and intonation define a worldview and group identity that is every bit as enforced and taken for granted in the hospital as the shop talk of shipping clerks is in a wallpaper warehouse or raw bluster is in a wrestling locker room. The language my students spoke when I first started teaching high school struck me as fresh and urgent, but after a while I recognized how much its laws and limits defined what students could accept as normal or rule out as weird or "deep." In high-risk language environments, whether in Cleveland or Huehuetenango, individuality fades into the background and the collective comes to the fore. In those pressured situations, I didn't read for distinction. I read to join the action along with everybody else.

Using what Yeats dismissed as "kitchen gabble"—the way regular people habitually speak—seemed at first a violation of my commitment to poetry. However, slowly I entered standard ways of speaking ("A fifty-five-year-old white male presented with classic joint pain associated with gout"), common idioms ("Deepness is everywhere—"), and nationally inflected swear phrases ("*Hijo de la Gran . . . Madre!*"). The onslaught of collective speech—infused with sexuality and oppression, physical violence and elation, disease and hope—challenged my cultivated preciousness but did not discourage my devotion to choosing the right word. If you're performing a dissection or interpreting news of an army massacre, you want to be as precise as Shelley writing about Monte Blanc or Stevens about blackbirds. I did, however, slowly stop mortgage payments on my isolated poet's garret. I let go of unique expression as the single goal and conceded that the expected phrase can be eloquent in its place.

Without my seeking it, Jewishness came back to me when I returned from Mexico. About halfway through my first year teaching for Anthony, he heard me say something in black English for emphasis. He looked at me with his peculiarly small eyes that narrowed even further when he was amused or disgusted. "Eli," he said, "why don't you stop trying to be black and start trying to be Jewish?" At first his judgment stung, but soon I realized he'd correctly called me out. My students didn't need a white teacher trying to be black. They needed an adult being real with them, no matter what my ethnicity. I had gone far away after Sylvie and I broke up, but in order to return, I had to come all the way back. I could not be my father's father's version of a Jew, but I could discover what my tradition was for me. What I did in the world defined me as Jewish, too. Rather than run out to a yeshiva to please the Goldblatt side or join a Reform temple to please the Kushner side, I simply needed to accept Judaism as I lived it. I performed a diminished bar mitzvah the week after my father died, and that stood as my bar mitzvah. I learned to pray in Hebrew so I could mourn my father in the year following the funeral, much as I learned Christian theology so I could read Milton and Dante. My mental image of textual interpretation arises from the passage in the Passover Haggadah when *rebbes* argue through the night over the meaning of the story of exile from Egypt until their students come at dawn and announce: "Rabbis, it's time for morning prayer." Judaism and my intimate relationships among the Jews I love define my writing life more than any other cultural stream. Yet Jewishness does not determine what I write or to whom I speak. Perhaps this is what it means to assimilate in America, to be a diasporic Jew. Ethnicity, no matter how thick or thin, need not limit one's reach across the human sea.

The Western focus on the individual has produced striking achievements I don't wish to demean. I wanted my work read as distinctive when I first started writing poems, and I want that still. But I do not accept literacy as an isolating, discrete skill. When I discovered the concept of the social nature of literacy in the essays of composition scholars like David Bartholomae and Patricia Bizzell, I embraced the idea like a new word for an unnamed emotion. Writers cannot live immersed in words defined exclusively by private experience; the fountain of language is shared and refreshed by common origins. At the same time, characterizing literacy as purely a phenomenon of societies and groups erases the individual writer in the rush to see collective experience in language. My personal experience reinforces for me the dialectic of individual and group, in writing as in every other human interaction. Dialectic leads to conflict as much as or more than harmony. The public world demands unflagging attention and, sometimes, the sacrifice of private energies. Real people are burned alive; language both frames the execution order and tells the tale from multiple vantage points in historical accounts. Meanwhile, the collective can be greedy for a person's time and insensitive to his or her gifts. For a writer, the solitary joys of the writing room are hard-won from a culture that rewards good work too seldom, but lone scribes should not pity themselves too easily.

## The Language for Language Is Language

Native speakers of American English have a very hard time believing that people in other parts of the world actually speak languages other than English. We're not even convinced that Brits aren't putting on that accent just to act superior. Despite all the traveling my family did in Europe during our three years stationed in Germany, I clung to my American blindness like most others. As a young adult, I studied Hebrew, Latin, and German with a compulsion to know the codes, and yet I didn't apprehend language as a communicative tool or an environment in which multiple local populations carry on their business, make love, and declare their faith. I wanted to participate in the strangeness of other languages in other times but never learned any one language well enough to embrace its daily character. Especially in school, languages appear to be tests of intelligence, markers of sophistication, or storage bins for arcane knowledge. The closest I came to appreciating the human heft of foreign words was in committing certain lines to memory so I could experience the music of consonants and vowels in my mouth and ear. A year of living in Spanish woke me up to the materiality of language, the sheer bewilderment of not knowing how to find the public toilet or what friendship could get you killed.

I still speak Spanish clumsily, understand rapid Spanish conversation imperfectly, and inscribe its sentences with the labored earnestness of a fourth grader. Yet this language broke through my ethnocentricity and convinced me that each language etches dreams in its own way while all languages form the thick atmosphere humans breathe at work and in love. I sat in a café in San Cristobal de las Casas, hung over and ashamed of myself for my dumb showing at a marvelous party the night before, and at that moment I realized language was a gift I needed to earn if I wanted to live among others in an unfamiliar country. My continuing struggle to acquire Spanish reminds me that those labeled "illiterate" must wrestle with symbols others recognize on sight. My tiny humiliations in conversation with *hispanohablantes* in Philadelphia and Costa Rica reinforce for me the pleasure of an easily accessible word-hoard in the common or esoteric spheres of one's "native" culture. As I get older, I don't take any language facility for granted. Finding the words to say what I mean—or unearthing what I mean through the words I say—continues to be a challenge in English or Spanish, even in speaking with intimate friends.

Here, poetry has helped me my entire adult life. The view of art as the mode by which the familiar becomes strange and the strange familiar became a crucial way for me to picture words assembled into poems. When a familiar word becomes estranged from common meaning, it discloses meanings obscured by heavy social use. Meanwhile, every phrase must account for its sound as well as its sense. I have only seldom composed in any other language but English—a few Kafkaesque stories in German and a handful of lines in Spanish—but if you treat English in poetry as an alien tongue, you need a dictionary for the simplest words. A poem develops in the sifting and reimagining process from initial composition through subsequent revisions to more or less finished form. Even in the plainest language, images form along a leading edge of long and short syllables arrayed against the usual way of speaking. In this way, literacy in poetry differs from other reading and writing in other genres. At least as I learned it from my American masters, the poet is in the business of discovering what cannot be known or said except by way of the poem. Other forms can pass along data or observations in a number of ways with little loss, but poetry (even if it is written in prose lines) must appear just nonnative enough to surprise you in your bed.

I'll use a piece of a poem from my late friend Gil Ott as an example. In my favorite of his books, a long poem entitled *Traffic*, he presents a short lyric at the top of the page and matches it with a few lines of prose at the foot. The result is like Jewish biblical commentary or the explanation of a hexagram in the Chinese *I Ching*, continually fresh but simultaneously familiar and strange. Here is a single page, with both the verse and prose lines:

When the cold had
fully penetrated he began to shiver

lake
he'd circled on foot.


What does it mean, "to shiver"? Shivering, the yard seemed tamed, the
lake a circle.                                                    (19)

The character's circumstance is defined by weather, by the geometry of fatigue, by the susceptibilities of flesh. When cold invades,
the human house trembles. But the mind grows impatient with the
excuses of the body and cannot accept weakness or mortality. The
mind forms questions, domesticating the wild into a "yard" and the
irregular lake into a perfect form, the O traced in a map of the poem.
Gil worked his poems but let his words work him, let them take him
places he could not plot on a standard sea chart. The poem's concision follows the logic of investigative music, a bird song by Olivier
Messiaen or a slanting folk tune whose dissonance burns lyrics into
the brain.

We don't need art to distance us momentarily from language.
Estrangement in language can happen to anyone at any time. Like the
phrase repeated too often or the word whose familiar spelling suddenly
looks wrong, the tide can momentarily withdraw and leave us standing
naked on the sand, looking out at a hostile sea. Because the comforting saltwater bath of common speech or private diary can lull us into
forgetting how foreign we are to ourselves, we must be grateful for a
little understanding and awe outside of the maxims we are always telling each other. Every sentence we form implies a speaker and a time, a
historical context and a palpable reality for reference. In a minute, our
usual grounding can disappear. I take syntax as the ultimate human
consolation, even if all grammar depends on a necessary fiction: we
trust that once the sentence has begun, it will be pronounced to its
satisfying end. Good poetry tests that faith.

When I left Mexico to return to the States after eight months away, I carried in my knapsack more than twenty books, two journals, and a scratch pad for notes and addresses. Written material far outweighed clothes. Scholars debate the differences between writing and speaking, literacy and orality, but my burden bore witness to one mark of written words: they're heavy to transport. Writing emphasizes the materiality of language while speaking reinforces the sound of the human voice. No matter how much at home a writer might be with vocabulary or print, he or she cannot forget that writing isn't merely an extension of the mouth or the mind but always a conscious production that involves energy and effort to create. All those books on shelves behind authors in book jacket photographs attest to the substance of what they have "said" inside their novels or histories. Of course, writing may be burned, misplaced, shredded, spoiled in the rain, or scanned into digital form and then deleted. But the material being of text is itself a metaphor for the promise of relationship that language offers one human with or among others. The palpable social fact of paper, envelope, and government stamp conjures up the chance for an exile to write his or her way home, if only for a moment.

## Baseball, Community Arts, and School

In the neighborhoods of Philadelphia where I work with local nonprofits focused on literacy development, children and adults need activities through which they can express, critique, imagine, investigate, and enjoy elements of their lives. Many community-based literacy centers publish kids' writing, put on shows, or hold meetings for adults to focus their concerns into political activity. In these projects, the goals of organizers and educators intersect. New writers need a lot of practice writing. They need to feel a sense of normalcy and taken-for-granted consistency in the written language they use so that, as writers or readers or actors, they can advocate forcefully for themselves. At the same time, as I have said about poetry, distinctive language and ambition for discovery must rumble through any kind of writing that stands out as vibrant and confident.

I'm always aware that my own literacy solidified in school without my noticing, and yet most of my understanding about writing came at painful and joyful moments away from classrooms. School isn't always so good at widening your perspective and stretching your vision. Walls regularly divide and categorize types of knowledge within our departmentalized educational system. As I worked through my journals and letters for this book, I noticed that school seldom served as the site of my greatest learning experiences—most of the time I didn't even see they were "learning experiences" until long afterward. For me, the classroom was a safe place because I was good at being a pupil even when I stuck out as a newcomer. I learned how to gain the teacher's attention but also how to fight other kids after class as the price for her approval.

School never mattered as much to me as my various projects outside: building structures with my Erector set, playing guns in the woods or ball on the sandlot, writing my first poems, reading history to make sense of Pound's pronouncements. I began to see my life's work independent of school assignments or major requirements, and what I regarded as "my work" sustained me where assignments could not. Medical school combined academic learning and hands-on training, and yet even there, hospital life outside the classroom taught me the most about how knowledge becomes action. In hospitals, you see the irresponsibility of segregating practice from theory while people die of gunshot wounds, hypertension, anorexia, or economic repression. I started teaching biology because my knowledge of science got me a job; I ended up in English because I wanted to connect with students through a subject I loved. Because I grew to locate myself in relation to others through writing and reading in school and outside its bounds, I try to help others along a similar path in community-based learning, but there's no denying that pure experience matters. History, chemistry, painting, and prosody all shaped my thinking, but no books I read mean more to me than my memories of Paul cursing across the vineyard, the Mexico City shopgirls in their high heels hosing down the street before opening time, or the lingering fragrance at the cosmetics factory when I climbed into the vat to scoop out a failed batch of cold cream.

In the summer of 2009, I volunteered to assist a friend I'll call Maury with a baseball team of eleven- and twelve-year-olds he was coaching. I had coached in this league for many years, including three seasons after my son no longer played the sport, and I knew how deeply involved coaches get with their players and teams. Maury had a son on the team, but he coached with even-handedness and accepted every kid who tried. You can't help but want to win, and yet, unless you're a jackass, you mostly hope the players fall in love with the game as you did yourself. In the process, maybe they learn something about failure when they strike out or success when they catch a fly ball, but their learning is really up to them. It's a simple, maddening game, and many have written better than I about its sorrows and pleasures.

One Saturday afternoon near the end of the season, we were playing a team we needed to beat for a better position in the playoffs. As usual at this age level, the momentum in the game shifted from one team to the other, depending on whether the kid on the mound could throw strikes. Late in the game we were ahead, and a big guy on our team I'll call Sol, short for Solomon, hit a single that the other team misplayed. Sol found himself standing proudly on second base, and in the dugout our kids yelled and pounded on the bench. The parents on our bleachers screamed and whistled. Sol got cocky and began to dance off the bag every time the pitcher threw to the plate. He had no intention of trying to steal third, but he liked the idea that he was giving the other team grief. I was coaching first base at the time and called over to Sol to stay on base. We had a ball game to win. Sol kept mocking the pitcher with every pitch, and darned if the pitcher didn't get mad, whirl around, and peg the ball to his second baseman so that Sol just barely beat the throw. I could see Maury growing angrier and angrier in the dugout. Why didn't Sol stay on the bag? When Sol stepped off base again on the next pitch, Maury asked the umpire for time and stalked out across the field. Everyone in the stands on both sides grew quiet. As in every league, a few coaches berate their players in front of parents and kids, but Maury was known as an honorable man who praised good plays, used mistakes to teach better technique, and urged kids to forget their errors. No one knew what Maury would do, but he sure looked mad. Sol hadn't made a playing error; he was just acting foolish and putting the team in jeopardy. Sol himself was standing meekly on second, shrunk from his full height but unable to hide in the middle of the field. Maury finally arrived at second and looked at Sol, put out his upraised palm and high-fived the boy, turned around, and strode back to the dugout. The crowd cheered, Sol stayed on second till a hit scored him, and we won the game handily two innings later.

If you didn't follow the jargon in the story above, I apologize, but this is part of my point. If you understood the story, then you're already inscribed in the Book of Baseball. Perhaps you imagine yourself in the dugout, in the coach's box on first base, in the parents' bleachers, or striding across the field or shrinking on second base. Especially in the case of rule-bound and traditional games, everyone involved has a role, and listeners to the story months or years later take up a position on the field in their minds to experience the poignancy of the action. Shirley Brice Heath, among other literacy researchers, might classify this as a literacy event, even though a written text wasn't directly involved. The customs of baseball governed the actions of Sol and the pitcher and Maury's and the spectators' reactions as they watched Maury cross the field. Baseball is played on a diamond of grass and dirt, but writing in newspaper reports and tall tales and rhyming poems keep the game alive in our imaginations, even while we're watching the drama unfold.

Maury told me later that he started out to yell at Sol for being silly at a serious moment, but halfway there he realized the wide-open stage, and Sol's particular history of behavior on the team would not have supported a public scolding. He had coached the kid for years with no problems. It would have seemed simultaneously harsh and bizarre to stop the game and dress down a sweet kid who'd hardly ever made trouble except for an occasional sulk, and it would have sent the wrong message to the rest of the team about the direness of our situation. Besides, no coach at any level calls a time-out to talk to a runner at second base! Mid-inning conferences are reserved for moments when a pitcher loads the bases and now faces the cleanup hitter. His high five with Sol surprised everybody, including Sol. The simple act defused the situation, restored good feeling, and yet placed the coach firmly in charge. Brilliant and funny, his improvisation clicked perfectly within the script of "runner in scoring position, no outs, up by a run in the fourth." Not to mention that the coach was a white man old enough to be the boy's grandfather and the player was a black adolescent tall enough to stare in his coach's eyes and heavier than his coach by fifty pounds. A little more than half the players on the field and parents in the stand were African American. The high five itself is a gesture introduced to baseball in 1977 by a black player named Glenn Burke, professional baseball's first openly gay alumnus, who died of AIDS in

1995. All of this or none of it may figure into how a given spectator, or Solomon himself, might remember the event. The official record of the game simply notes, inside Sol's box for the inning, that he hit a single (1B), took second on an error by the opposing team's center fielder (E8), and scored before the last out (blackened diamond indicating a run).

As I think about Maury's action now, I'm struck by the intense moment of recognition that man and boy exchanged in front of fifty people on a Saturday afternoon. Had Maury yelled at Sol, we might have written it off as a case of nerves in the heat of a game. Even in our laid-back league, coaches confront players publicly now and then. A scolding in front of the crowd would have locked Maury and Sol into the usual power differential between coach and kid, teacher and student, parent and child. Maury's performance enlarged us and recast the baseball game in a different key. Was this a literate act? I can't speak for anyone else, but I experienced their drama on second base in the context of my own reading and writing life. Martin Buber might interpret a coach's scolding as an I-It encounter, where neither acknowledges the other as anything more than a functional piece in a game. A surprise mutual meeting in the ritual gesture of a high five, however, represents an I-Thou relationship between two individuals. In an instant, they recognized, with the rest of us as witnesses, that they stood together on the same field and the same planet. That recognition between Maury and Sol reminds me of the struggle—as palpable for individual writers composing a text as for individual athletes playing a game—to act simultaneously out of personal and collective consciousness. Maury showed Sol that a player stands alone on the field but always in the company of others.

Baseball and other sports teach physical invention within a harness of rules, but other activities also allow bodies and minds to engage in organized actions. Most have definite endpoints, like musical performances or public protests or garden harvests, but all group projects involve what John Dewey calls "joint action" (16). In recent years, I have become particularly excited about the possibilities for people in marginalized or under-resourced neighborhoods through community-based arts organizations. I've seen the exuberant and focused way that local groups respond to the challenge of putting on a show, painting a mural, developing an interactive website, or producing a video. Setting out to make a new thing in the world, unconnected to school and off the grid of conventional power differences, writers and other artists can build intimate relationships through meaning-making media with students, neighborhood participants, and the eventual audience. In the fury of art making, literacy shrugs off correctness or diction as its defining qualities just as music transcends the demand for flawless performance or painting the expectation to "look like the real thing."

My colleague and friend Karen Malandra noted that a community-based approach to the arts "works intentionally to move ideas back and forth from individual voice to community voice, from self to text to other to image" (6). Malandra studied a year-long performance project called *Reflections in Brown: Separate/Unequal/Still?* sponsored by Art Sanctuary, an organization founded by novelist Lorene Cary to bring high-quality arts experiences to the people of North Philadelphia. In collaboration with a class taught by Billy Yalowitz at Temple, high school students sang, acted, and danced about the history and results of the *Brown vs. Board of Education* Supreme Court decision that banned de jure racial segregation in US schools. Malandra emphasized in her study "a beneficial landscape of tensions" (228) in the development of *Reflections in Brown*. What she doesn't say, because dissertations must invariably leave the personal out of the story, is that she herself did much of the video production and training to make the show a stunning experience for the hundreds of community people who attended. She died of cancer soon after that dissertation was bound in the library.

I sat in the audience for *Reflections in Brown* at the Church of the Advocate, six blocks from my English department office, and felt so grateful for the opportunity to witness the event. The show represented a confluence of efforts from academic disciplines like performance art, theater, and history mixed with the Art Sanctuary's characteristic mix of jazz, poetry, and African dance within the tradition of civil rights activism at this particular Episcopal church. Teens from Philadelphia and college kids from a wide variety of urban and suburban environments energized the whole and made it happen. Together, a crew of over thirty produced a work far richer than any one faction could have mounted alone. This grand performance could be seen as challenging the individualist vision that first drew me to poetry, and yet it's really not so far from the John Berryman reading that compelled me so many years ago. In both cases, the poet and the performers enact their personal struggles in words and signs embedded in valued cultural traditions. The individual striving of a given artist becomes consecrated by the collective effort of artists over time. Indeed, all kinds of writing inscribe the writer and immerse the reader, for better or worse, in history that humans accrete with every text. This apparent fact can stultify or liberate us, depending on the concept of literacy we embrace.

As I am finishing this chapter, my son, Leo, is completing his senior year at the university where I teach. He's never been an enthusiastic student, and even though he finally thinks a few of the courses he takes are relevant to work he might do in the world, he remains profoundly unconvinced by classes and papers and lectures. They often seem to him like utter wastes of his time. In one of our first honest talks since he started college, he told me, "Dad, I sit in these lectures, and the guy on one side of me is playing a game on his computer, and the girl on the other side of me is texting. We get nothing from what the professor is saying up there, and his exams don't match what he covers in class! Most of my friends can't understand why we need most of what we're required to do. College interferes with my life." I can accept that he's bored by the institution I spend most of my time perpetuating, but I'm no longer able to explain the dead time as an unfortunate artifact of this bad teacher or that ignorant student attitude. Instead, I'm haunted by the image of classes camped out in the ruins of an ancient Roman public forum, endlessly rehearsing information that makes no sense of the world students face in their personal lives. Not that all the books in our libraries have suddenly lost their relevance or that professors truly don't care that their students learn anything, but the very structures in which we teach tend to render our utterances hollow and our assignments the arbitrary tasks for prisoners serving out life sentences.

When I think about the experience of the college students Malandra followed in her study, I can't help but compare their enthusiasm and sense of accomplishment to my son's detachment from school assignments. My son has taught me many lessons along the way, but this may be the starkest. I have learned how to judge health by the consistency and color of baby poops, how to tolerate a child's frightening wheeze from croup at three in the morning, how to pretend a baseball in the ear doesn't hurt when a line drive screams back at me in batting practice, how to put up with silence in a car full of teenage boys coming home from the movies, and how to talk a young man out of burning his girlfriend's letters when the romance ends. But his deep distrust of school stings more than a baseball to the ear. I've taught for years that schools aren't congenial to everyone and that students come to classes with an array of multiple intelligences and learning differences. I just wasn't prepared for my own kid to convince me that, for many kids, school just doesn't digest well. As I finish this book and Leo finishes undergraduate school, I'm coming to a new stage with teaching and learning. I don't mind earning my living from a university, but the old wariness is back in force. One of the central preoccupations of my teaching these days is to enhance learning by freeing the learner whenever possible from the dulling influence of school.

## A Final Phase

Literacy connects the writer with the living and those coming after, but writing cannot reach the dead. My mother and father are gone, along with Gil and Karen and other dear friends; the roster of people I can't speak to grows longer each year. Of course I want to address the dead, but the desire remains unsatisfied. No matter how many books or poems I write, on some midnights I glimpse myself shouting down an empty hole in the ground. Writing can connect the dead to the living, but not the other way round.

I've found some relief from the rhetorical problem of mortality through fatherhood. Whether I was holding my son in a cloth pouch on my chest, walking hand-in-hand with him to daycare, entering a pizza shop arm-in-arm, or waving to him as he drove away to his apartment downtown, I have always recognized my son with an immediacy I imagine my father knew in me. Sometimes I speak to Leo as I wish my father had spoken to me. And yet, if Leo reads these words, he will still have to imagine what I feel about him, just as I have had to imagine for years what my father felt about me. I can conjure with the emotion and thought necessary to cast words into sentences and sentences into print, and thus I enact that intimate and public drama I experience as literacy. My attitudes toward literacy may or may not be peculiarly Jewish, or American, or male, or a product of the late twentieth and early twenty-first centuries, although clearly I partake in all these social identities. Like every other writer, I'm both a creature of the composing moment and one among many persons in my time.

Recently, I came across a reprint of a little essay called "The Practice" that William Carlos Williams published in 1951, the year before I was born. I welcomed his voice again. In his tone, I hear a characteristic mixture of fierce love for the unheeding fellow beings around him and utter disdain for their inevitable cruelties: "there is no need for us to be such strangers to each other, saving alone laziness, indifference and age-old besotted ignorance" (30). Williams always reminds me why I can't quit poems, even if I chafe at the academic fetishism of Literature and the American tendency to isolate its poets in shrines to individual talent. He was more acutely aware than any other poet I know, with the possible exception of Langston Hughes, of the precious commonness in speech that can be hammered into poems. No matter how removed the emotion, how steep the idea, the poem for him had to be wrought in words you could hear in the five and dime. Although the "practice" in this essay ostensibly refers to his daily physician's rounds, the word applies equally well to his particular poetics: "For under that language to which we have been listening all our lives a new, a more profound language, underlying all the dialectics offers itself. It is what they call poetry. That is the final phase" (30). Not final, really, but a fundamental place from which to launch our practice.

I've tried in this book to tell stories that represent literacy in action among the pains and pleasures of relationships, self-deceptions, ambitions large and small, gradients of power, and the political debris that falls like sediment on the shoulders of time-bound people traveling together. Williams teaches us to listen, and that act requires something more than natural talent or an expensive education. He wants us to hear, within the urgencies of the day, a communally generated murmur below, a music jointly made. Amid histories, dreams, and assertions, this literacy anchors me home.

# Bibliography

Ammons, A. R. *Collected Poems 1951–1971*. New York: Norton, 1972.

Ammons, A. R., et al. *The First Anthology*. Ithaca: Society for the Humanities, 1974.

Bakhtin, M. M. *The Dialogic Imagination*. Ed. Michael Holquist. Trans. Caryl Emerson and Michael Holquist. Austin: U of Texas P, 1981.

Bate, Walter Jackson. *John Keats*. Cambridge, MA: Harvard UP, 1963.

Berryman, John. "The Ball Poem." *Norton Anthology of Modern Poetry*. Ed. Richard Ellman and Robert O'Clair. New York: Norton, 1973. 893.

Blake, William. *The Complete Poetry and Prose of William Blake*. Ed. David Erdman. New York: Random House, 1965.

Borges, Jorge Luis. *Labyrinths: Selected Stories and Other Writings*. New York: New Directions, 1964.

Buber, Martin. *Hasidism and Modern Man*. Ed. and trans. Maurice Friedman. New York: Harper and Row, 1958.

———. *I and Thou*. New York: Scribner's, 1958.

Césaire, Aimé. "Notebook of a Return to the Native Land." Trans. Clayton Eshleman and Annette Smith. *Montemora* 6 (1980): 9–37.

Coe, Michael D. *The Maya*. London: Thames and Hudson, 1966.

Crane, Hart. *Hart Crane: Complete Poems and Selected Letters and Prose*. Ed. Brom Weber. Garden City, NY: Anchor/Doubleday, 1966.

Creeley Robert. *For Love*. New York: Scribner's, 1962.

Daly, Mary. *Beyond God the Father*. Boston: Beacon, 1973.

Dewey, John. *Democracy and Education*. 1916. New York: Free, 1944.

Doolittle, Hilda. *H. D.: Collected Poems 1912–1944*. Ed. Louis Martz. New York: New Directions, 1983.

Duberman, Martin. *Black Mountain: An Exploration in Community*. New York: Dutton, 1972.

Eliot, T. S. *Four Quartets*. New York: Harcourt, Brace, and World, 1943.

Goldblatt, Eli. *Round My Way: Authority and Double-Consciousness in Three Urban High School Writers*. Pittsburgh: U of Pittsburgh P, 1995.

Harrison, Jane Ellen. *The Myths of Greece and Rome*. 1928. Charleston, SC: Forgotten Books, 1970.

Hayden, Robert. *Words in the Mourning Time*. New York: October House, 1970.

Hertz, Joseph H. *The Authorized Daily Prayer Book*. New York: Bloch, 1948.

Hesse, Hermann. *Siddhartha*. Trans. Hilda Rosner. New York: Bantam, 1971.

Huntington, Samuel. *The Soldier and the State*. Cambridge, MA: Belknap, 1957.

Ives, Charles. "The Circus Band." *114 Songs by Charles Ives*. Merion Music, 1975.

Jung, C. G. *Memories, Dreams, Reflections*. Trans. Richard and Clara Winston. New York: Vintage, 1963.

Kandinsky, Wassily. *Concerning the Spiritual in Art*. Trans. M. T. H. Sadler. New York: Dover, 1977.

Koch, Kenneth. *Thank You and Other Poems*. New York: Grove, 1962.

Lakoff, George, and Mark Johnson. *Metaphors We Live By*. Chicago: U of Chicago P, 1980.

Lee, Don L. *Don't Cry Scream*. Detroit: Broadside, 1969.

Levertov, Denise. *O Taste and See*. New York: New Directions, 1962.

Lowell, Robert. *Notebook*. New York: Farrar Strauss and Giroux, 1967.

Malandra, Karen. "Interrupting Habitus and Community-Based Arts: Pedagogical Efficacy in a University/Community Collaboration." Diss. Temple University, 2007.

Miller, Valerie. *Between Struggle and Hope: The Nicaraguan Literacy Crusade*. Boulder: Westview, 1985.

Moore, Marianne. *Observations*. New York: Dial, 1924.

O'Hara, Frank. *The Selected Poems of Frank O'Hara*. Ed. Donald Allen. New York: Vintage, 1974.

Olson, Charles. *Selected Writings*. Ed. Robert Creeley. New York: New Directions, 1966.

Oppen, George. *New Collected Poems*. Ed. Michael Davidson. New York: New Directions, 2002.

Ott, Gilbert. *Traffic*. Tucson, AZ: Chax, 2001.

"Politics Highlights Student Parley." *Baltimore Sun* Nov. 1, 1969: A10.

Pound, Ezra. *ABC of Reading*. New York: New Directions, 1960.

———. *The Cantos of Ezra Pound*. New York: New Directions, 1972.

———. *Guide to Kulchur*. New York: New Directions, 1968.

———. *Personae*. 1926. New York: New Directions, 1971.

Rothenberg, Jerome. *Technicians of the Sacred*. Berkeley: U of California P, 1968.

Valéry, Paul. *Selected Writings of Paul Valéry*. New York: New Directions, 1964.

Whalen, Philip. *On Bear's Head*. New York: Harcourt, Brace, and World, 1969.

Williams, William Carlos. *The Autobiography of William Carlos Williams*. New York: New Directions, 1967.

———. *The Collected Earlier Poems of William Carlos Williams*. New York: New Directions, 1966.

———. *The Collected Poems of William Carlos Williams*. Vol. 2, 1939–62. Ed. Christopher MacGowan. New York: New Directions, 2001.

———. "The Practice." *American Poetry Review* 38.6 (Nov./Dec. 2009): 29–30.

———. *A Voyage to Pagany*. New York: New Directions, 1970.

Yeats, William Butler. *The Collected Poems of W. B. Yeats*. New York: Macmillan, 1956.

**Eli Goldblatt**, a professor of English at Temple University, is both a composition/literacy researcher and a published poet. He is the author of eight books, including *Because We Live Here: Sponsoring Literacy beyond the College Curriculum*, four volumes of poetry, and two children's books.